The 2012
Presidential Campaign

Communication, Media, and Politics

SERIES EDITOR
ROBERT E. DENTON, JR., VIRGINIA TECH

This series features a range of work dealing with the role and function of communication in the realm of politics, broadly defined. Including general academic books and texts for use in graduate and advanced undergraduate courses, the series encompasses humanistic, critical, historical, and empirical studies in political communication in the United States. Primary subject areas include campaigns and elections, media, and political institutions. *Communication, Media, and Politics* books will be of interest to students, teachers, and scholars of political communication from the disciplines of communication, rhetorical studies, political science, journalism, and political sociology.

Recent Titles in the Series

The 2012 Presidential Campaign

A Communication Perspective

Edited by Robert E. Denton, Jr.

ROWMAN & LITTLEFIELD PUBLISHERS, INC.
Lanham • Boulder • New York • Toronto • Plymouth, UK

Published by Rowman & Littlefield Publishers, Inc.
A wholly owned subsidiary of The Rowman & Littlefield Publishing Group, Inc.
4501 Forbes Boulevard, Suite 200, Lanham, Maryland 20706
www.rowman.com

10 Thornbury Road, Plymouth PL6 7PP, United Kingdom

British Library Cataloguing in Publication Information Available

Library of Congress Cataloging-in-Publication Data
The 2012 presidential campaign : a communication perspective / edited by Robert E.
Denton, Jr.
    pages cm.
  Includes bibliographical references and index.
  ISBN 978-1-4422-1673-0 (cloth : alk. paper)—ISBN 978-1-4422-1674-7 (pbk. : alk.
paper)—ISBN 978-1-4422-1675-4 (electronic : alk. paper) 1. Presidents—United States—
Election—2012. 2. Presidential candidates—United States—History—21st century.
I. Denton, Robert E., Jr.
  JK5262012 .A18 2013
  324.973'0932—dc23   2013015722

∞™ The paper used in this publication meets the minimum requirements of
American National Standard for Information Sciences—Permanence of Paper
for Printed Library Materials, ANSI/NISO Z39.48-1992.

Printed in the United States of America

Contents

Tables

Preface

Every four years a gong goes off and a new presidential campaign surges into the national consciousness—new candidates, new issues, a new season of surprises. But underlying the syncopations of change is a steady, recurrent rhythm from election to election, a pulse of politics that brings up the same basic themes in order, over and over again.

—James David Barber[1]

Over thirty years ago, as a graduate student, I was struck by the above quotation by noted political science scholar James David Barber. Every modern presidential campaign is different yet the same. Since 1992 I have edited a volume on every presidential election. In all the previous volumes I have noted that every presidential election is historic from policy, issues, and cultural perspectives. Even in the shadows of the 2008 presidential campaign the 2012 contest was equally unique. For example:

The reelection of Barack Obama is the first time in two hundred years that American citizens have elected three two-term presidents in a row when Thomas Jefferson, James Madison, and James Monroe were each elected.

President Obama is the third Democrat in 180 years to win a majority of the popular vote twice. The others were Grover Cleveland and Franklin D. Roosevelt.

Both candidates broke tradition and campaigned on Election Day. Governor Romney visited two battleground states—Ohio and Pennsylvania—while President Obama did a number of radio and television interviews.

This is the first election since World War II in which neither candidate had served in the military.

Interestingly, this is the first election since 1976 in which no Bushes or Clintons were running for president or vice president.

After the 2012 election Democrats had won the popular vote in five of the last
   six elections. Prior to that Republicans had won the popular vote in five of six
   elections.
2012 was the first election since 1972 (before campaign finance reforms following
   the Watergate scandal) in which neither candidate accepted public funds and
   limits on spending.
The 2012 contest was the most expensive in American history. It was the first race
   to break the one billion dollar spending mark. Governor Romney spent $992
   million while President Obama spent $1.07 billion.[2]

And yet, from an electoral perspective, the 2012 race was very similar to 2008's.
Regionally President Obama maintained his support in the Northeast and Pacific
West and a slim advantage in the Midwest. Republican support was once again
strongest in the Greater South, the plains, and the inner West.[3] President Obama
held the same advantages within previous constituency groups: African Americans,
Hispanics, eighteen- to twenty-nine-year-olds, and nonmarried and professional
women. Governor Romney did well among men (especially white males), middle-
and older-aged citizens, and married women. Nationally the 2012 contest was virtually a status-quo election with overall voting down 5 percent and President Obama
receiving about 2 percent less of the popular vote—or six million votes. Governor
Romney ran about three hundred thousand fewer votes than McCain's total in 2008.
North Carolina was the only state to change its vote from 2008.

However, it is important to note that 2012 was still a very partisan and polarizing
election. Despite the electoral-college number advantage, the race pivoted on just a
handful of states. President Obama won 62 percent of the electoral-college votes but
just 22 percent of all the counties in the nation. In fact, according to one analysis,
without the huge margins of minority and young voters in Broward County, Florida;
Cuyahoga County, Ohio; and Philadelphia County, Pennsylvania, President Obama
would have lost those states and the electoral-college winning vote.[4] Governor Romney actually won 52 percent of all congressional districts.

For communication scholars, the essence of politics is talk or human interaction.
The interaction may be formal or informal, verbal or nonverbal, public or private,
but it is always persuasive, forcing us to interpret, to evaluate, and to act.

I have argued for years that presidential campaigns are our national conversations.
They are highly complex and sophisticated communication events: communication of issues, images, social reality, and personas. They are essentially exercises in
the creation, re-creation, and transmission of significant symbols through human
communication. As we attempt to make sense of our environment, political bits
of communication comprise our voting choices, worldviews, and legislative desires.

The purpose of this volume, as it was with my previous publications, is to review
the most recent presidential campaign from a communications perspective. The
analyses presented here go beyond the quantitative facts, electoral counts, and poll
results of the election. Each chapter focuses on a specific area of political-campaign

communication: the conventions, the social and political contexts, the debates, candidate strategies, popular culture, political advertising, the use of new media, and an analysis of the vote. All the contributors are accomplished scholars. Most have participated in my past volumes.

Rachel L. Holloway begins the volume analyzing the nomination conventions. She first offers a theoretical and historical review of American Dream narratives in presidential convention rhetoric. Over time divergent views of the American Dream have emerged, one emphasizing the role of the individual, the other emphasizing societal values like justice, fairness, and community. The Republican narrative for America's future was based on individual ambition and achievement made possible by the opportunity America provides. Democrats, rather, offered an American Dream balanced between individual and communal responsibilities within a broad conception of citizenship. Holloway concludes by examining the role convention discourse plays in defining the American Dream.

In the second chapter Gwen Brown reveals the roles of candidate wives in their campaigns—specifically during the national conventions. Since 2004 spouses of both presidential nominees have given convention addresses. After providing a rich history of convention spousal speeches, Brown builds upon the work of Elizabeth Petre. Petre is one of the few scholars who have focused on the speeches of women at political conventions. She notes the ceremonial nature of the addresses and views them as epideictic in form. Brown identifies five strategies of the spouse/First Lady convention speech—praising America's past, use of narrative to personalize her husband, creation of a sense of intimacy, listing the accomplishments of her husband, and defining the candidate as a reflection of his wife. Spouses also provide a strong presence in the campaign films shown at conventions. At each of the 2012 conventions, Michelle Obama and Ann Romney in their speeches and films directly address the overarching political problems each spouse faced, a new twist to their roles.

In chapter 3 Ben Voth provides insightful analysis into the 2012 presidential debates. He finds these most recent debates most noteworthy for three reasons: they attracted the largest television audiences in fifty years, President Obama overcame one of the worse performances in presidential-debate history to win reelection, and moderators and candidates alike widely disregarded the predetermined rules for engagement. Voth furthermore reveals great disparity between total candidate speaking time and interruptions of each candidate by either the moderator or the other candidate. His analysis is unique and compelling, concluding with recommendations for improving future presidential debates.

In chapter 4 Craig Allen Smith argues that presidential campaigns are essentially rhetorical puzzles, solvable where challengers eke out pluralities in enough states to defeat the incumbent and win the electoral-college vote. Utilizing Allan Lictman's thirteen true/false keys to the White House, Smith develops a framework for reelection campaigns, requiring challengers to attack incumbents so as to convince voters that six or more of the keys are false, and simultaneously requiring incumbents to proclaim and defend that only five or fewer keys are false. When applying his framework to the 2012 campaign, Smith concludes that President Obama's defeat was not probable or even likely, as some analysts had suggested. Smith also discusses alternative campaign strategies that would have improved Governor Romney's chances of defeating an incumbent.

John C. Tedesco and Scott W. Dunn cover the advertising in the 2012 presidential campaign in chapter 5. They report the expenditures of the campaign and Super PAC ads, types and issues of the ads, types of attack ads and accuracy in the ads and conclude with a discussion on the impact of Super PACs and the Supreme Court ruling of *Citizens United*. Going beyond the statistics, Tedesco and Dunn note the extreme negativity of the campaign ads despite record spending, the incredible influence of wealthy contributors, and the savvy early advertising and market segmentation of the Obama campaign.

Despite all of Governor Romney's business experience, the Obama campaign was most successful in defining him as an individual whose personal wealth was obtained at the expense of putting people out of work and not paying his fair share of taxes. And so in chapter 6 Joseph M. Valenzano III and Jason A. Edwards examine how Governor Romney handled his tax returns and find it illustrative of his larger strategy for shaping his image as a business leader. The authors argue that Romney managed the tax-return issue well during the primaries but that during the summer prior to the general election he was never able to overcome and neutralize the attacks, raising questions about his business experience and potential leadership. They conclude by noting the risks of using surrogates to address candidate criticisms and the importance now of the summer between conventions and the general election in determining candidate image.

For Jeffrey P. Jones the 2012 presidential election represents the complete convergence of politics with popular culture, the latter of which was an integral part of every campaign moment and event. In chapter 7 Jones assesses the myriad ways the campaigns—from the Republican primary debates to Election Day—were intertwined in popular culture in mainstream media, niche media, and social media. Presidential campaigns are cultural events where each campaign's and each voter's challenge is to maintain an understanding of what is real and what is fake.

Mass media and politics have gone hand-in-hand since the forming of our nation, with campaigns always utilizing the newest communication technologies. Perhaps the most dramatic use of new media was by the Obama campaign in 2008, where they set the standard for powerful usage of new media in politics. In chapter 8 John Allen Hendricks examines how the 2012 campaigns utilized new media—especially social media and the Internet. While both campaigns took advantage of the new technologies, it was the Obama campaign that dominated in all areas. The accumulation of potential voter technology behavior and the expansion of all types of social media outlets, applications, and devices allowed more targeting and tailoring of messages than ever before. Social media provided a platform for citizen engagement. Mobile devices, Facebook, Twitter, YouTube, Pinterest, and Tumblr became important tools of the campaigns. The magnitude and scope of the new technologies have become an essential component of all campaigns.

In the final chapter, as has become tradition, Henry C. Kenski and Kate M. Kenski analyze the vote in 2012, focusing on the overall political environment, rules of the game and the electoral college, salience of party identification, messenger, messages and strategies, channels of communication, and the demographic base of the presidential vote. President Obama won despite campaigning for re-election in a very negative political environment. Democrats enjoyed a six-point party-voting edge over Republicans, despite Romney's having won independents by 5 percentage points. Obama was clearly a more successful messenger, framing the campaign as a choice between him and Romney rather than a referendum on his first-term performance. The Obama campaign mastered the attack strategy, especially in eleven critical electoral-vote battleground states. According to Kenski and Kenski, the election was essentially over by September. Without question, newspapers, radio, and traditional mainstream media continue to lose influence and audience in every election year, while new media and the Internet continue to show impressive growth in audience and electoral strategy. As already noted, demographic group support in the 2012 election did not change dramatically from 2008. According to Kenski and Kenski, not only must Republicans address internal divisions and appeal to more diverse voting groups, they also need to improve technical skill and campaign talent.

Presidential campaigns communicate and influence, reinforce and convert, motivate and educate. Bruce Gronbeck argues that campaigns "get leaders elected, yes, but ultimately they also tell us who we as a people are, where we have been, and where we are going; in their size and duration they separate our culture from all others, teach us about political life, set our individual and collective priorities, entertain us, and provide bases for social interaction."[5]

As I have argued in the past, I believe strongly that political-communication scholars should remember that *more* communication does not mean *better* communication. More technology does not mean more effective communication. For well over two hundred years America has moved toward a more inclusive democracy: greater participation of women, minorities, and the young. We have also witnessed unparalleled advances in communication technologies. Yet for more than a quarter of a century, during a time of increased opportunity for participation and information, we have seen a decline in citizen political awareness, knowledge, and understanding. Fortunately in 2004 and 2008 voting, across the board, in every demographic group, increased to levels of the 1970s.

The central question is how we are to cultivate an active, democratic citizenry. Civic responsibility and initiative should once again become a keystone of social life. It is my hope that perhaps by better understanding the role and process of communication in presidential campaigns we may somehow improve the quality of our national conversations.

NOTES

1. James David Barber, *The Pulse of Politics* (New York: W. W. Norton, 1980), 3.

2. Jeremy Ashkenas, Matthew Ericson, Alicia Parlapiano, and Derek Willis, "The 2012 Money Race: Compare the Candidates," *New York Times*, November 26, 2012, http://elections .nytimes.com/2012/campaign-finance.

3. Larry J. Sabato, Kyle Kondik, and Geoffrey Skelley, "Closing the Book on 2012," *Sabato's Chrystal Ball*, UVA Center for Politics, December 20, 2012, www.centerforpolitics.org/ crystalball/articles/closing-the-book-on-2012/.

4. Jennifer Duffy, "25 Interesting Facts about the 2012 Elections," *Cook Political Report*, December 20, 2012, accessed January 1, 2013, http://cookpolitical.com/story/5219.

5. Bruce Gronbeck, "Functions of Presidential Campaigns," in *Political Persuasion in Presidential Campaigns*, ed. Lawrence Patrick Devlin (New Brunswick, N.J.: Transaction Books, 1987), 496.

Acknowledgments

I have had the privilege to edit several volumes over the years. Despite the ever-present challenges inherent in working with a very smart, busy, and diverse group of scholars, I have actually come to enjoy the process. This project was no exception. This project brought together colleagues and friends, new and old. I am most fortunate to work with such an outstanding group of scholars. Once again, the contributors have made this a most rewarding and enjoyable endeavor. I genuinely appreciate their participation in this volume. I also value their friendship.

I thank my colleagues in the Department of Communication at Virginia Polytechnic Institute and State University (Virginia Tech) for their continued collegiality and encouragement for the rich environment they create that supports differing thoughts, views, and scholarship. I appreciate the opportunity to serve as department head yet once again in my career and their support as we navigate the challenges of higher education. I thank Richard Sorensen, dean of the Pamplin College of Business, who for fifteen years has been incredibly supportive of my administrative, professional, and scholarly activities. He has served as a most valuable mentor and outstanding leader. I wish him the very best on his retirement and will miss his insights, skills, and leadership. Thanks are also due to Sue Ott Rowlands, dean of the College of Liberal Arts and Human Sciences. Together the deans have understood the importance of the right mix to making my job a privilege and pleasure. I am genuinely fortunate to have worked for years for two such outstanding administrators whom I admire.

Finally, as always, it is family members who sustain us, encourage us, and provide a sense of belonging, love, and security that frees us to read, write, think, and pursue projects of interest. Thankfully, they provide the joys of life well beyond academe. They keep me grounded, protected, and simply happy. Of course, countless thanks to my wonderful wife, Rachel, a true blessing, friend, colleague, and partner in my life. We are a good team and enjoy our life together, along with wonderful friends. Life simply could not be any better or filled with more blessings. And also to my now-grown sons, Bobby and Chris, who are good people and have grown into fine citizens. I am very proud of them. In Bobby's case, it helps to have a wonderful wife, Christen. And Chris, recently engaged, has found a magnificent partner in Sarah. The boys and Rachel have always been tolerant of my countless hours in the study— perhaps too tolerant and too many hours. Together those three—plus our precious dogs, Daisy and Abby—enrich and fulfill every moment of my life.

1

The 2012 Presidential-Nominating Conventions and the American Dream: Narrative Unity and Political Division

Rachel L. Holloway

Presidential-nominating conventions mark the end of tough primary battles and the beginning of the general-election campaign. They serve multiple functions: energizing party delegates and volunteers, introducing and promoting the party's future leaders, establishing party platforms and issue positions, and formalizing the nomination of the presidential and vice presidential candidates.

And much about nominating conventions is highly predictable. Speakers deliver a carefully scripted campaign message focusing on themes and issues central to the campaign's strategy. Producers use physical and digital stagecraft to support the message and the candidates within the parameters of shrinking network-television coverage, the editorial selectivity of cable-news channels, and the hyperconnected space of Web-based news and editorial outlets. The convention strategists deploy the latest in social media to connect party volunteers and voters in geographically disbursed networks. If all goes well, the nominating convention reintroduces the nominees to the voting public, stakes out the party's issue positions for the coming election, produces a bump in public-opinion polls, and builds momentum for the campaign.

Despite their predictable, staged nature, political nominating conventions play an important rhetorical function as the epideictic—the articulation and reinvigoration of the party's values, inviting the public's support.[1] The conventions offer a focused opportunity for each political party to shape the public's perception of the present political moment within a compelling story of the nation, the American Dream narrative. Each party's narrative calls on voters to come together to elect a president and vice president who will secure the American Dream in the present and for future generations.[2]

The purpose of this chapter is to analyze the competing visions of the American Dream constructed at the 2012 presidential-nominating conventions. I offer a brief theoretical and historical review of American Dream narratives in presidential-convention rhetoric to provide a context for the 2012 conventions. Then the American Dream narratives articulated at the Republican National Convention and the Democratic Convention are presented. Finally I explore the role of convention discourse in what Rowland and Jones describe as one of the core issues in American politics—"control of the American Dream."[3]

THE AMERICAN DREAM IN PRESIDENTIAL ELECTIONS

In the *Cycles of American History*, Arthur M. Schlesinger, Jr., interprets American political change as a predictable pendulum swing between the nation's commitment to private interest and its commitment to public purpose. While both sets of values are central to American thought and share commitments to individual liberty, constitutional government, and the rule of law, he says, the role of government flowing from the values is quite different. In periods of public purpose, Schlesinger believes that people come together to reform government and society, based on democratic values of equality, social responsibility, and the common good. In these times public concerns outweigh commitment to individual prosperity, and government action emphasizes policies aimed at improving the conditions for all citizens.

The resulting growth of government and continuous reform during periods of public purpose, however, eventually test the nation's commitments to freedom, says Schlesinger, and a belief in the individual's right to self-determination and produce a desire for change. Free enterprise, individual ambition, and voluntary associations become the preferred agents of change, and government should stay out of the way, the people say. Over time the emphasis on private concerns highlights divisions within society, Schlesinger believes, and as people feel cut off from one another and disparities in income, education, and opportunity become increasingly evident, a renewed sense of community and public purpose emerges as the remedy.[4] And then the cycle begins again.

The conflicting value sets embedded within American political thought and the resulting divergence in belief about the role of government produce what Walter Fisher has described as competing American Dream myths—one a materialistic myth focused on self-reliance, achievement, and success and the other a moralistic myth centered on equality, tolerance, and cooperation to create a public good. As candidates adopt one myth over the other, voter choice becomes a statement of "how Americans want to conceive of themselves, the particular myth they want to live by."[5]

Robin C. Rowland and John M. Jones extended Fisher's work, identifying the American Dream as a subform of myth, the political romance based in the ideology of classical liberalism. Rowland and Jones identify three defining features in the American Dream romance—"a scene defined by opportunity, agency defined by personal and societal values that allow for the opportunity to be fulfilled, and a protagonist who enacts the personal values in order to achieve a better life."[6] Progress, the motivating force in a romance narrative, is achieved both individually and communally by those willing to strive, work hard, and accept individual responsibility for their own lives and those of others. While individual actions and responsibility are key components of the American Dream narrative, so too are communal values of fairness, compassion, and community. Rowland and Jones contend that the protagonists in the American Dream narrative serve as "a kind of rhetorical proof that commitment to the values inherent in the American Dream will lead to its achievement."[7] Thus, in Rowland and Jones's conceptualization of the American Dream myth, both the materialistic and moralistic, the personal and societal, are always present within the American Dream.

The primary difference between the Republican and Democratic conceptions of the American Dream is a matter of emphasis of agency. Conservatives (and thus the majority of Republicans) emphasize the role of the individual in fulfilling the American Dream: Hard work, strong families, and voluntary associations lead to a stronger society and nation, they say, and the role of government is to do only what individuals cannot do for themselves. Liberals (and therefore most Democrats), on the other hand, emphasize the importance of justice, fairness, inclusivity, and community, arguing for the removal of systemic barriers to individual success. In a liberal conception of the American Dream, government's role is to create a scene that supports and empowers individuals seeking a better life: federal responses to societal problems can protect individuals against the vagaries of local or regional attitudes and inequality of prosperity produced in competitive markets.

Rowland and Jones explain the "conservative ascendancy" in America over the last twenty-five years not as an ideological victory but as a "narrative victory" in which the individualist version of the American Dream narrative dominated political discourse and became closely associated with President Ronald Reagan and the Republican Party. When in 1980 Reagan accepted his party's nomination, he gave an address promoting an American Dream narrative based on individualistic values in which ordinary Americans willing to work hard could achieve a better life for themselves and their families and create a peaceful and free society. The "conservative romance" appealed to the traditional conservative base but also drew Reagan Democrats into a Republican coalition. Eventually the dominance of the narrative made it difficult for Democrats to offer a compelling alternative vision. Later, in 1992, President Clinton won the White House in part by a move to the middle as a "new" Democrat, embracing individualistic values traditionally associated with conservatives. President George W. Bush returned to the conservative romance in 2000, adding a dose of "compassion" to his expression of individualistic values. Presidential candidates clearly recognized the need to balance the personal and societal elements of agency within the American Dream myth to offer a myth to live by that was attractive to a majority of voters.

In 2004, as keynote speaker at the 2004 Democratic National Convention, Barack Obama began articulating an alternative American Dream. He proposed what Rowland and Jones call a "balanced recasting" of the narrative, thereby "reclaiming the narrative center of American politics for the Democratic Party."[8] Obama spoke of an America of limitless opportunity for all people, using his personal story as rhetorical proof of the American Dream, saying, "I stand here knowing that my story is part of the larger American story, that I owe a debt to all of those who came before me, and that in no other country on Earth is my story even possible."[9]

He characterized the challenges of the time—increasing unemployment, lowering income status, increasing health-care and education costs—as evidence that the American Dream was slipping away from many Americans. He embraced America's commitment to individualistic values: "Now, don't get me wrong—the people I meet in small towns and big cities and diners and office parks, they don't expect government to solve all of their problems. They know they have to work hard to get ahead. And they want to." But he balanced personal with societal responsibility explicitly: "For alongside our famous individualism, there's another ingredient in the American saga, a belief that we are all connected as one people." The commitment to each other, to shared achievement, is essential to the American Dream narrative constructed by Obama. He asserted that "it is that fundamental belief *I am my brother's keeper, I am my sister's keeper* that makes this country work. It's what allows us to pursue our individual dreams yet still come together as a single American family: *E pluribus unum,*—Out of many, one." Obama carefully transcended divisions traditionally associated with the Republican and Democratic parties.

In the end, Obama encapsulated his recasting of the American Dream narrative as "the audacity of hope," a careful balancing of personal and social values.[10] Obama's narrative featured individuals who worked hard, persevered, and had strong commitments to family and country but needed the support of their fellow Americans to achieve the American Dream. He argued that society and government were failing many and thus called for a "slight change in priorities" to restore America's promise, to preserve the American Dream.

By 2008 Obama's call for a "slight change in priorities" had become a "defining moment" in American history. In his acceptance address at the 2008 Democratic National Convention, he said the election was "our chance to keep, in the twenty-first century, the American promise alive."[11] Obama painted a stark picture of the nation's challenges. He said that "more Americans are out of work and more are working harder for less. More of you have lost your homes, and even more are watching your home values plummet. More of you have cars you can't afford to drive, credit card bills you can't afford to pay, and tuition that's beyond your reach." He blamed "broken politics" and the "failed policies of George W. Bush."

His solution was a return to communal values, arguing that the country was more "decent," "generous," and more "compassionate" than the last eight years had evidenced and then characterized the Republican philosophy as old and discredited, where big companies and the wealthy were favored with a trickle-down theory of economics and where those struggling the most in a tough economy had been abandoned. Obama argued that "what it really means is, you're on your own. Out of work? Tough luck. No health care? The market will fix it. Born into poverty? Pull yourself up by your own bootstraps, even if you don't have boots. You're on your own."

The alternative Obama promised was a return to the "American promise." He articulated his vision in a series of statements in which he balanced individual effort and communal values with the conjunction *but*, clearly indicating the nation was failing in its commitment to societal values:

> It's a promise that says each of us has the freedom to make of our own lives what we will but that we also have the obligation to treat each other with dignity and respect.
>
> It's a promise that says the market should reward drive and innovation and generate growth but that businesses should live up to their responsibilities to create American jobs, look out for American workers, and play by the rules of the road.
>
> That's the promise of America, the idea that we are responsible for ourselves but that we also rise or fall as one nation, the fundamental belief that I am my brother's keeper, I am my sister's keeper.

Obama's articulation of the American Dream narrative in 2008 refined his integration of individual and communal values to support policy positions consistent with the traditional Democratic narrative. Rowland contends that Obama's rhetoric was particularly effective in responding to a political scene marked by increasingly desperate economic conditions for many Americans. His articulation of the American promise that included both "working hard and working together" responded to the "fierce urgency of now," asking voters to adopt his American story.[12]

Four years later "the fierce urgency of now" had turned into a protracted period of economic distress for the American people. Obama had promised to bring change and relief to those feeling abandoned and left behind. As the two parties marked the beginning of the general election, the Republicans hoped measuring the president's performance against his promises would lead voters to make a different choice in 2012.

THE AMERICAN DREAM IN 2012

Republican Party delegates gathered in Tampa, Florida, from August 27 through 30 to nominate their presidential candidate, former Massachusetts governor Mitt Romney, and their vice presidential candidate, Wisconsin congressman Paul Ryan. The Democratic Party assembled the following week, September 4 through 6, in Charlotte, North Carolina, to reaffirm their support for President Barack Obama and Vice President Joe Biden. The two visions for the future of the nation articulated at the two conventions would lay the groundwork for the tough general election ahead.

The Republican National Convention

Hurricane Isaac formed in the Gulf of Mexico just as the Republicans prepared to gather in Tampa for their convention. The storm's potential physical impact on the convention site and its competition for precious news coverage leading up to and during the convention disrupted Republicans plans. While they officially opened the convention as planned that Monday, they ended up canceling all but essential activities. They adjusted the speaking schedule, omitting many speakers and retaining a key lineup of the party's rising stars and key leaders during broadcast network coverage from 10 to 11 P.M., EST.[13]

A month earlier, while at a campaign stop, President Obama had contributed to the Republican's convention message while delivering his stump speech to an enthusiastic crowd in Roanoke, Virginia, saying, "If you've got a business, you didn't build that. Somebody else made that happen."[14] Of course, Obama said much more than that, but the Republicans seized on the phrase, suggesting it revealed Obama's "true" disdain for American individualism. GOP chairman Reince Priebus said, "That makes me think that Barack Obama has a problem with the American dream."[15] Attempting to capitalize on Obama's statement, the RNC chose "We Built It" to be the convention theme. Priebus said the convention speakers would "remind American that we are a nation made great not by Washington but by the men and women who summoned the inner drive, discipline, and persistent effort to achieve their dreams within the free-enterprise system."[16] In other words, the Republicans intended to return to Reagan's conservative romance.

Prominent speaking roles at the Republican convention were filled by rising stars and key leaders within the party—Florida senator Marco Rubio, New Jersey governor Chris Christie, and former secretary of state Condoleezza Rice, among others—along with the presidential nominee's wife, Ann Romney, vice presidential nominee Paul Ryan, and presidential nominee Mitt Romney. They charged President Obama and Democrats with endangering the American Dream through the administration's failed policies and unfulfilled promises. They responded to what they called a disappointed and disillusioned electorate with a message focused on freedom of choice and self-determination through the creation of opportunity for individuals so they could rise to a better life through their effort and God-given abilities.

The Republicans also needed to inoculate voters against the Democrat's traditional charge that Republicans were uncaring, dispassionate, and committed only to the survival of the fittest. To complicate matters, Romney's wealth, his connections to big business and Wall Street, and his career as a venture capitalist easily fed into the Democrats' narrative. And Romney's difficulty personally connecting with voters reinforced the Democrats' contention that he "just didn't get" the struggles of the American people.

The convention's primetime slot from 10 to 11 on the convention's first night paired Chris Christie, the straight-talking governor of New Jersey, with Ann Romney. Ann Romney's speech featured an unusual political theme—love. She spoke of her love for her husband, the love of a mother for her children and grandchildren, and the love "we all share for Americans, our brothers and sisters, who are going through difficult times, whose days are never easy, nights are always long, and whose work never seems to be done."[17] The opening section of Ann Romney's speech addressed the challenges the American people faced, giving special attention to the struggles of the "moms of the nation," a significant group of voters in the coming election.

She also shared her personal story as the daughter of a Welsh immigrant, told of meeting Mitt Romney, described their early years of marriage as college students, and countered the description of the marriage as "storybook," saying "in the storybooks I read, there were never long, long, rainy winter afternoons in a house with five boys screaming at once. And those storybooks never seemed to have chapters called *MS* or *breast cancer*." She described her husband as "good and decent, a "warm and loving and patient" man who "has tried to live his life with a set of values centered on family, faith, and love of one's fellow man." While acknowledging their success as "beyond their dreams," she said their success allowed them to care for their family and "to help others in ways that we could never have imagined." Although their capacity to give was far greater than others, she again identified with the motivations of people who share their values, saying, "we're no different than the millions of Americans who quietly help their neighbors, their churches, and their communities." Ann Romney certainly echoed Obama's belief that "we are our brother's keeper."

She also spoke of "communal good" within the business environment, discussing Mitt Romney's success as a businessman. The success of one extends to the prosperity of others: "But because this is America, that small company which grew, has helped so many others lead better lives. The jobs that grew from the risks they took have become college educations, first homes. That success has helped fund scholarships, pensions, and retirement funds. This is the genius of America: dreams fulfilled help others launch new dreams."

Ann Romney's speech framed the conservative romance of individual success and achievement with a focus on caring for others. She offered "rhetorical proof" for the validity of the conservative romance in the story of her immigrant father and others like him who she says laid the foundation on which she and her husband built lives "beyond their dreams," enabling them to then extended the American dream to their own children and to others. Her strong emphasis on the family and the importance of economic opportunity for families was consistent with the traditional conservative romance, while attempted to overcome the distance created by wealth and privilege associated with the Romney's story by identifying with women through her lived experience as a mother.

New Jersey governor Chris Christie's keynote speech followed Ann Romney's, creating a jarring contrast. Christie's theme might be characterized as "tough love." Christie said of all the lessons his mother ever taught him, the greatest was that "there would be times in your life when you have to choose between being loved and being respected. She told me that love without respect was always fleeting but that respect could grow into real and lasting love."[18] Christie applied her lesson to the present political environment: "I believe we have become paralyzed, paralyzed by our desire to be loved. . . . Our leaders of today have decided it's more important to be popular, to say and do what's easy, and say yes rather than to say no, when no is what is required." Christie's approach veered sharply away from the positive, can-do spirit usually associated with the conservative romance.

Christie accused Democrats of pandering and dividing the American people in order to be loved. Republicans, he said, would tell the American people the hard truths about fiscal realities, make tough choices about entitlement reform, and take on powerful teacher's unions to reform a failing education system. He said, "We believe that if we tell the people the truth that they will act bigger than the pettiness we see in Washington, D.C." Democrats on the other hand, said Christie, believe the American people need to be "coddled by big government" and would prey on, scare, divide, and misinform them in order to win the election. Leadership in Christie's terms required a president who would "tell us the hard truths we need to hear to put us back on a path to growth and create good-paying private-sector jobs again in America." Of course, much of the hard truth Republicans felt the public needed to hear was a series of noes to government programs that voters considered essential in hard economic times.

Unfortunately for the Republicans, Christie's choice of language and examples reinforced the image of Romney as someone who "likes being able to fire people," a Romney quotation used in the primary period and into the general election to cast Romney as a heartless venture capitalist who closed plants and shipped jobs overseas to increase his personal wealth.[19] At the very least, Christie's tone—attacking, tough—undermined Ann Romney's emphasis on compassion, exposing a lack of consistency in the Republicans' convention message.

The second and third nights of the convention featured inspirational leaders of the party and the nominees. Former secretary of state Condoleezza Rice and vice presidential nominee Paul Ryan spoke on Wednesday night. Florida governor Mark Rubio's speech on Thursday night led into the nominee Mitt Romney's speech, which closed the convention.

As the convention progressed that week, Republicans painted a national picture very similar to the one Democrats had described four years earlier. Vice presidential nominee Paul Ryan delivered the Republicans' foundational argument calling for a change in leadership: "The recovery that was promised is nowhere in sight. Right now twenty-three million men and women are struggling to find work. Twenty-three million people, unemployed or underemployed. Nearly one in six Americans is living in poverty. Millions of young Americans have graduated from college during the Obama presidency, ready to use their gifts and get moving in life. Half of them can't find the work they studied for or any work at all. So here's the question: without a change in leadership, why would the next four years be any different from the last four years?"[20]

Ironically, the Republican description of the contemporary scene sounded strikingly similar to Obama's message four years earlier. The opportunity central to the American Dream was slipping away from most Americans.

A key failure of Obama's first term, according to Republicans, was the federal government's role in diminishing "freedom," a central value of the individualist version of the American Dream. Florida senator Mark Rubio asserted that the federal government's role "is to protect our rights and serve our interests," nothing more.[21] Yet the American scene was dominated by big government, a weakened economy, less security for older Americans, and less opportunity for the young, in the Republican construction. Rubio accused Democrats of limiting choice in health care, imposing excessive rules and regulations, and using "tired and old big-government ideas." Vice presidential nominee Paul Ryan characterized "Obamacare" as "more than two thousand pages of rules, mandates, taxes, fees, and fines that have no place in a free country." Democratic proposals were, according to Rubio, "ideas that people come to American to get away from, ideas that threaten to make America more like the rest of the world, instead of helping the world become more like America."

In contrast to the Democrats' desire to create opportunity through governmental action, Republicans reiterated the American narrative in which ordinary people do extraordinary things because of the opportunity created through the free-enterprise system. America's prosperity, Rubio argued, didn't happen "because our government simply spent more. It happened because our people used their own money to open a business. And when they succeed, they hire more people, who then invest or spend their money in the economy, helping others start a business and create jobs." The importance of small business, fueled by individual dreams and work, was central to the Republican message.

The Republican narrative also celebrated the small-business owner in very human terms, honoring the hard work, sacrifice, and courage of ordinary people. Ryan humanized the Republican theme, We Built It, saying, "if small-business people say they made it on their own, all they are saying is that nobody else worked seven days a week in their place. Nobody showed up in their place to open the door at five in the morning. Nobody did their thinking and worrying and sweating for them." At the convention that night an individual's work was given greater value than any external assistance the person might have had in building a business.

The convention celebrated communal values with multiple speakers following Ann Romney's introduction to the theme, reaffirming Reagan's core values of "family, community, faith"[22]: Families take care of each other, neighbors help neighbors, and good people come together in their communities to help others. Ryan directly answered Obama's contention that Republicans in charge would abandon those in need. Ryan said, "We have responsibilities, one to another—we do not each face the world alone. And the greatest of all responsibilities is that of the strong to protect the weak. The truest measure of any society is how it treats those who cannot defend or care for themselves." Yet Republicans clearly prefer private responses to address communal values, turning to government solutions only for those situations private action cannot address adequately.

Indeed the Republicans offered a clear choice, Ryan said, between "more freedom or more government." Ryan turned directly to the American-journey metaphor, saying the Democrats and Republicans offered very different journeys through life: The Democrats offered "a dull, adventureless journey from one entitlement to the next, a government-planned life, a country where everything is free but us. Listen to the way we're spoken to already, as if everyone is stuck in some class or station in life, victims of circumstances beyond our control, with government there to help us cope with our fate." Ryan shifted the emphasis in the Democratic construction to a scene constraining the individual and denying progress. The Republicans, on the other hand, offered the journey Ryan had experienced, "an American journey where I could think for myself, decide for myself, define happiness for myself. That's what we do in this country. That's the American Dream. That's freedom, and I'll take it any day over the supervision and sanctimony of the central planners." Government "supervisors" and "elites," in Ryan's terms, take away individual freedom from the common people.

Freedom was also central to the Republican view of foreign policy. Former secretary of state Condoleezza Rice asked, "Where does America stand?" and answered unequivocally, "We stand for free people and free markets. We will defend and support them. We will sustain a balance of power that favors freedom."[23] She noted the ultimate sacrifice of men and women in the military and also noted how important it was that the United States "speak for those who would otherwise not have a voice." She tied the nation's leadership internationally to its economic challenges domestically, saying that "the world knows that when a nation loses control of its finances it eventually loses control of its destiny. That is not the American that has inspired people to follow our lead." She highlighted the need for energy independence and called for trade agreements to support an open global economy with free and fair trade.

Rice also spoke to two key domestic issues: immigration and education. She said, "More than at any other time in history greatness is built on mobilizing human potential and ambition" and calls for immigration reform to "welcome the world's most ambitious people." Rice defined education as "the civil-rights issue of our day," calling for greater school choice, "particularly for poor parents, whose kids, very often minorities, are trapped in failing neighborhood schools." She said failing to address the issue of education would "condemn generations to joblessness and hopefulness and life on the government dole. If we do anything less we will endanger our global imperative for competitiveness. And if we do anything less we will tear apart the fabric of who we are and cement the turn toward entitlement and grievance." The need for high standards, ambition, and achievement was captured in Rice's compelling personal story.

Over the course of two nights Republican leaders described an American Dream that was slipping away: Obama-administration policies had not restored the dream. Rather, the "tired, old big-government solutions" stifled freedom and economic growth. The Republicans offered an alternative path focused on individual freedom to achieve within a free-enterprise system, focusing on the dreams, work, and risk of small-businesses owners who built the American economy.

On the final night of the convention, after Rubio articulated the conservative romance—and a bizarre interlude where actor Clint Eastwood dialogued with an empty chair—nominee Mitt Romney's challenge was to pull together the key themes from across the convention in his acceptance address, chart the course for the general-election campaign, and establish his image as a caring and capable leader. He began his speech looking back to 2008 and a "fresh excitement about the possibilities of a new president."[24] He said the optimism and confidence for the future evident after Obama's election was uniquely American and part of the immigrant spirit that defines the country, one defined by freedom: "Freedom of religion. Freedom to speak their mind. Freedom to build a life. And, yes, freedom to build a business. With their own hands." Yet four years later, Romney said, President Obama's "promises gave way to disappointment and division."

Romney said that in the face of this division and disappointment, the Republicans offered a choice, including a choice of leadership. Most of the speech told his own life story—first his personal story and then the story of his success as a business-man. He talked of his immigrant father who worked as a carpenter, then as a leader of a Detroit automobile company, and finally as governor of Michigan. Romney's parents, he said, had provided a loving home and an "everyday example" as true partners. And he left Detroit because he needed to prove himself away from his fa-ther's influence, working long hours and weekends, often leaving Ann to guide their five sons through homework and school. A community of friends and their church supported them. Romney said their story was indicative of America: "We look to our communities, our faiths, our families for our joy, our support, in good times and bad. It is both how we live our lives and why we live our lives. The strength and power and goodness of America has always been based on the strength and power and goodness of our communities, our families, our faiths."

Romney then told his professional story, focusing on the creation of Bain Capital. He spoke of starting a company with some friends, not certain of their success, and eventually growing a business that is a "great American success story." He said he and his partners weren't always successful, "but no one ever is in the real world of business. That's what this president doesn't seem to understand: Business and grow-ing jobs is about taking risk, sometimes failing, sometimes succeeding, but always striving. It is about dreams." Romney highlighted the role of risk played in the con-servative romance and the ever-present possibility of failure.

Romney then tied the American Dream to the opportunity created in a free-enterprise system: "The genius of the American free-enterprise system," he said, is "to harness the extraordinary creativity and talent and industry of the American people with a system that is dedicated to creating tomorrow's prosperity rather than trying to redistribute today's." His answer to the nation's problems was therefore "lots of jobs." He promised to secure energy independence, reform education, forge new trade agree-ments, cut the deficit and balance the national budget, and champion small business by reducing taxes, simplifying and modernizing regulations, and repealing Obama's health care–reform legislation. Romney said he would not raise taxes on the middle class, would protect the sanctity of life, honor the institution of marriage, and protect freedom of religion. He said he would return to the bipartisan foreign-policy legacy of Truman and Reagan because "a free world is a more peaceful world."

In the end Romney called for a "united America" to unleash the economy, uphold constitutional rights, care for the poor and the sick, honor and respect the elderly, and give a helping hand to those in need. He said he would work "to restore America, to lift our eyes to a better future. That future is our destiny. That future is out there. It is waiting for us. Our children deserve it, our nation depends upon it, the peace and freedom of the world require it. And with your help we will deliver it."

As the Republican National Convention closed, the nation was offered an alternative vision for the future, one based squarely in the traditional conservative romance focused on individual ambition and achievement made possible by the opportunity America provided. Republicans promised that once in power they would restore freedom and opportunity by reducing the burden of government on Americans and American business. By making tough choices in order to balance the budget, repealing Obama's health-care reform, and empowering small-business owners through reduced and modernized regulation, the Republicans said they would unleash the economy, create jobs, and offer greater prosperity to Americans. They would restore "opportunity" to the American scene.

The Democratic National Convention

Four days after the close of the Republican National Convention, Democrats gathered in Charlotte, North Carolina, to see their own lineup of rising stars and party leaders—San Antonio mayor Julian Castro, U.S. senate candidate Elizabeth Warren, Massachusetts senator John Kerry, and former president Bill Clinton, among others, along with First Lady Michelle Obama, Vice President Joe Biden, and President Barack Obama. Unlike in 2008, this time as the incumbent President Obama had to defend his record and inspire voters to give him four more years to pursue his agenda. While he remained true to the American promise he'd articulated in 2008, subtle changes in that promise, along with pointed attacks on the Republican alternative vision, created a somber tone at the 2012 Democratic National Convention, where he called for patience, perseverance, and sacrifice to complete the long and difficult journey ahead.

The first night of the convention featured two skilled speakers, Julian Castro, mayor of San Antonio, and the first lady, Michelle Obama, who together reinforced President Obama's articulation of the American promise.

Echoing Obama's 2004 keynote address at the convention, Castro told "his American story" of a grandmother who emigrated from Mexico to the United States and worked as a maid, a cook, and a babysitter to support his mother so that she in turn could provide a better life for Castro and his twin brother, Joaquin. He then placed their story within the greater American story, "where my grandmother's generation and generations before always saw beyond the horizons of their own lives and their own circumstances."[25] The work they did—building infrastructure, creating higher-education systems, and securing civil rights—created opportunity "for a decent job, a secure retirement, the chance for your children to do better than you did." Castro's examples featured communal, societal contributions to the American scene, not individual achievements.

Michelle Obama similarly retold the Obamas' stories, placing a clear emphasis on sacrifice. She said, "Barack and I were both raised by families who didn't have much in the way of money or material possessions but who had given us something far more valuable: their unconditional love, their unflinching sacrifice, and the chance to go places they had never imagined for themselves."[26] She poignantly recounted her father's struggle to work as he fought against the debilitating effects of multiple sclerosis and spoke of her parents' determination to give her "the kind of education they could only dream of," sharing the financial challenges of their education in detail: "And when my brother and I finally made it to college, nearly all of our tuition came from student loans and grants, but my dad still had to pay a tiny portion of that tuition himself. And every semester he was determined to pay that bill right on time, even taking out loans when he fell short." She honored her father's work and contribution and yet noted that his work alone could not have provided the education he dreamed of giving his children. Castro used the bootstrap metaphor to make the image vivid: "Now, in Texas we believe in the rugged individual. Texas may be the one place where people actually still have bootstraps, and we expect folks to pull themselves up by them. But we also recognize there are some things we can't do alone." The Democrats saw communal effort as essential to individual achievement for many Americans.

Castro reinforced this theme by contrasting his friends from high school in San Antonio with his classmates at Stanford and Harvard, saying that "the difference wasn't one of intelligence or drive. The difference was opportunity." And opportunity doesn't just happen, the Democrats insisted; it requires government action. Michelle Obama listed the investments in opportunity made during her husband's first term: commitments to equal pay for equal work, saving the auto industry, cutting taxes for working families and small businesses, saving the economy from the brink of disaster, securing health care for all citizens, and increasing financial aid for education and lowering rates for student loans. All of these measures, she said, were communal investments to promote greater success for individuals, families, communities, and the nation. In the Democratic worldview, Michelle Obama said, "when we invest in people we're investing in our shared prosperity. And when we neglect that responsibility we risk our promise as a nation."

Castro and Michelle Obama both extended the time frame for achieving the broad-based prosperity of their dream. Castro insisted that "the American dream is not a sprint, or even a marathon, but a relay," with each generation handing off "the fruits of its labors" to the next. Michelle Obama adopted a generational story as well, extending the narrative beyond any one administration, asserting that "if they could raise beams of steel to the sky, send a man to the Moon, connect the world with a touch of a button, then surely we can keep on sacrificing and building for our own kids and grandkids, right?" And so she called for perseverance.

Thus the first night of the Democratic convention called voters to stay true to the communitarian Democratic vision, one grounded in a long story of struggle.

Both Castro and Michelle Obama framed the election in generational terms, thus recasting the current economic conditions as a stage in a long story of sacrifice that ultimately would lead to greater prosperity, if not for the current generation then for the one that follows.

On the second night the Democrats attacked the Republican vision of the American Dream and described their own policies as "investments in opportunity" designed to produce fairness, to give all citizens access to the American promise. They argued that Republican policies create inequity, less opportunity, and greater division between the wealthy and the middle and lower classes. Their argument for fairness was articulated clearly by Massachusetts Senate candidate Elizabeth Warren and former president Bill Clinton. Warren stated it quite simply: "People feel like the system is rigged against them. And here's the painful part: They're right. The system is rigged."[27] Warren said Republicans protected large corporations, did the bidding of Wall Street CEOs, and gave tax breaks to millionaires and billionaires, all while proposing tax hikes for the middle class and planning to "pulverize financial reform, voucherize Medicare, and vaporize Obamacare." She said the Republican vision was clear: "I got mine; the rest of you are on your own."

The Republicans received a slightly more generous attribution of motives from former president Bill Clinton, who said they "were honorable people who believed what they said" and would keep their commitments, but his summary of their commitments was as devastating as Warren's. Clinton said, "they want the same old policies that got us in trouble in the first place."[28] Clinton gave his accounting of the last four years, contrasting Obama's accomplishments with the Bush administration's, with Congressional Republican action, and with Romney's positions. In each comparison Obama and the Democrats earned positive numbers while the Republicans scored "zero." In the end, Clinton said the decision was between two strikingly different views of the future: "If you want a winner-take-all, you're-on-your-own society you should support the Republican ticket. But if you want a country of shared opportunities and shared responsibility, a we're-all-in-this-together society, you should vote for Barack Obama and Joe Biden." Clinton offered the key communitarian values as a campaign theme: "a nation of shared opportunities, shared responsibilities, shared prosperity, a shared sense of community."

Senator John Kerry addressed foreign policy and offered quite a different picture from the one painted by former secretary of State Condoleezza Rice. Kerry said that at the beginning of his first term in 2005 President Obama had inherited "disaster and disarray": "A war of choice in Iraq had become a war without end, and a war of necessity in Afghanistan had become a war of neglect. Our alliances were shredded. Our moral authority was in tatters. America was isolated in the world. Our military was stretched to the breaking point, Iran marching towards a nuclear weapon unchecked, and Osama bin Laden was still plotting."[29]

He said President Obama subsequently restored the nation's moral authority and kept his promises to end the war in Iraq, to end the war in Afghanistan, and to destroy Al Qaeda, noting the success of his order to kill Osama bin Laden. He gave the president credit for "unprecedented" security cooperation with Israel, signing a historic treaty with Russia to reduce the threat of nuclear weapons, and leading a coalition to free the people of Libya. He compared Obama, "a president who has made America lead like America again," to Romney and Ryan, an "extreme and expedient candidate who lacks the judgment and the vision so vital to the Oval Office, the most inexperienced foreign-policy twosome to run for president and vice president in decades." Kerry said President Barack Obama had delivered on his promises in foreign policy during his first term, restoring America's promise as a leader for peace and stability in the world.

Vice President Joe Biden served as a "character reference" for the president, reinforcing both Michelle Obama's testimony to the president's courage, compassion, and decisiveness and Kerry's characterization of the president as a strong commander-in-chief. Biden's speech focused on two stories: Obama's decision to bail out the auto industry and his decision to order the attack on Osama bin Laden.

Biden mirrored Clinton's attacks on the Republicans, excoriating them for looking backward to failed policies, and contrasted Obama's decisions with what Romney purportedly would have done faced with the same situation. He said that for Romney the decision about the auto industry was reduced to "balance sheets and write-offs."[30] For President Obama, on the other hand, Biden insisted the decision was about "restoring America's pride." He reported that when Romney was asked about bin Laden in 2007 he'd said that "it's not worth moving heaven and earth and spending billions of dollars just to catch one person." Biden believed that Obama, by contrast, understood that the search for bin Laden "was about a lot more than taking a monstrous leader off the battlefield. It was about so much more than that. It was about righting an unspeakable wrong. It was about—literally, it was about, it was about healing an unbearable wound, a nearly unbearable wound in America's heart." Biden characterized Romney as "calculating," again feeding the impression that Romney "didn't get it," while the president, on the other hand, had an emotional understanding of what Americans needed.

The Democrats deftly set the stage for the president. They rearticulated the American Dream using communitarian values, upholding hard work and individual effort within a context of fairness, and contrasted their calls for investment in opportunity with rapacious, selfish, and destructive Republican policies. Yet at a time when Americans were frustrated, fearful, and impatient for relief from the economic downturn, the Democrats were also asking voters to sacrifice and persevere in order to build a foundation for a future generation's prosperity.

President Obama's 2012 acceptance speech extended the American Dream narrative he first articulated in 2004 and reaffirmed in 2008, defining the American promise as "the basic bargain at the heart of America's story, the promise that hard work will pay off, that responsibility will be rewarded, that everyone gets a fair shot and everyone does their fair share and everyone plays by the same rules, from Main Street to Wall Street to Washington, D.C."[31] He reprised his analysis of Republican policies that had led to the economic crisis in 2008 and called the Republican proposals for 2012 the "same prescriptions they've had for the last thirty years." Obama contrasted the backward-looking policies of the Republicans with his call to move forward. He outlined his plans in corporate-regulation, energy, education, foreign, deficit-reduction, and tax policy. He reaffirmed his commitment to protect the poor and middle class and to sustain the social safety net of Medicare and Social Security.

Given the ongoing challenges in his first administration and the uncertainty for the future, Obama needed to motivate his voters to stay the course, which he did by introducing a new concept to his American Dream narrative—citizenship.

The word *citizenship* does not appear in either Obama's 2004 keynote or his 2008 acceptance address. Yet in his 2012 speech citizenship played a pivotal role and was fundamental to his American Dream narrative. He used the idea of citizenship to transform individual responsibilities into communal responsibility, thereby moving away from a careful balance between personal and societal responsibility to a narrative fully grounded in communal responsibility. He first reasserted individualism as central to the American promise, reasserting the American belief in "inalienable rights, that no man or government can take away." He spoke of personal responsibility, individual initiative, and the belief that success is earned and not an entitlement. He said, "we honor the strivers, the dreamers, the risk takers, the entrepreneurs who have always been the driving force behind our free-enterprise system, the greatest engine of growth and prosperity that the world's ever known." After this expression of America's individualist spirit, he signaled a response to individualism using the conjunction *but*: "But we also believe in something called citizenship—a word at the very heart of our founding, a word at the very essence of our democracy, the idea that this country only works when we accept certain obligations to one another and to future generations."

He then elaborated the concept of citizenship by intertwining individual, communal, and national interests: "We believe that when a CEO pays his autoworkers enough to buy the cars that they build, the whole company does better." Obama deftly transformed a business decision, one typically considered part of the free market, into a political act, one of citizenship. He then insisted that regulation that stops lenders from enticing families into mortgages they cannot afford protects the family from unsustainable debt, protects the values of neighbors' homes, and supports the housing economy of the nation. The communal good provides for private security. And then he spoke of a child rising above poverty with the combined support of good teachers, academic achievement, and financial aid, which supports her college attendance, allowing her to perhaps rise to become a national leader creating a communal good. Thus, for Obama, teaching well and doing homework are a form of citizenship. Obama then acknowledged communal obligations outside of government action—"churches and charities can often make more of a difference than a poverty program alone"—and emphasized that responsibility and fairness are both individual and communal obligations—"We don't want handouts for people who refuse to help themselves, and we certainly don't want bailouts for banks that break the rules." Individual effort is important, Obama insisted, because it serves society as well as self-interest. So in Obama's narrative neither individual effort alone nor government action exclusively would move the nation forward. Both were central to his American Dream narrative.

Having embedded the individual into the communal, Obama then gave voice to the communitarian vision of the American Dream: "We the people recognize that we have responsibilities as well as rights; that our destinies are bound together; that a freedom which asks only What's in it for me?, a freedom without a commitment to others, a freedom without love or charity or duty or patriotism, is unworthy of our founding ideals and those who died in their defense." By implication, those who fail in their commitment to others, a charge made frequently against Republicans throughout the Democratic convention, are failing as citizens to uphold the American Dream.

In addition, Obama asserted that citizenship calls voters to action because "we understand that America is not about what can be done for us. It's about what can be done by us, together through the hard and frustrating but necessary work of self-government." Governing, thus, is the work done by citizens. Obama then shifted the election outcome back to the people: "So you see, the election four years ago wasn't about me. It was about you. My fellow citizens, you were the change."

Within this framework of citizenry, Obama then credited the citizenry for the major achievements of his first administration, starting each paragraph with the phrase, "you're the reason" and ending with "you did that" or "you made that possible." The citizenry, he said, provided health care, financial-aid funding, access for immigrants, repealed the Don't Ask Don't Tell policy for gays in the military, and ended the war in Iraq.

This transition from an election decision to a shared journey, one the citizenry began four years earlier, was the foundation of Obama's campaign theme, Forward. To elect Romney, then, would constitute a negative action, a turning away from the progress Obama insists was made *by the people* over the previous four years. And so he called for perseverance because he "never said this journey would be easy, and I won't promise that now. Yes, our path is harder, but it leads to a better place. Yes, our road is longer, but we travel it together." To vote for Romney, then, would be to abandon commitments, to turn away from progress, and to renege on a promise *the people* had made in 2008.

As Obama built to the final crescendo of the speech, he called citizens to continue the journey toward a more perfect union: "We don't turn back. We leave no one behind. We pull each other up. We draw strength from our victories. And we learn from our mistakes. But we keep our eyes fixed on that distant horizon knowing that providence is with us and that we are surely blessed to be citizens of the greatest nation on earth."

NARRATIVE DOMINANCE IN AMERICAN POLITICS

Back in 2007 Rowland and Jones argued that Obama had possibly reclaimed the American Dream narrative for liberals, as his 2004 keynote address at the Democratic National Convention "forecast the possibility of a sea change in political ideology based not on policy but on narrative preference."[32] The 2012 election possibly confirmed their prediction, when the majority of citizens chose President Obama's American promise, a story balancing individual and communal responsibilities within a broad conception of citizenship. Resonance with Obama's narrative was perhaps especially strong for the middle class as they saw a lifetime of work slipping away in an extended period of economic distress. Obama's discourse gave them solace, suggesting that the system itself was the cause of their struggle and offering a new way forward if they were willing to sacrifice for the next generation.

Republicans, meanwhile, continued to embrace the conservative romance that had dominated political discourse for most of the previous twenty-five years: They promised that Republican principles and policies would support individual achievement and self-determination within a free-enterprise system. Their stories acknowledged that self-determination involved risk taking and possible failure. However, they believed the trade-off between freedom and risk was essential to the American story. When they upheld communal values of compassion and generosity, they usually focused on individual and private generosity—of neighbors helping neighbors or faith-based organizations reaching out to help others—rather than on the social safety net of entitlements. They acknowledged government's role in helping "those who cannot help themselves." Yet even their expressions of commitment to others emphasized individual responsibility. Although they pledged to preserve Medicare and Social Security, their overall narrative presented a vulnerability Obama exploited—a fear of abandonment.

President Obama and the Democrats reversed this emphasis, moving what had been Obama's "balanced" approach to the American Dream closer to the traditional emphasis on the "public good." Given the prevailing economic conditions of 2012, Obama was unable to point to a clear positive record of restored opportunity and prosperity during his first term. His convention challenge was to position his first administration and its achievements as part of a "longer journey," asking voters to sacrifice and persevere in order to move forward within the long American story of progress.

His American Dream narrative more clearly spoke of a communitarian vision of the American journey through his definition of citizenship, where a woman showing up to work, a student doing homework, or a businessperson setting a pay scale became acts of citizenship. Rather than balancing individual responsibility against social responsibility, Obama redefined individual responsibility as participation within social responsibility, where decisions ought not be made because they benefit the self or even those closest to us but ought to reflect a commitment to a broader public good. In Obama's construct the decision or action itself might not change, but the justification for the choice or action does.

In so framing of the nation's challenges, Obama acknowledged the slow progress of his first term without accepting failure. Focusing on equality, on helping those left behind, he called for self-sacrifice for the greater good, which justified government action meant to help those struggling, certainly a resonant message in 2012 for those who felt hard work and striving were simply insufficient to achieving the American Dream.

For all the thematic differences evident in the two parties' political nominating conventions of 2012, each turned to the American Dream narrative as a central rhetorical trope, thereby affirming its motivating force in American political thought and discourse. Both parties made stories of the nation's progress a central theme, accusing their opponents of proposing "old and tired" policies, of looking backward rather than moving toward a better society. Both called for a "united America," drawing on the American Dream's promise to form a "more perfect union." Stories of ordinary people achieving great things filled both conventions, with each convention emphasizing "journeys" of Americans across generations. Republican senator Marco Rubio remembered a father who worked as a bartender in the back of the room so he one day would stand in the front of a room. Democratic congressional candidate Julian Castro told a similar story, honoring the work across two generations that moved his family from a mop to a microphone on a national stage. The stories credited America as exceptional, the only place these stories were even possible, contrasting America with the birthplaces of immigrant ancestors who had come to America seeking a better life. The stories offered the "rhetorical proof" for the American Dream narrative, perpetuating its influence as a rhetorical vision for the nation.

Thus, even though in the months that followed the conventions the parties and their candidates engaged in divisive campaigning with unprecedented negative attacks, the political nominating conventions had reaffirmed the American Dream narrative, perpetuating a mythic vision of a nation and its people on a journey toward a more perfect union. Ironically the divisions that emerged within the campaign were energized by the inherent tension within the shared narrative vision of the American Dream. But whether the nation prefers one emphasis or the other at any given time does not lesson the mythic force of the American Dream in American political discourse.

NOTES

1. Chaim Perelman and L. Olbrechts-Tyteca, *The New Rhetoric: A Treatise on Argumentation* (Notre Dame, Ind.: University of Notre Dame Press, 1969), 47–50. See also Elizabeth A. Petre, "Understanding Epideictic Purpose as Invitational Rhetoric in Women's Political Convention Speeches," *Kaleidoscope* 6 (2007): 21–37.

2. Craig Allen Smith describes this process as "constitutive"; audiences are invited to accept an identity created through the candidate's rhetoric. See his "Constituting Contrasting Communities: The 2008 Nomination Acceptance Addresses," in *The 2008 Presidential Campaign: A Communication Perspective*, ed. Robert E. Denton, Jr. (Lanham, Md.: Rowman & Littlefield, 2009), 48–67.

3. Robert C. Rowland and John M. Jones, "Recasting the American Dream and American Politics: Barack Obama's Keynote Address to the 2004 Democratic National Convention," *Quarterly Journal of Speech* 93 (2007): 443.

4. Arthur M. Schlesinger, Jr., *The Cycles of American History* (Boston: Houghton-Mifflin, 1985), 23–38.

5. Walter R. Fisher, "Reaffirmation and Subversion of the American Dream," *Quarterly Journal of Speech* 59 (1973): 160.

6. Rowland and Jones, "Recasting the American Dream, 431–32.

7. Rowland and Jones, "Recasting the American Dream," 431.

8. Rowland and Jones, "Recasting the American Dream," 435.

9. "Keynote address by Barack Obama, Democratic Candidate for Senator of Illinois, at the Democratic National Convention," Federal News Service, July 27, 2004. Retrieved from LexisNexis Academic database. All subsequent references to Obama's 2004 keynote address are attributed to this source.

10. Rowland and Jones detail the rhetorical strategies Obama used to create his alternative balancing of personal and communal values in "Recasting the American Dream and American Politics."

11. "Remarks by Senator Barack Obama (D-IL), Democratic Party Nominee for President, at the 2008 Democratic National Convention; Location: Invesco Field at Mile High, Denver, Colorado," Federal News Service, August 28, 2008. Retrieved from LexisNexis Academic Database. All subsequent references to Obama's 2008 acceptance address are attributed to this source.

12. Robert C. Rowland, "The Fierce Urgency of Now: Barack Obama and the 2008 President Election," *American Behavioral Scientist* 54 (2010): 218.

13. David Grant, "Hurricane Isaac delays start of Republican National Convention in Tampa," *Christian Science Monitor*, August 25, 2012, www.csmonitor.com/USA/Elections/President/2012/0825/Hurricane-Isaac-delays-start-of-Republican-National-Convention-in-Tampa.

14. Office of the Press Secretary, "Remarks by the President at a Campaign Event in Roanoke, Virginia," the White House, www.whitehouse.gov/the-press-office/2012/07/13/remarks-president-campaign-event-roanoke-virginia/.

15. "Republican Officials Release Tuesday Convention Schedule," *PR Newswire*, August 21, 2012, www.prnewswire.com/news-releases/republican-officials-release-tuesday-convention-schedule-166912296.html.

16. "Republican Officials Release Tuesday Convention Schedule."

17. "Remarks by Ann Romney, Wife of Former Massachusetts Governor Mitt Romney (R), at the 2012 Republican National Convention Location: *Tampa Bay Times* Forum, Tampa, Florida Time: EDT Date: Tuesday, August 28, 2012," Federal News Service, August 28, 2012. Retrieved from LexisNexis Academic database. All subsequent references to Ann Romney's speech are attributed to this source.

18. "Remarks by New Jersey Governor Chris Christie (R) at the 2012 Republican National Convention Location: *Tampa Bay Times* Forum, Tampa, Florida Time: 10:35 P.M. EDT Date: Tuesday, August 28, 2012," Federal News Service, August 28, 2012. Retrieved from LexisNexis Academic database. All subsequent references to Christie's speech are attributed to this source.

19. S. A. Miller, "Rivals Rip Crack about Liking to Ax Folks Romney in Line of 'Fire,'" *New York Post*, January 10, 2012, 6. At a campaign stop in Nashua, New Hampshire, candidate Romney, in discussing health-insurance providers, said, "If you don't like what they do, you can fire them. I like being able to fire people who provide services to me." The excerpted statement was used by opponents in the Republican primary to attack Romney for not caring for working people.

20. "Remarks by Representative Paul Ryan (R-WI), Republican Nominee for Vice President, at the 2012 Republican National Convention Location: *Tampa Bay Times* Forum, Tampa, Florida Time: 10:26 P.M. EDT Date: Wednesday, August 29, 2012," Federal News

Service, August 29, 2012. Retrieved from LexisNexis Academic database. All subsequent references to Ryan's speech are attributed to this source.

21. "Remarks by Senator Marco Rubio (R-FL) at the 2012 Republican National Convention Location: *Tampa Bay Times* Forum, Tampa, Florida Time: 10:14 P.M. EDT Date: Thursday, August 30, 2012," Federal News Service, August 30, 2012. Retrieved from LexisNexis Academic database. All subsequent references to Ryan's speech are attributed to this source.

22. Henry Z. Scheele, "Ronald Reagan's 1980 Acceptance Address: A Focus on American Values," *Western Journal of Speech Communication* 48 (1984): 51–61.

23. "Remarks by Former Secretary of State Condoleezza Rice at the 2012 Republican National Convention Location: *Tampa Bay Times* Forum, Tampa, Florida Time: 9:55 P.M. EDT Date: Wednesday, August 29, 2012," Federal News Service, August 29, 2012. Retrieved from LexisNexis Academic database. All subsequent references to Rice's speech are attributed to this source.

24. "Remarks by Former Massachusetts Governor Mitt Romney (R), Republican Nominee for President, at the 2012 Republican National Convention Location: *Tampa Bay Times* Forum, Tampa, Florida Time: 10:36 P.M. EDT Date: Thursday, August 30, 2012," Federal News Service, August 30, 2012. Retrieved from LexisNexis Academic Database. All subsequent references to Mitt Romney's speech are attributed to this source.

25. "Remarks by San Antonio, Texas Mayor Julian Castro (D) at the 2012 Democratic National Convention Location: Time Warner Cable Arena, Charlotte, North Carolina Time: 10:08 P.M. EDT Date: Tuesday, September 4, 2012," Federal News Service, September 4, 2012. Retrieved from LexisNexis Academic Database. All subsequent references to Castro's speech are attributed to this source.

26. "Remarks by First Lady Michelle Obama at the 2012 Democratic National Convention Location: Time Warner Cable Arena, Charlotte, North Carolina Time: 10:39 P.M. EDT Date: Tuesday, September 4, 2012," Federal News Service, September 4, 2012. Retrieved from LexisNexis Academic database. All subsequent references to Michelle Obama's speech are attributed to this source.

27. "Remarks by Elizabeth Warren, Democratic Candidate for U.S. Senate, Massachusetts, at the 2012 Democratic National Convention Location: Time Warner Cable Arena, Charlotte, North Carolina Time: 10:15 P.M. EDT Date: Wednesday, September 5, 2012," Federal News Service, September 5, 2012. Retrieved from LexisNexis Academic database. All subsequent references to Warren's speech are attributed to this source.

28. "Nominating Speech by Former President Bill Clinton at the 2012 Democratic National Convention Location: Time Warner Cable Arena, Charlotte, North Carolina Time: 10:34 P.M. EDT Date: Wednesday, September 5, 2012," Federal News Service, September 5, 2012. Retrieved from LexisNexis Academic database. All subsequent references to Clinton's speech are attributed to this source.

29. "Remarks by Senator John Kerry (D-MA) at the 2012 Democratic National Convention Location: Time Warner Cable Arena, Charlotte, North Carolina Time: 8:42 P.M. EDT Date: Thursday, September 6, 2012," Federal News Service, September 6, 2012. Retrieved from LexisNexis Academic Database. All subsequent references to Kerry's speech are attributed to this source.

30. "Remarks by Vice President Joseph Biden at the 2012 Democratic National Convention Location: Time Warner Cable Arena, Charlotte, North Carolina Time: 9:29 P.M. EDT Date: Thursday, September 6, 2012," Federal News Service, September 6, 2012. Retrieved from LexisNexis Academic database. All subsequent references to Biden's speech are attributed to this source.

31. "Remarks by President Barack Obama at the 2012 Democratic National Convention Location: Time Warner Cable Arena, Charlotte, North Carolina Time: 10:24 P.M. EDT Date: Thursday, September 6, 2012," Federal News Service, September 6, 2012. Retrieved from LexisNexis Academic database. All subsequent references to Obama's speech are attributed to this source.

32. Rowland and Jones, "Recasting the American Dream," 428.

2

Change in the Communication Demands of Spouses in the 2012 Nominating Convention

Gwen Brown

> She is widely considered to be one of the most powerful people in Washington, yet we know little about her responsibilities or her predecessors. Her name has routinely appeared atop the annual Gallup poll of America's most admired women in the world, but there exists little systematic study of what she has done to deserve this attention. It could be argued that she is the second most powerful person in the world, even though some scholars dismiss the effort to formalize a field of study of her as "trivial" or unworthy of serious academic attention. However, recent scholarship on the matter is beginning to reverse long-standing assumptions about her and is raising some provocative and important questions. Yet many of these questions remain largely unexamined let alone answered. Indeed she is the missing link in our study of the presidency, and a strong case exists for formal study of the "unknown institution" of the office of the president: the first lady.
>
> —Robert P. Watson[1]

When Robert P. Watson offered his assessment of the literature on the role of the first lady in 1997, some scholars had already begun turning more of their focus to the study of that subject,[2] and certainly since then more work has seen publication in political science and communication journals as well as in a number of books. Some of the more recent work has focused on individual first ladies,[3] while other scholarship has analyzed media treatment of those women,[4] the roles and duties of first ladies,[5] perceptions of them,[6] and first ladies and feminism.[7] And one recent article provides us with a historical treatment of the rhetoric of first ladies and argues that we have seen "The Rise of the Rhetorical First Lady."[8]

Seldom covered in the literature is any analysis of the role that the first lady or aspiring first ladies play in the political campaigns of their spouses, and what is noticeably lacking in the literature is much in the way of critical treatment of the roles contemporary presidential candidates' spouses—both first ladies and aspiring first ladies—play at nominating conventions.[9] This is particularly surprising given the changing and increasingly important part they take in the transition from the close of the primary season of the campaign, through the nominating phase, and on to the general election campaign. As Trent and Friedenberg tell us, it is in the nominating phase that we see four important communication functions occur: (1) the electoral process is reaffirmed and legitimized, (2) the party's candidate gains legitimacy as nominee and spokesperson for the party, (3) the party demonstrates unity in general and specifically in support of its nominee, and (4) the nominee and the campaign themes and issues are introduced to the nation.[10] The nominating convention marks a critical, liminal stage in our political process; once that stage is concluded it is time for the general campaign, time to "close the sale"; it is—as Trent and Friedenberg also remind us—"electing time."[11] Thus the performance of the party leaders and the candidates as well as their surrogates at the nominating convention can become a key factor in our voting decisions.

Myra Gutin, who has written extensively on first ladies, tells us that "the tradition of a political spouse speaking at a national convention is relatively new."[12] In fact, prior to 1992 only three first ladies ever gave speeches to national nominating conventions. In 1940 when Eleanor Roosevelt, at her husband's request, gave the first speech by a presidential spouse at a convention her goal was not so much to endorse her husband's candidacy as it was to bring about unity and shore up support for his vice presidential choice. Giving more traditional remarks were Patricia Nixon in 1972 and Nancy Reagan in 1984. In 1992 Barbara Bush spoke, but Hillary Clinton did not, and in 1996 both Hillary Clinton and Elizabeth Dole were featured speakers. In 2000 Laura Bush spoke, and Tipper Gore introduced a video in which she narrated a series of family photographs, but she did not give a traditional, formal address to the convention. From 2004 to the present the spouses of both presidential nominees have given featured speeches: Laura Bush and Teresa Heinz Kerry in 2004, Michelle Obama and Cindy McCain in 2008, and Michelle Obama and Ann Romney in 2012. As Gutin says, "Today it is expected that spouses will deliver a speech to the nominating conventions. . . . Today political spouses are both seen and heard— they are silent no more."[13] Indeed the role of the spouses at the nominating convention has changed, and they are more prominent; they are "seen and heard," and two moments during the convention are the focus of their appearances: the convention address and the convention film. Together these two events, I contend, demonstrate an evolving role for presidential spouses, and while the 2012 convention films and wives' speeches meet the generic expectations of earlier speeches and films, they also mark an important change in the communication functions they fulfill. To set the stage for understanding that change, we begin with the genre of the spouse's convention address during the period in which it became an expected part of the nominating convention—from Barbara Bush in 1992 to Michelle Obama and Ann Romney in 2012. We then briefly survey the role the spouses played in convention films in that same period. Finally, we focus on the marked change in the communication function of spouses' remarks and film appearances in the 2012 campaign.

THE CONVENTION ADDRESS

Limited attention has been paid in the communication literature to convention rhetoric, and most of the extant work focuses on the acceptance speeches of individual presidential and vice presidential candidates or analyzes keynote addresses.[14] And while convention rhetoric has received some attention, only a scant portion of that work has focused on the speeches of women at conventions. A notable exception is Elizabeth A. Petre's "Understanding Epideictic Purpose as Invitational Rhetoric in Women's Political Convention Speeches."[15] Petre analyzes the speeches of eight women at the 2004 conventions of both parties; those eight include two candidates' wives (Laura Bush and Teresa Heinz Kerry), four daughters (Jenna and Barbara Bush and Vanessa and Alexandra Kerry), Senator and former first lady Hillary Clinton, and Senator and spouse of a former presidential candidate Elizabeth Dole. Petre notes the ceremonial nature of the occasions and classifies the women's speeches as epideictic in form and purpose—that is, speeches praising the candidate the rhetor endorses and, by either overt comparison or through silence, implying blame on the opponent. Then through the lens of Foss and Griffin's concept of "invitational rhetoric,"[16] Petre demonstrates how the epideictic purpose is fulfilled. "Invitational rhetoric," according to Foss and Griffin, is a distinctly feminist perspective that describes women's rhetoric often as "an invitation to the audience to enter the rhetor's world and see it as the rhetor does."[17] Petre adds that "invitational rhetoric takes the form of offering perspectives and of creating external conditions [that] allow others to present their ideas openly and without judgment."[18] Thus, to complete its epideictic purpose women rhetors engage in "invitational" rhetorical forms that encourage the audience to understand and participate in the perspectives of the rhetor, to see the world as she does, to "try on" vicariously her points of view—regardless of whether or to what degree that point of view is found to be persuasive.

Petre identifies two distinct strategies that embody the invitational style in the women's speeches from the 2004 convention—praising America's past and the use of narratives to personalize—and she provides examples of both strategies. In praising the nation's past, the speakers provide the audience with a sense of shared heritage and values and indicate that the candidate understands, identifies with, and celebrates that heritage and those values. Narratives, Petre notes, are often used to suggest speakers' personal perspectives and to "reveal the 'softer side' of themselves and their respective candidates."[19] Among those Petre included in her study were two spouses—Laura Bush and Teresa Heinz Kerry—who used those two strategies. Bush and Kerry, though, were not unique in employing the strategies. These same elements were also routinely present in the recent convention speeches of presidential candidates' spouses (first ladies and contenders for that role) and thus can be counted as strategic responses to the rhetorical demands they face in their participation in the genre of the spouse's convention speech.

The reiteration of the nation's past as praiseworthy and exemplary of shared values came in multiple ways from spouses. For example, Barbara Bush[20] (1992) praised the nation's family values that "extended to neighbors, even the community itself," the many "points of light" (vignettes that were interspersed throughout the convention that highlighted positive and charitable actions, or deeds by ordinary citizens) that "made me really proud to be an American," and the values of "integrity, courage, strength" the nation requires of its leaders. Like Barbara Bush, Hillary Clinton[21] (1996) also praised the family and family values and described the nation as individuals who are all part of the "American family." That family is composed, she asserted, of moms and dads and teachers and coaches and police officers and doctors and nurses and volunteers and others who are "all responsible for ensuring that children are raised in a nation that doesn't just talk about family values but acts in ways that values families." Elizabeth Dole[22] (1996) identified the values the nation expects from a leader and noted that these were the values passed on to her husband by his family: "values like honesty, decency, respect; values like personal responsibility, hard work, love of God, love of family, and patriotism." In her first convention speech in 2008, Michelle Obama[23] praised her husband for reminding the nation of the "great American story," the story of "men and women gathered in churches and union halls, in high school gyms, and people who stood up and marched and risked everything they had, refusing to settle, determined to mold our future into the shape of our ideals." In that same year, Cindy McCain[24] praised the "uniquely American faith in and compassion for each other's neighbors. A helping hand and friendly support has always been our way. It's no surprise that Americans are the most generous people in history." And in 2012 Ann Romney[25] singled out American moms for praise ("You are the best of America. You are the hope of America. There would not be an America without you.") and recalled that her father had often "reminded my brothers and me how fortunate we were to grow up in a place like America." Implicit in all the speeches given by spouses was the idea that their husbands' characters and careers were emblematic of and contributed to the shared heritage and values that were so praiseworthy.

Petre's second strategy, the use of narratives to highlight the personal, is also routinely included in the speeches. For example, in 2012 First Lady Michelle Obama[26] described her husband as a man who, despite his lofty office, remained unchanged in important ways, a humble man, a man who cared little for himself and more for others. She verified these characteristics with a narrative that recalled their early relationship. He remained, she says, "still the guy who'd picked me up for our dates in a car that was so rusted out, I could actually see the pavement going by through a hole in the passenger-side door . . . he was the guy whose proudest possession was a coffee table he'd found in a dumpster and whose only pair of decent shoes was half a size too small." In a section of her speech that touted her husband's accomplishments with family and medical-leave legislation and his goals of passing flex-time legislation and health-insurance legislation, Hillary Clinton (1996) sought to establish empathy and identification as she described a time when their only child, Chelsea, had to spend the night in a hospital following tonsil surgery: "Bill and I couldn't sleep at all that night." The Clintons, then, can clearly understand the stress parents undergo who might benefit from such legislation. Barbara Bush (1992) included a comical narrative that, in the end, turned serious and illustrated the qualities of leadership, respect, and compassion she thought her husband possessed:

> Thank heavens George didn't expect our kids to be perfect. They weren't. Once, when one of the boys hit a baseball through the Vanderhoff second-story window, I called George to see what dire punishment should be handed out, and all he said was, "The Vanderhoff second-story window, what a hit." I don't believe that George ever had to punish the children. He had a quiet way of making them want to do right and give reverence to God. And it made such a difference having his wise hand guiding them. You know, to us, family means putting your arms around each other and being there.

Ann Romney (2012) attempted to replace the image of a wealthy and privileged background enjoyed by Mitt Romney with a more down-to-earth image of the two of them struggling to make ends meet in mean circumstances. She did so by telling the story of their early life together: "We were very young. Both still in college. There were many reasons to delay marriage, and, you know? We just didn't care. We got married and moved into a basement apartment. We walked to class together, shared the housekeeping, and ate a lot of pasta and tuna fish. Our desk was a door propped up on sawhorses. Our dining room table was a fold-down ironing board in the kitchen. Those were very special days."

And lest anyone believe that they had a "storybook marriage," she recalled "long, long, rainy winter afternoons with five boys screaming at once" and spoke of her bouts with multiple sclerosis and breast cancer. Instead of having a storybook marriage, she argued that she has had a "real marriage," and clearly a narrative one with which many in her audience might identify. Finally, in 2000 speech Laura Bush's speech[27] was almost exclusively narratives of her life and marriage to George Bush, all used to illustrate the personal qualities and humble nature of her husband.

The strategies Petre identified in the women's speeches in the 2004 conventions were also clearly at work in the convention speeches given by the wives of presidential candidates since 1992. Those two, though, are not the only strategies at work. At least three other distinct strategies that comport with the invitational style are present in spousal addresses. Those three complement the strategies identified by Petre and function to fulfill the generic requirements of the spouse/first lady speech.

The first of the three is the creation of a sense of intimacy. Foss and Griffin describe *invitational rhetoric* as "an invitation to understanding as a means *to create a relationship* rooted in equality, immanent value, and self-determination" (emphasis added). Relational communication is not formal and presentational in style; it is informal and "conversational" in style and encourages the development of a rapport between participants. It suggests an interpersonal involvement and an informal exchange of ideas and experiences. It encourages a sense of closeness and identification. For example, Hillary Clinton (1996) attempted to conjure up just such a setting when she said "I want to talk about what matters most in our lives and in our nation—children and families. I wish we could be sitting around a kitchen table, just us, talking about our hopes and fears about our children's futures." Clinton was not alone in attempting to establish a setting of intimacy and speaking of subjects appropriate for that setting.

In her 1992 speech Barbara Bush declared that her purpose was not to "give a speech" but rather to "have a conversation" with the audience about what she "and George" had experienced during his term in office. The informal "conversation" and the familiar tone set by the use of President Bush's first name called to mind a more intimate setting rather than a public, televised address to thousands in the immediate audience and millions in the mediated audience. The experiences of which she spoke weren't described in lofty terms or as earth-shattering events of the leader of a nation; rather, they were everyday experiences—"shared moments" with families, gaining help from neighbors and friends. Her sentences were filled with informal contractions and often began with casual, conversational phrases such as "You know . . .", reminiscent of the conversational style and tone of interaction with a friend. Her "conversation" ended with the invitation to meet her family—all twenty-two of them.

Barbara Bush's daughter-in-law, Laura,[28] also created a sense of intimacy in her 2004 address. She asked her audience for the opportunity to speak to them as if they were in an informal setting of friends chatting, as though "we sat down for a cup of coffee or ran into each other at the store." As other first ladies also did in their speeches, Mrs. Bush described her sense of the private moments she shared with her husband:

> I remember some very quiet nights at the dinner table. George was weighing grim scenarios and ominous intelligence about potentially even more devastating attacks. I listened many nights as George talked with foreign leaders on the phone or in our living room or at our ranch in Crawford.
>
> I remember an intense weekend at Camp David. George and Prime Minister Tony Blair were discussing the threat from Saddam Hussein. And I remember sitting in the window of the White House, watching as my husband walked on the lawn below. I knew he was wrestling with these agonizing decisions that would have such profound consequence for so many lives and for the future of our world.

Mrs. Bush took her audience into her confidence as we often do with close friends and shared with them the private moments and thoughts that perhaps even her husband was unaware of. This sharing of the private moments suggests the conversation of intimates, of friends who trust one another enough to exchange confidences.

Elizabeth Dole (1996) not only spoke in informal and intimate ways but also enacted the sense of intimacy by leaving the speaker's platform, joining the audience, and using her speech to introduce a number of individuals who had known presidential candidate Robert Dole in one capacity or another: a nurse who worked with him when he returned home with war wounds and was hospitalized for three years, a doctor who'd helped Dole face the reality of his physical condition and provided medical treatment for him without charge, a couple of disabled young people who inspired Dole to begin a foundation for those with disabilities, these and more were introduced. Standing side by side with them, Elizabeth Dole introduced them to the audience as one might introduce a friend to another. Diminishing the distance from the audience, leaving the elevated setting of the dais to join the audience at their level, and filling her speech with introductions and personal anecdotes about her and her husband's warm and personal relationships with those she introduced—all contributed visually and rhetorically to a sense of intimacy. And in that setting Dole provided her audience witnesses to verify her husband's character and qualifications.

Developing a sense of relationship, of intimacy, and of trust complements the strategy of the narrative that Petre describes. It also complements the second of the three additional strategies: the sense of positional advantage. The underlying premise of this strategy is that the spouse is uniquely positioned to know and verify the candidate's character and qualifications. More than colleagues, more than friends, and more than other family members, the spouse knows the candidate. She sees the private moments to which no one else has access. She may well hear his immediate and personal responses to the problems he faces and see the difficulties he faces when he must make decisions in uncertain situations. As witness to and confidante in these situations, the spouse is positioned better than anyone to know the candidate.

Barbara Bush (1992) directly pointed out the advantage she enjoyed as spouse when she said, "With all my heart I say—*and I know him best*—you have made a superb choice" (emphasis added). After telling her audience that her speech would largely focus on children and families, Hillary Clinton (1996) verified, from her position as spouse and mother, her husband's ability to understand and act in the best interest of children and families: "It takes a president who believes not only in the potential of his own child but of all children, who believes not only in the strength of his own family but of the American family, who believes not only in the promise of each of us as individuals but in our promise together as a nation. It takes a president who not only holds these beliefs but acts on them. It takes Bill Clinton." Elizabeth Dole (1996) suggested the depth of the insight she had concerning her husband when she said that she "could go on and on sharing stories about this loving husband and father, this caring friend," and Laura Bush (2004), like her mother-in-law, directly asserted her advantaged position in answer to a hypothetical question: "You know him better than anyone, you've seen things no one else has seen; why do you think we should reelect your husband as president?" Cindy McCain (2008) spoke of the personal commitment, sense of history, and ideas for the future that were important qualifications for the presidency and then identified her husband as the sole individual who had met those qualifications: "I know of no one who better defines how to do that, whose life is a better example of how to go about that than the man I love, whom [*sic*] I've shared almost thirty years of my life, my husband, John McCain."

In the reelection campaign, first ladies tend to list the accomplishments of their husbands and ascribe that success to the personal qualities and leadership skills they have observed firsthand in their spouses. Michelle Obama, for example, can even tell her audience at the 2012 convention what it was that her husband was thinking that led him to take certain actions: "So when it comes to rebuilding our economy, Barack is thinking about folks like my dad and like his grandmother. He's thinking about the pride that comes from a hard day's work. That's why he signed the Lilly Ledbetter Fair Pay Act to help women get equal pay for equal work." Some spouses even forecast the greatness of their husbands by seeming to equate them with revered figures or to place them in a line of succession of other presidents who have had to make similarly difficult decisions. Laura Bush (2004), for example, noted that "no American president ever wants to go to war. Abraham Lincoln didn't want to go to war, but he knew saving the Union required it. Franklin Roosevelt didn't want to go to war, but he knew defeating tyranny demanded it. And my husband didn't want to go to war, but he knew the safety and security of America and the world depended on it." And quoting the "mystic cords of memory"/"better angels of our nature" section of Lincoln's first inaugural, Teresa Heinz Kerry[29] (2004) predicted that "the better angels of our nature are just waiting to be summoned. We only require a leader who is willing to call on them." Unsurprisingly, Mrs. Kerry believed that she had found that leader; she happened to be married to him.

Often first ladies will include in their speeches an account of what they have accomplished and focused on during their husband's first term in office and what they have learned as a result; similarly, those who aspire to be first ladies comment on their experiences on the campaign trail or as a result of the offices their spouse has held and what lessons they have taken from those experiences. Additionally a familiar theme in spouses' remarks is some history of their own—where they were born, what valuable lessons they took from their parents or grandparents, what life-changing experiences they've had, how they met their husbands, and a sense of the life they have formed together. These themes of personal accomplishments and life history serve a valuable function in the addresses and constitute the final strategy that recurs in the typical spouse's speech: defining her husband by defining herself. Suggesting that she is uniquely positioned to know and verify the qualities and character traits of her husband makes the spouse's convention speech an important testimonial about the candidate and his abilities. To some extent, though, the spouse must also define and defend herself. After all, it is perfectly reasonable to believe that we see a reflection of him in her; that is, our image of the spouse affects our image of the candidate.

Barbara Bush (1992) made families her theme and recalled the many single moms and dads and families that "George and I have met" and noted many similarities to her own family: "I car pooled, was a den mother, and went to more Little League games than I can count. We went to church; we cheered at Fourth of July picnics and fireworks, and we sang carol . . . carols [sic] together at Christmas." Mrs. Bush's family, she argued, shared the same concerns, worries, and joys that all families experience: "No family is perfect, and no family is without pain and suffering. We lost a daughter; we almost lost a son, and one child struggled for years with a learning disability." What she had seen and experienced her husband had also seen and experienced, she implied, and so the audience was asked to draw the conclusion that the family, and the values associated with the family, were important to her and, by extension, to him: "Both George and I believe that while the White House is important, the country's future is in your house, every house, all over America."

Hillary Clinton (1996) also made families her theme and singled out actor Christopher Reeve's speech at the same convention for his description of the nation as "one family, the American family." Mrs. Clinton vouched for her husband's similar interest in the family when she listed his accomplishments that were connected to and benefitted families, and she then reminded the audience that she too had an accomplishment and expertise to share regarding family. The reminder came in the form of a pointed mention of the title of her book—*It Takes a Village*: "It takes all of us. Yes, it takes a village. And it takes a president." In both Mrs. Bush and Mrs. Clinton's remarks, their focus on families was reflected in their husbands' understanding of the important role family plays and in the family-oriented legislation that they supported.

Teresa Heinz Kerry (2004) focused very nearly half of her speech on her own background and upbringing in South Africa, her sense of what makes America so great, and why the American spirit is so important: "It is the America the world wants to see, shining, hopeful, and bright once again. And that is the America that my husband, John Kerry, wants to lead." She argued that Senator Kerry loved the nation as she did and that this love would lead him to focus on a specific agenda were he elected.

Much as she did in her first convention address, Michelle Obama (2012) rehearsed for the audience what she described as a fairly modest upbringing, the sacrifices her parents made for her and her brother, and the values those parents instilled in their children. As she also did in her first convention speech, she asserted that her husband shared those same values and repeatedly assured the audience that he was the "same man" that she had always known. In fact, her speech seemed so very reminiscent of her 2008 address that the underlying argument of the 2012 speech seemed to be, What you saw and liked in us then has not changed.

And finally, Ann Romney (2012) began her speech by saying she would focus on the subject of love—"the deep and abiding love I have for a man I met at a dance many years ago. And the profound love I have, and I know we share, for this county." And after telling the audience about her marriage and her husband's accomplishments, she gave perhaps the most direct and forceful endorsement possible: "I can't tell you what will happen over the next four years. But I can only stand here tonight, as a wife, a mother, a grandmother, an American, and make you this solemn commitment: This man will not fail. This man will not let us down. This man will lift up America!" Her certainty, she hoped, would become the nation's certainty.

Praising the nation, use of compelling narratives, setting a tone of intimacy, the positional advantage of a spouse, and defining the candidate as a reflection of his wife are all recurring strategies in the convention addresses of spouses. However, the convention address is not the only role the spouse plays. A second appearance often occurs in the convention films that have become a regular feature of nominating conventions.[30]

THE CONVENTION FILM

In her thorough and much-cited work *The Presidential Campaign Film: A Critical History* Joanne Morreale provides an authoritative history of the campaign film as well as explanation and extensive analysis of the films from 1952 (when conventions were first televised) through 1992—from Eisenhower's campaign film, *Report to Ike*, to Bill Clinton's convention film, *The Man from Hope*.[31] Morreale makes the case that the campaign film constitutes a rhetorical genre, documentary in nature, and divides the films into three subgenres: "the biographical film, concerned with establishing a candidate's identity; the résumé film, concerned with reiterating a candidate's accomplishments; and the visionary film, concerned with articulating a candidate's concepts of America's future."[32] Challengers for the presidential office tend to emphasize biographical elements, while incumbents tend to focus on résumé. She notes that the genre has changed over time and specifically points to the Ford and Carter films of 1976 as the first indication of a structural shift from the "narrative-expository" format of the documentary genre to the hybrid genre of the "documentary-advertisement" that included the more "poetic" format of advertising and film techniques such as "implication, juxtaposition, and association of words, images, and music [to] impress the candidate's virtues upon viewers."[33] And with Ronald Reagan's 1984 film, *A New Beginning*, the hybrid genre came into its own as an alternative to the nominating speech that served to introduce the candidate at the party's convention. These generic elements and formats have continued to be utilized through the years and, for the most part, still form the basis of more recent convention and campaign films.

Where Morreale leaves off, Parmelee picks up the history of convention films and tells us that Clinton in 1996 focused on issues in his thirty-second television advertising and used the convention film "to tell a personal story that connected Clinton to the average American."[34] Instead of telling the nation that he still believed in "a place called Hope," as he did in his first campaign in 1992, Clinton told us that he believed in "a place called America," a place that still has its "best days" ahead of us. If Clinton focused on his personal story and linked it to the future of the country, his 1996 opponent, Senator Bob Dole, used his film (*Portrait of a Man*) to look back and to the present—to his upbringing in Kansas, his service in the military, the agony of his long recovery from war wounds, the values he learned from his family, and his life in the Senate and with his wife, Senator Elizabeth Dole. In fact, Parmelee notes that both candidates focused heavily on their wives, children, and families. Dole's focused on the past and the present in his campaign film and promised in his acceptance speech to "be the bridge to an America that only the unknowing call myth . . . to a time of tranquility, faith, and confidence in action,"[35] allowing Bill Clinton to quip, "We do not need to build a bridge to the past; we need to build a bridge to the future."[36] The outcome of the election indicated that the nation clearly agreed with Mr. Clinton.

In 2000 several changes in the use and structure of convention films were apparent. First, Tipper Gore, as noted above, did not give a formal speech at the convention but instead narrated a film consisting solely of family photographs she had taken. The film was largely biographical and served to tell Gore's personal and political story and frame his character. A second change was that a separate film about Gore and his family was produced just weeks before the convention by director Spike Jonze (most notably, the director of *Being John Malkovich*).[37] Following the Gores and capturing what seemed to be the routines of their daily life in cinema-verité style, Jonze provided what some thought a much more intimate, charming, and human portrait of Gore. As the *New York Times* noted, though, "the Jonze film was almost sneaked on the air at an especially off time, 7:30 Tuesday night, as if it were being tested [and] was carried only by MSNBC and C-SPAN."[38]

On the Republican side in 2000, change was also evident. Not only was a film used to introduce Governor George Bush (a film titled *The Sky's the Limit*), but a short, biographical film of Laura Bush was also used. This was the first time since the film tribute to Patricia Nixon was used in 1972 that a spouse was featured in her own film. Another change in the use of convention films was also noted by Edwards and Smith, who pointed out that both the Bush and Gore films took a turn away from the traditional "mythic" style that emphasizes power, strength, and the masculine and instead were more illustrative of what the authors call an "antimythic" style that focuses more on the personal, on familiar relationships, on identification, and on a message that is "'feminized' by an intimate relational tone or content."[39] So in not giving a separate convention speech but instead narrating her husband's convention film Mrs. Gore shifted the role of the spouse in the 2000 campaign; and by giving a speech endorsing her husband, being featured in a separate convention film about her own life and possible pursuits as first lady, and taking a supporting role in George Bush's film, Mrs. Bush also altered the role of the spouse.

2004 saw a return to both wives—Laura Bush and Teresa Heinz Kerry—giving convention speeches in support of their spouses as well as appearing in a supporting capacity in the films about their husbands. With events such as the 9/11 terrorist attack and the Iraq and Afghan wars looming large and defining his presidency, Bush's film, *The Pitch* (narrated by former actor and Senator Fred Thompson), unsurprisingly emphasized the mythic features of the presidency and the strength of the American spirit. Kerry's *A Remarkable Promise* balanced his biography with his résumé to introduce himself as loving father and husband, both war hero and skeptic, and public servant, and focused on his senatorial credentials to make the case for his election.[40] And while Mrs. Bush's role was understandably minimal in a film focused almost exclusively on featuring her husband as a strong, brave, and responsive leader, Mrs. Kerry took on a larger role, as she was integral to John Kerry's biography. Moreover Mrs. Kerry was herself the subject of a separate convention film.

Both Michelle Obama and Cindy McCain used their convention speeches to make the case for the election of their spouses in 2004, and they also used generous portions of those speeches to introduce themselves to the nation. This probably accounted for the lack of any campaign film specifically about either woman. Additionally Mrs. Obama could rely on her brother's introduction of her to fill in some biographical and personal information. Barack Obama's film, *A Mother's Promise*, seemed to meld Morreale's three subgenres—biography, résumé, and visionary—while John McCain's untitled film complemented the convention theme, "Country First," and focused on biography, military service, and heroism, as well as his public service as a senator. Again, both wives served in supporting roles in their husband's films.

In 2012 the roles played by Mrs. Obama and Mrs. Romney were a continuation of past campaigns. Both wives gave speeches of support for their husbands, and Mrs. Obama was featured in her own campaign film that reminded the audience of her upbringing and recalled the projects she had taken on as first lady. President Obama made brief appearances in the film to focus on the personal: Mrs. Obama's skills as a parent, her devotion to her children, and her support of her husband. Both conventions featured candidate films. President Obama's film focused heavily on résumé and relied on former president Bill Clinton and Vice President Joe Biden to testify to the wisdom of the decisions the president made during his first term, his strength as a leader, his work ethic, his accomplishments, and his willingness to take unpopular positions in which he nonetheless believed. And Mrs. Obama made appearances to speak of his family life. Mrs. Romney took a prominent role in Governor Romney's film primarily to tell stories of his generosity to others, his care for her when she suffered from multiple sclerosis and cancer, the values his father taught him, and his devotion to their large family. Others with whom Romney worked as governor of Massachusetts, as chief executive of the winter Olympics in Salt Lake City, and in his business capacity with Bain Capital provided evidence of his leadership skills, but the film returned again and again to Mrs. Romney to establish the personal qualities. In the contemporary presidential campaign, the role of the spouse has evolved, gaining attention and become more prominent, and 2012 illustrates those changes well.

THE SPOUSES' ROLE IN 2012: A DIFFERENT STRATEGY

As noted above, in many ways Michelle Obama and Ann Romney took on roles that had come to be expected and that fit into the trend of more participation by spouses in the nominating conventions. Each spouse gave a major convention address that made use of an invitational style and employed strategies that fulfilled the generic requirements of the spouse address. As has been the case for some years, convention films that focus on the candidate are expected, and participation in the film by the spouse has also become the norm; both Mrs. Obama and Mrs. Romney participated in their husbands' films. And as was the case in many recent conventions, the spouses' remarks and their participation in their husbands' films (and, in the case of Mrs. Obama, in her own film) not only met what had become traditional and expected but also seemed to work in concert either to reinforce or supplement the messages of one another. For example, President Obama's introductory convention film in 2012 focused on his accomplishments in the office, burnished his image as a leader, and included others assessing the skills he brought to the office; Mrs. Obama's speech, while mentioning his work in office, tended to focus more on the personal—their relationship, her husband's values, and his strengths as a father and husband.

What makes the 2012 election unusual and marks an important change in the communication functions of the spouse's addresses and film appearances is that the remarks and films didn't simply meet the traditional expectations of supplying biographical, personal, and professional qualifications or of putting forward the issues the candidate believed were central or of identifying a vision for the nation that was compatible with the nation's sense of its history and its future possibilities. Rather, the addresses and films in 2012 overtly tackled the overarching political problem that each candidate faced at that point.

All communication from the candidate or his surrogates can be said to have political functions. In that sense, spouses' addresses and the use of candidate films have always been broadly aimed at the political ends of gaining support for a candidate. In the 2012 election, though, the spouses' speeches and candidates' films clearly targeted the specific political weaknesses of their respective candidates and attempted to use the speeches and films to refute the claims lodged against the candidates or to reframe their images more positively.

By late spring in 2012, when it became clear that Mitt Romney would be the Republican nominee, he had already taken a pummeling from his primary opponents and in media reports and the broadsides from the Obama campaign were ramping up. The main focus of their criticisms was that Romney was a plutocrat, used to getting his own way, a wealthy man who could never understand the problems of the average American. Romney's Bain Capital was accused of shutting down businesses and causing the loss of jobs;[41] Romney was labeled insensitive to the middle class because "he wants to cut jobs for firefighters, police, and teachers";[42] his wealth—for example, spending $55,000 for a car elevator in his garage—put him out of touch with the average person;[43] and he had engaged in questionable business dealings involving offshore accounts.[44] His insensitivity was not limited to the business world, though; Romney was also accused of bad judgment in several ways ranging from the treatment of pets[45] to bullying behavior as a young student in his private school[46] and boorish behavior abroad.[47] And as these attacks mounted during the early summer, Romney faced the problem of not having enough money to be able to respond to the accusations in targeted advertising, so the accusations went unanswered.[48] Without the ability to advertise broadly until after the nominating convention when the general-election campaign would begin, Romney was saddled with the negative stories. The next opportunity he would have to reframe the negative image was the convention. As the *Washington Post*'s Dan Balz reported, "There is much more that Romney's team wants to say about his biography: his days at Bain Capital, certainly, but also his one term as governor of Massachusetts; his role in turning around the 2002 Olympics; his family as the center of his life; the role his Mormon faith has played in his life; and the role he has played through his church in helping others."[49]

And so wherever possible in the convention schedule, organizers inserted testimony by friends, fellow church members, classmates, and colleagues to tell stories of Romney's generosity and friendship.[50] For example, poignant stories were told of Romney helping a dying child, paying for someone's college education, making a surprise delivery of Christmas gifts to a family in need, bringing his sons to help clean a park—all described as spontaneous acts of charity.[51] Additionally, the *New York Times* reported that prior to Romney's speech "his campaign started a Web site . . . devoted almost entirely to his years at the investment firm Bain Capital" that argued the firm "'was about fixing companies that were broken and giving new companies a shot at success.'"[52] And certainly Ann Romney's speech and participation in the Romney film was central to that effort.

Mrs. Romney's speech told the story of two people who had come from parents of modest means and background, and who began their life together in meager circumstances. She told family stories of their five boys and Romney as a devoted father. She told stories that she said "Mitt doesn't like to talk about," stories of friendship when her husband would "drop everything to help a friend in trouble" and of his being available to help "when late-night calls of panic came from a member of our church whose child had been taken to the hospital." She told stories of her husband's success in business, in government, and with the Olympics, and she chalked it all up to hard work that paid off. She told stories of her illnesses and her husband's steadfastness throughout. Every part of Ann Romney's speech functioned to reframe the image of Mitt Romney and offer proof that the narrative of Romney as an insensitive and out-of-touch millionaire was at odds with the reality she knew. And, in a sense, the Romney film was the visual version of Ann Romney's speech. Many of the themes that she had introduced in her speech were repeated, reinforced, and verified in the video by Ann Romney herself, along with friends, family members, business associates, and others who had known or worked with Romney.

President Obama also had political problems plaguing his campaign, chief among them the all-consuming and constantly looming problem of the economy's poor performance. From January through August of 2012 the unemployment rate held fairly steady at above 8 percent, ranging from 8.1 percent to 8.3 percent.[53] And as the Democratic convention came to a close, the *New York Times* reported that "the nation's employers eased up on hiring in August, making it clear that the economy was stuck in low gear. The pace of job creation, disclosed in government figures released on Friday, fell far short of the stronger showing at the start of the year. It presents a fresh challenge to President Obama just two months before the election."[54]

Adding to the economic woes felt by the nation, in early August of 2012 gas prices were reported to have "surged in recent weeks, and analysts predict they'll keep rising."[55] And adding still more concern related to the economy was the fact that the president's signature accomplishment, the Patient Protection and Affordable Care Act—or Obamacare, as it became known—was meeting with mixed reviews. Gallup reported that "Americans see more economic harm than good in Health Law," and the much-sought-after independent voters seemed to "help tilt the balance to the negative."[56] Finally the fear arose in the Obama campaign that they might be losing the voting bloc that had done them so much good in 2008—the votes of young people. The *New York Times* reported that young, first-time voters were concerned about the economy and also were "significantly more likely to identify as conservative and cite a growing lack of faith in government in general, according to interviews, experts, and recent polls."[57]

Concern about the economy as a political issue rose among Democratic strategists in the early summer of 2012, and one group, Democracy Corps, headed by pollster Stan Greenberg and campaign consultant James Carville, argued that the Obama campaign's message was "out of touch with the daily pain voters are feeling." Moreover, they predicted, "we will face an impossible head wind in November if we do not move to a new narrative, one that contextualizes the recovery but, more importantly, focuses on what we will do to make a better future for the middle class."[58] Perhaps it wasn't exactly the change that the strategists had called for, but First Lady Michelle Obama's convention address, and the film focused on her, as well as the film focused on President Obama, certainly changed the message. Whereas Mrs. Romney attempted to handle her husband's image problem by offering a different and more positive image to replace it, Mrs. Obama downplayed or ignored the problems her husband was faced with and returned instead to the strategies, themes, and topics that had worked well in 2008.

Mrs. Obama's 2008 speech and 2012 speech are remarkably similar. In both she talks about her modest upbringing, the values her parents instilled in her and her brother, and the bravery of her father as he faced a battle with multiple sclerosis. In both she identifies Barack Obama as having grown up in similar circumstances and with similar family values. Both use the same words to describe her husband being raised by "a single mother who struggled to pay the bills"; both pay tribute to families who "work hard"; both honor the military. In the 2008 speech Mrs. Obama praised her husband for seeing "the world as it is" and wanting "the world as it should be"; and in the 2012 speech she seemed to revive that image of the world as it is versus the world as it should be when she describes moments of seeing her husband "poring over the letters people have sent him" that described their concerns and worries, and she sees "that's what drives Barack Obama every single day" to effect change. He is, she assures the audience repeatedly, the "same man" he has always been. He "knows the American Dream because he's lived it . . . and he wants everyone in this country to have that same opportunity." In her paper at the 2009 National Communication Association meeting, Jaclyn Howell makes the case that Michelle Obama "crafted her [2008 convention] speech in the image of the American Dream";[59] the "American spirit" and the "American Dream" not only make appearances in the 2012 speech but were arguably its central theme.

The film devoted to Mrs. Obama set a positive tone before the first lady's speech. It opened, as did her speech shortly thereafter, with a summary of her background and upbringing, featuring family pictures and her brother and mother adding commentary. The focus then shifted to record her work as first lady and included testimony by her husband and White House staffers addressing her effectiveness in that role. The film ended with her husband paying tribute to her as wife and mother. Her appearance in her husband's film was brief, serving to verify his character and his concern for the nation and its citizens. The problems the nation might have been facing (and expecting to be addressed by the president) were alluded to only at the beginning and end of the film, and only in an abstract and generalized fashion; with the admonition that "We've been through a lot together," we've seen "tough times before," and we've got "a long way to go," the president seemed to suggest that Americans would overcome any current or future problems, and the remainder of the film then moved on to praise the president for doing the "right thing" regardless of the political peril, for making it a principle of his leadership to focus on what was in the nation's best interest, and for having the determination and courage to make tough decisions regarding the safety of the nation. The film ended with a tribute to the "resilience, strength, and character of the American people." Robert Ivie and Oscar Giner argue that Obama's 2008 acceptance speech was rooted in "American exceptionalism" that would lead to the American Dream.[60] The case might well be made that the president's 2012 acceptance speech mirrored that same construction and that Mrs. Obama's speech and the president's convention film were both forecasts of and complements to that argument.

In sum, both the convention speeches and appearances in films by First Lady Michelle Obama and aspiring first lady Ann Romney in 2012 marked a change in the communication functions employed previously. While meeting the expectations that traditionally accompany those events, they also became a rhetoric of apologia, a defense of their husbands in the face of political peril. Ann Romney chose the strategy of redefinition; Michelle Obama placed her husband in the role of guarantor of the American Dream.

CONCLUSION

With participation by the candidate's spouse now an expectation, we will probably see continued use of the convention speech and campaign films. Scholars should continue to expand the literature on those spouses and certainly should provide more work on their convention discourse. Will the generic qualities of the spouse's convention speech and film appearances remain the same if the day comes when the spouse is a man? In what other ways might the spouse's participation change in its communication functions? How much elasticity is possible in discourse bound up with generic expectations? These questions and more should be on our minds as 2016 approaches.

NOTES

1. Robert P. Watson, "The First Lady Reconsidered: Presidential Partner and Political Institution," *Presidential Studies Quarterly* 27 (Fall 1997): 805.

2. See, for example, Lewis L. Gould, "Modern First Ladies and the Presidency," *Presidential Studies Quarterly* 20 (Fall 1990): 677–83; Lewis L. Gould, "Modern First Ladies in Historical Perspective," *Presidential Studies Quarterly* 15 (Summer 1985): 532–40; Karen O'Connor, Bernadette Nye, and Laura Van Assendelft, "Wives in the White House: The Political Influence of First Ladies," *Presidential Studies Quarterly* 26 (Summer 1996): 835–53; Kathy B. Smith, "The First Lady Represents America: Rosalynn Carter in South America," *Presidential Studies Quarterly* 27 (Summer 1997): 540–48; Faye Lynd Jensen, "An Awesome Responsibility: Rosalynn Carter as First Lady," *Presidential Studies Quarterly* 20 (Fall 1990): 769–75; Leesa E. Tobin, "Betty Ford as First Lady: A Woman for Women," *Presidential Studies Quarterly* 20 (Fall 1990): 761–67; Betty Houchin Winfield, "Anna Eleanor Roosevelt's White House Legacy: The Public First Lady," *Presidential Studies Quarterly* 18 (Spring 1988): 331–45.

3. See, for example, Elizabeth Watts, "Eleanor Roosevelt: Transformative First Lady," *Journalism History* 37 (Summer 2011): 123; Judith L. Weaver, "Edith Bolling Wilson as First Lady: A Study in the Power of Personality, 1919–1920," *Presidential Studies Quarterly* 15 (Winter 1985): 51–76.

4. See, for example, Jenna Swan, "Newspaper Coverage of Cindy McCain and Michelle Obama in the 2008 Presidential Election," *Media Report to Women* 38 (Spring 2010): 6–21; Erica Scharrer, "An 'Improbable Leap': A Content Analysis of Newspaper Coverage of Hillary Clinton's Transition from First Lady to Senate Candidate," *Journalism Studies* 3 (August 2002): 393–406; Ralina L. Joseph, "'Hope Is Finally Making a Comeback': First Lady Reframed," *Culture and Critique* 4 (March 2011): 56–77; Janis L. Edwards and Rong-Chen Huey, "The First Lady/First Wife in Editorial Cartoons: Rhetorical Visions Through Gendered Lenses," *Women's Studies in Communication* 23 (Fall 2000): 367–91.

5. See, for example, J. K. Muir and M. L. Benitez, "Redefining the Role of First Lady: The Rhetorical Style of Hillary Rodham Clinton," in R. E. Denton, Jr., and R. L. Holloway, *The Clinton Presidency: Images, Issues, and Communication Strategies* (Westport, Conn.: Praeger, 1996); Mary L. Kahl, "First Lady Michelle Obama: Advocate for Strong Families," *Communication and Critical/Cultural Studies* 6 (September 2009): 316–20; Keith V. Erickson and Stephanie Thomson, "First Lady International Diplomacy: Performing Gendered Roles on the World Stage," *Southern Communication Journal* 77 (July 2012): 239–62.

6. See, for example, Jeffrey E. Cohen, "'The Polls': Public Attitudes toward the First Lady," *Presidential Studies Quarterly* 30 (June 2000): 374–81; Valerie A. Sulfaro, "Affective Evaluations of First Ladies: A Comparison of Hillary Clinton and Laura Bush," *Presidential Studies Quarterly* 37 (September 2007): 486–514.

7. See, for example, Kristy Maddux, "Feminism and Foreign Policy: Public Vocabularies and the Conditions of Emergence for First Lady Rosalynn Carter," *Women's Studies in Communication* 31 (Spring 2008): 29–55; Tasha N. Dubriwny, "First Ladies and Feminism: Laura Bush as Advocate for Women's and Children's Rights," *Women's Studies in Communication* 28 (Spring 2005): 84–114; Charlotte Templin, "Hillary Clinton as Threat to Gender Norms: Cartoon Images of the First Lady," *Journal of Communication Inquiry* 23 (January 1999): 20–37.

8. Shawn Parry-Giles and Diane M. Blair, "The Rise of the Rhetorical First Lady: Politics, Gender Ideology, and Women's Voices," *Rhetoric and Public Affairs* 5 (Winter 2002): 565–600.

9. For an exception, see Jaclyn Howell, "Recasting Femininity within the American Dream: Michelle Obama's 2008 Democratic National Convention Address," presented at the National Communication Association Conference, 2009, accessed January 5, 2013, Communication and Mass Media Complete.

10. Judith S. Trent and Robert V. Friedenberg, *Political Campaign Communication: Principles and Practices*, 6th ed. (Lanham, Md.: Rowman & Littlefield, 2008), 59–65.

11. Trent and Friedenberg, *Political Campaign Communication*, 6th ed., 66.

12. "Roles Grew as Women's Influence Rose," *New York Times*, September 5, 2012, accessed January 5, 2012, www.nytimes.com/roomfordebate/2012/09/04/do-we-need-to-hear-from-the-candidates-spouse/roles-grew-as-womens-influence-rose.

13. "Roles Grew as Women's Influence Rose."

14. See, for example, Sharon E. Jarvis, "Campaigning Alone: Partisan versus Personal Language in Presidential Nominating Convention Acceptance Addresses, 1948–2000," *American Behavioral Scientist* 44 (August 2001): 2152–72; David A. Frank and Mark Lawrence McPhail, "Barack Obama's Address to the 2004 Democratic National Convention: Trauma, Compromise, Consilience, and the (Im)Possibility of Racial Reconciliation," *Rhetoric and Public Affairs* 8 (Winter 2005): 571–93; Robert C. Rowland and John M. Jones, "Recasting the American Dream and American Politics: Barack Obama's Keynote Address to the 2004 Democratic National Convention," *Quarterly Journal of Speech* 93 (November 2007): 425–48; Larry David Smith, "Convention Oratory as Institutional Discourse: A Narrative Synthesis of Democrats and Republicans of 1988," *Communication Studies* 41 (Spring 1990): 19–34; Larry David Smith, "The Nominating Convention as Purveyor of Political Medicine: An Anecdotal Analysis of the Democrats and Republicans of 1984," *Central States Communication Journal* 38 (Fall/Winter 1987): 252–61; Katie Gibson and Amy L. Heyse, "'The Difference between a Hockey Mom and a Pit Bull': Sarah Palin's Faux Maternal Persona and Performance of Hegemonic Masculinity at the 2008 Republican National Convention," *Communication Quarterly* 58 (July 2010): 235–56; Takako Sano, "A Rhetoric of Superb Craftsmanship: A Stylistic Analysis of Adlai E. Stevenson's 1952 Campaign Speeches," *Speech Education* 6 (July 1978): 80–87; Michael William Pfau, "Conventions of Deliberation? Convention Addresses and Deliberative Containment in the Second Party System," *Rhetoric and Public Affairs* 9 (Winter 2006): 635–54; Craig R. Smith, "Richard Nixon's 1968 Acceptance Speech as a Model of Dual Audience Adaptation," *Today's Speech* 19 (Fall 1971): 15–22; Henry Z. Scheele, "Ronald Reagan's 1980 Acceptance Address: A Focus on American Values," *Western Journal of Speech Communication* 48 (Winter 1984): 51–61; Alvin R. Kaiser, "Style and Personal Appeal of Adlai E. Stevenson," *Western Speech* 18 (May 1954): 181–85; Robert T. Oliver, "The Speech that Established Roosevelt's Reputation," *Quarterly Journal of Speech* 31 (October 1945): 274–83; and Rebecca J. Cline, "Victory Rally Cheer versus Policy Statement on the Acceptance of Richard Nixon's 1986 Acceptance Speech," *Communication* 4 (July 1975): 186–211.

15. In *Kaleidoscope: A Graduate Journal of Qualitative Communication Research* 6 (Fall 2007): 21–37.

16. S. K. Foss and C. L. Griffin, "Beyond Persuasion: A Proposal for an Invitational Rhetoric," *Communication Monographs* 62 (1995): 2–18.

17. Foss and Griffin, "Beyond Persuasion," 5.

18. Petre, "Understanding Epideictic Purpose," *Kaleidoscope: A Graduate Journal of Qualitative Communication Research* 6 (Fall 2007): 22.

19. Petre, "Understanding Epideictic Purpose," 31.

20. For all references to Barbara Bush's 1992 RNC speech, see the transcript available at "1992 Speech RNC: Barbara Bush," Speeches-USA.com, accessed November 20, 2012, www.speeches-usa.com/Transcripts/039_bush.htm.

21. For this and all subsequent references to Hillary Clinton's 1996 DNC speech, see the transcript available at "First Lady Hillary Rodham Clinton Speaks at the Democratic National

Convention," *PBS Newshour*, accessed November 20, 2012, www.pbs.org/newshour/bb/politics/july-dec96/hillary-clinton.html.

22. For this and all subsequent references to Elizabeth Dole's 1996 RNC speech, see the transcript available at "Elizabeth Dole Speaking before the Republican National Convention," *PBS Newshour*, accessed November 20, 2012, www.pbs.org/newshour/convention96/floor_speeches/elizabeth_dole.html.

23. For this and all subsequent references to Michelle Obama's 2008 DNC speech, see the transcript available at "Transcript: Michelle Obama's Convention Speech," NPR, August 25, 2008, accessed November 20, 2012, www.npr.org/templates/story/story.php?storyId=93963863.

24. For this and all subsequent references to Cindy McCain's 2008 RNC speech, see the transcript available at "Transcript: Cindy McCain's Speech," NPR, September 4, 2008, accessed November 20, 2012, www.npr.org/templates/story/story.php?storyId=94301516.

25. For this and all subsequent references to Ann Romney's 2012 RNC speech, see the transcript available at "Transcript: Ann Romney's Convention Speech," NPR, August 28, 2012, accessed November 20, 2012, www.npr.org/2012/08/28/160216442/transcript-ann-romneys-convention-speech.

26. For this and all subsequent references to Michelle Obama's 2012 DNC speech, see the transcript available at www.npr.org/2012/09/04/160578836/transcript-michelle-obamas-convention-speech, accessed November 20, 2012.

27. For this and all subsequent references to Laura Bush's 2000 speech, see the transcript available at "Special Event: Republican National Convention: Laura Bush, Gen. Colin Powell Address Delegates," CNN, accessed November 20, 2012, http://edition.cnn.com/TRANSCRIPTS/0007/31/se.20.html.

28. For this and all subsequent references to the Bush 2004 speech, see the transcript available at "Text: Remarks by First Lady Laura Bush to the Republican National Convention," *Washington Post*, accessed November 20, 2012, www.washingtonpost.com/wp-dyn/articles/A50438-2004Aug31.html.

29. For this and all subsequent references to the Kerry 2004 speech, see the transcript available at "Teresa Heinz Kerry's Remarks to the Democratic National Convention," *New York Times*, July 27, 2004, accessed November 20, 2012, www.nytimes.com/2004/07/27/politics/campaign/27TEXT-TERESA.html.

30. For all references to convention films from 1992 to 2012, see the video available from the C-SPAN Video Library, Public Affairs Video Archives, Purdue University, School of Liberal Arts, West Lafayette, Indiana, available online at www.c-spanvideo.org/videoLibrary/organization.php?id=16501.

31. Joanne Morreale, *The Presidential Campaign Film: A Critical History* (Westport, Conn.: Praeger, 1996).

32. Morreale, *The Presidential Campaign Film*, 4–5.

33. Morreale, *The Presidential Campaign Film*, 15.

34. John H. Parmelee, "'A Better Man for a Better America': Presidential Campaign Films as a Mirror of Society," *Atlantic Journal of Communication* 17 (2009): 95.

35. See "Dole's Speech Accepting the Nomination for President," *New York Times*, August 16, 1996, accessed December 15, 2012, www.nytimes.com/1996/08/16/us/dole-s-speech-accepting-the-gop-nomination-for-president.html.

36. "Mr. Clinton's Bridge," *New York Times*, August 31, 1996, accessed December 15, 2012, www.nytimes.com/1996/08/31/opinion/mr-clinton-s-bridge.html.

37. The film is available at www.spike.com/video-clips/0kac69/unseen-al-gore-campaign
-video (accessed January 5, 2013). See also Ellen Gamerman, "Spike Jonze Films a Day in Gore's
Life," *Baltimore Sun*, August 18, 2000, accessed January 5, 2013, http://articles.baltimoresun
.com/2000-08-18/news/0008180150_1_al-gore-gore-home-gore-campaign.

38. Caryn James, "The Lighter Side of the Candidate Still Largely Hidden from the Cam-
era," *New York Times*, August 18, 2000, 20.

39. Janis L. Edwards and Stacey M. Smith, "Myth and Anti-myth in Presidential Cam-
paign Films 2000," in *The Millennium Election: Communication in the 2000 Campaign*, ed.
Lynda Lee Kaid, John C. Tedesco, Dianne G. Bystrom, and Mitchell S. McKinney (New York:
Rowman & Littlefield, 2003), 20.

40. For a fuller treatment of the Bush and Kerry films, see Janis L. Edwards, "Presidential
Campaign Films in a Televisual Convention Environment: The Example of 2004," in *The
2004 Presidential Campaign: A Communication Perspective*, ed. Robert E. Denton, Jr. (Lanham, Md.: Rowman & Littlefield, 2005), 75–92.

41. "Special Report: Romney's Steel Skeleton in the Bain Closet," Reuters, January 6,
2012, accessed January 5, 2013, www.reuters.com/article/2012/01/06/us-campaign-romney
-bailout-idUSTRE8050LL20120106.

42. Halimah Abdullah, "Romney, Obama: Why They Have Trouble Connecting," CNN,
June 12, 2012, accessed December 6, 2012, www.cnn.com/2012/06/12/politics/obama
-romney-connecting/index.html.

43. "Mitt Romney Ordered $55,000 'Phantom Park' Car Elevator, Designer Says,"
ABC News, May 25, 2012, accessed December 5, 2012, http://abcnews.go.com/blogs/
politics/2012/05/mitt-romney-ordered-55000-phantom-park-car-elevator-designer-says/.

44. "Mitt Romney, Offshore Tax Accounts Entangled Since Bain Capital's Founding," *Huffington Post*, July 19, 2012, accessed January 8, 2013, www.huffingtonpost
.com/2012/07/19/mitt-romneys-offshore-tax-accounts_n_1686742.html.

45. Phillip Rucker, "Romney's Dog-on-the-Car-Roof Story Still Proves to Be His Critics'
Best Friend," *Washington Post*, March 14, 2012, accessed January 5, 2013, http://articles
.washingtonpost.com/2012-03-14/news/35450454_1_tagg-romney-romney-first-romney
-supporter.

46. Jason Horowitz, "Mitt Romney's Prep School Classmates Recall Pranks but Also Trou-
bling Incidents," *Washington Post*, May 10, 2012, accessed January 6, 2013, http://articles.
washingtonpost.com/2012-05-10/news/35456919_1_school-with-bleached-blond-hair-mitt
-romney-george-romney.

47. Bruce Crumley, "After Gaffe-Filled Foreign Tour, Europe Asks: 'Is Mitt Romney a
Loser?'" *Time*, July 31, 2012, accessed January 5, 2013, http://world.time.com/2012/07/31/
after-gaffe-filled-foreign-tour-europe-asks-is-mitt-romney-a-loser/.

48. Holly Bailey, "Romney: Lack of Primary Cash Has Limited Ad Spending," ABC News,
July 18, 2012, http://abcnews.go.com/Politics/OTUS/romney-lack-primary-cash-limited-ad
-spending/story?id=16805160 (accessed January 5, 2013).

49. Dan Balz, "Showtime Arrives for Romney Campaign," August 26, 2012, accessed
January 5, 2013, www.lexisnexis.com.

50. Jodi Kantor, "Convention Voices Hope to Add Texture to Romney's Faith," *New York
Times*, August 30, 2012, www.nytimes.com/2012/08/30/us/politics/romneys-mormon-faith
-in-convention-spotlight.html.

51. Gary Bauer and Daniel Allott, "An Appeal to See Romney's Softer Side," *Washington Post*, August 30, 2012, www.washingtonpost.com/blogs/guest-voices/post/an-appeal-to-see-romneys-softer-side/2012/08/30/8995c9c8-f20a-11e1-adc6-87dfa8eff430_blog.html.

52. Peter Lattman, "Before Romney's Big Speech, a Focus on Bain," *New York Times*, August 30, 2012, http://dealbook.nytimes.com/2012/08/30/on-eve-of-romneys-big-speech-a-focus-on-bain/.

53. Bureau of Labor Statistics, accessed January 5, 2013. For January2012 data see www.bls.gov/news.release/archives/empsit_02032012.htm. For February 2012 data see www.bls.gov/news.release/archives/empit_03092012.htm. For March 2012 data see www.bls.gov/news.release/archives/empit_04062012.htm. For April 2012 data see www.bls.gov/news.release/archives/empit_05042012.htm. For May 2012 data see www.bls.gov/news.release/archives/empit_06012012.htm. For June 2012 data see www.bls.gov/news.release/archives/empit_07012012.htm. For July 2012 data see www.bls.gov/news.release/archives/empit_08032012.htm. For August 2012 data see www.bls.gov/news.release/archives/empit_09072012.htm.

54. Nelson Schwartz, "Hiring Slows in U.S., Putting Pressure on Obama and Fed," *New York Times*, September 7, 2012, accessed January 5, 2013, www.nytimes.com/2012/09/08/business/economy/us-added-96000-jobs-in-august-rate-fell-to-8-1.html.

55. Ben Geman, "Rising Gas Prices Return to Haunt Obama," *The Hill*, August 5, 2012, accessed January 5, 2013, http://thehill.com/blogs/e2-wire/e2-wire/242249-rising-gas-prices-may-haunt-obama.

56. Frank Newport, "Americans See More Economic Harm than Good in Health Law," *Gallup,* July 5, 2012, accessed January 5, 2013, www.gallup.com/poll/155513/americans-economic-harm-good-health-law.aspx.

57. Susan Saulny, "Stung by Recession, Young Voters Shed Image as Obama Brigade," *New York Times,* July 1, 2012, accessed January 5, 2013, www.nytimes.com/2012/07/02/us/politics/economy-cuts-into-obamas-youth-support.html.

58. Karen Tumulty, "Obama Campaign's Rough Patch Concerns Some Democrats," *Washington Post*, June 12, 2012, accessed January 5, 2013, http://articles.washingtonpost.com/2012-06-12/politics/35460146_1_president-obama-david-plouffe-democracy-corps.

59. Howell, "Recasting Femininity."

60. Robert L. Ivie and Oscar Giner, "American Exceptionalism in a Democratic Idiom: Transacting the Mythos of Change in the 2008 Presidential Campaign," *Communication Studies* 60 (September/October 2009): 359–75.

3

Presidential Debates 2012

Ben Voth

GENERAL HISTORY REGARDING TELEVISED PRESIDENTIAL DEBATES

Since at least 1960 when Kennedy and Nixon debated, millions of prospective voters have tuned in to their television sets to gain a relatively unmediated sense of the political options for the presidency.[1] By comparison, televised presidential debates tend to dwarf the political conventions that take place in August and September. Viewership of the conventions has been declining for some time and contracted considerably in 2012. For 2012, the Democratic and Republican conventions were viewed by less than twenty million people. This is not the case for the televised presidential debates.[2]

The debates can make a significant difference for the two contestants. Since 1960 Gallup polling has indicated noticeable persuasive effects. Only in 1984 did the October debates fail to register a change in the polling of the two major candidates (Reagan and Mondale). Poll changes since 1960 range from twelve points for President Bush in 2000 to one point for President Bush Sr. in 1988.[3]

Presidential debates constitute a significant communication opportunity for candidates. Very few communication outlets offer a comparable audience. As a matter of comparison, the *Saturday Night Live* skit about the debates following on the Saturday after they take place will likely attract about three million viewers. *Saturday Night Live* drew its largest number of viewers in October 2008 when Sarah Palin joined Tina Fey on the show.[4] The Palin *SNL* attracted seventeen million viewers, which is exponentially larger than the average viewership of the NBC comedy show. Most of the news shows hosted by debate moderators attract between two and eight million viewers at the most.

THE PRINCIPLES OF DEBATE

Presidential debates pose a special analytical problem for academics. Presidential debates are a tool and vehicle for sharing valuable candidate and issue information for voters. However, from an academic perspective, the structure and components of a debate are critical for them to function as appropriate means of political communication. It is important to reflect on the well-established academic ideals of debates. Debates represent an ideal form of communication wherein two sides have an equal opportunity to present their viewpoints and a reasonably fair adjudication of those views by a relatively impartial party. The four essential ingredients of a debate according to most studies of the topic are:

1. a topic of controversy typically known as the *resolution*;
2. two sides to oppose one another on the topic—typically known as *affirmative* and *negative sides*;
3. equal time to speak assigned to both sides;
4. a judge to review and render a decision as to which side won the performed debate.

These four ingredients create a communication context of inherent fairness so that competing ideas on a matter can be reasonably compared. The ideals of debate for purposes of the presidential election are mediated by the Commission on Presidential Debates (CPD).[5] This organization has since 1988 established the ground rules of debate. The commission is composed of campaign representatives from the two major parties and academics interested in the process of debate within the presidential-election process. In 2012 the CPD produced twenty-one pages of rules governing the debate process, and those rules were the culmination of these three parties discussing and ultimately agreeing to these rules. The rules of these debates remain controversial despite various revisions. The CPD is presently the principal social fulcrum for mediating the expectations of a debate within the presidential-election process.

Incumbent candidates and challengers are not required by law or statute to participate in these debates. In fact, in 1964, 1968, and 1972 there were no presidential debates.[6] In many states governors do not participate in debates. In fact, incumbents face a peculiar strategic communication burden in that attending a debate with a new challenger will inherently elevate that challenger both in the public imagination and the polls themselves. Though many were stunned at the loss of President Obama in 2012's first debate, he actually followed tradition, where incumbents tend to stumble in the first debate. President Bush in 2004 and President Reagan in 1984 both ostensibly lost their first debates while recovering to win reelection.[7] Incumbents face serious risks in agreeing to debate.

With this understood, the CPD record of securing multiple debates among candidates since 1988 is both surprising and impressive. It does not remain without controversy both for politicians and academics seeking to further idealize the process. This analysis will conclude with some recommendations for further improving the CPD and presidential debate process.

ELECTION 2012 AND THE DEBATES

The rhetorical impact of the presidential debates in October of 2012 were noteworthy. Numerous aspects of the debates can and will be studied for some time. The presidential debates of 2012 were primarily noteworthy in that: (1) they attracted some of the largest audiences in the fifty years of televised debates, (2) the incumbent president overcame one of the worst losses in a debate to win the election, and (3) the degree of procedural transgressions regarding the rules of the debate continued to progress markedly.

PRESIDENTIAL DEBATE #1: OCTOBER 3 IN DENVER

Prior to the debates, polling suggested that President Obama had a lead and that he would likely win the first debate against Romney.[8] The media constructed a view that the Democratic National Convention had left a more powerful rhetorical effect on the public—particularly through the efforts of Bill Clinton's convention address.[9] By an almost two-to-one margin, the public expected Obama to win. The low-expectations gambit made famous in 2000 by Karl Rove did not deter the Obama campaign from agreeing to these high expectations. The polling situation was so acute that some pundits were suggesting the race was functionally over because the Obama campaign had locked up strong leads in key states such as Ohio and Florida.[10] Several polls suggested that double-digit leads might exist in key swing states. Republicans and conservatives were complaining that the polls were skewed and relying on 2008 turnout assumptions that favored Democrats. In any case, the Romney campaign was certainly on the defensive going into the first debate.

Nielsen surveys of the viewing audience suggest that sixty-seven million viewers tuned in to presidential debate number one between President Obama and Mitt Romney on the night of October 3. This viewing audience was the second largest in history—surpassed only by the 1980 debate between Carter and Reagan that attracted eighty-one million viewers.[11] The Nielsen ratings did not include viewers who watched or listened to the debate from sources such as the Internet, NPR, and C-SPAN. This leads many experts to agree that the viewing audience was likely in excess of seventy million.

The size of the audience is rhetorically suggestive. The public was interested in seeing the debate. The audience was much larger than those for debates in 2000, 2004, and 2008. Public viewing of the conventions in August and September was down to well under twenty million for each convention and was part of a long-term downward trend. Public interest in that form of political communication is generally waning. But that was not the case for the first presidential debate of 2012. The public was increasingly frustrated with the media and its coverage of politics—with public trust in the media at record lows in the fall of 2012.[12] The public likely saw the debates as a relatively unobstructed view of the candidate messages and arguments.

This provides a rationale for the large audience in debate one. Gallup recorded a record lopsided public perception of the debate, with 70 percent indicating that Romney won compared to 20 percent believing President Obama won.[13] Polls typically register much more ambiguous results along partisan lines with strong performances showing a 55–35 split. The October 3 event was a unique communication event.

The resulting change in poll position was arguably one of the largest in fifty years of televised debates. A Pew poll became the rhetorical lightning rod of analysis the week after the debate. According to their poll of likely voters, Romney reversed a 51–43 deficit to Obama from September 16 to a 49–45 advantage on October 7.[14] There is no record of such a sharp swing from any other debate. In 2000 president Bush netted a large twelve-point swing during the month of October against Vice President Gore. Amid the polling data from Pew was a rather shocking report in the area of gender: Prior to the debate President Obama had a seventeen-point lead over Romney among women. After the debate the two were tied. The seventeen-point lead had completely evaporated. The poll led columnists such as Andrew Sullivan to lament that President Obama had lost the election by losing the debate.[15]

Democrats also agreed that President Obama had lost the debate, and independents strongly agreed with Republicans that Romney had won—both in flash polling after debate one and more methodical polling within forty-eight hours of the debate. It was unquestionably a striking win among presidential debates and perhaps the most decisive single win in presidential-debate history.

The substance of the debate revolved on two key concerns: (1) the weak delivery of the president versus the strong style of the challenger and (2) the focused attacks of the challenger and the lack of rebuttals from the president. Those two points tended to dominate critiques of debate number one. There were also criticisms made about the moderator, Jim Lehrer. Many commentators felt that he let the debate get out of control, and some partisans felt he should have done more to help President Obama fend off the vigorous attacks of Romney.[16] At one point Obama did ask Lehrer to move on, and Lehrer did occasionally ask the president if he specifically wanted to respond to Romney. The most lively exchange for the moderator came when Romney directly challenged government funding for public broadcasting. He specifically mentioned the character Big Bird from *Sesame Street* and Jim Lehrer at NPR. Romney used humor to joke that he liked Jim but was not sure we should be borrowing from China to pay for such broadcasts. The exchanges and the concerns after the debate suggest that revision may be in order for the process of moderators in presidential debates. Ultimately the Obama campaign went on to create TV political ads defending Big Bird.[17]

The fascinating collapse of women voters is arguably the most striking rhetorical effect of the debate. Polling data suggests that women were more drawn than men to the messages of the president during the event.[18] But something transpired in the ultimate understanding of the event to collapse the president's gender advantage. In the closing minutes of the debate, an interesting exchange emerged about bipartisanship. The two candidates compared their efforts to pass health-care laws at the federal level and in Massachusetts. Romney noted that the president got zero votes from Republicans in his bill while he had gotten more than eighty Democrats to sign his bill when he was governor of Massachusetts. The argument had resonance and may have been the kind of argumentative warrant that female voters were ready to acknowledge in a quest for cooperation rather than further political conflict.

VICE PRESIDENTIAL DEBATE: OCTOBER 11

The vice presidential debate was watched by more than fifty million viewers—which was down considerably from when Sarah Palin debated Joe Biden in 2008. It was however a large audience. By the time of the debate the public sense of Obama's loss in debate number one was evident and there was considerable pressure to turn the fortunes of the campaign around. Vice President Biden was exceedingly aggressive in the debate and cut off Congressman Ryan more than eighty times.[19] Prior to the debate it was discovered that the moderator, Martha Raddatz, had hosted President Obama as a guest at her wedding. As moderator she was more aggressive than Lehrer had been in the first debate. The nonverbal differences of the debaters were striking, and Biden grinned and laughed continually regardless of the remarks made by Paul Ryan.

PRESIDENTIAL DEBATE #2:
OCTOBER 16, TOWN-HALL FORMAT

The town-hall debate represents one of the more recent format adaptations of the presidential debates. Moderator Candy Crowley indicated that she would not abide by the agreements established that she should take a passive role in the debate.[20] Both campaigns publicly resisted her announcement, but she pressed forward with a plan to redirect candidates as she saw fit. She was guided by a committee in selecting questions created by the town-hall participants.

The most striking moment of the debate came in discussion of a controversy over the death of an American ambassador in Libya. Romney challenged the president on when exactly he had called the event a terror attack. In the exchange that featured considerable direct eye contact and emotional gravity, the president asserted that he termed the incident an "act of terror" the next day, rather than taking weeks to figure that out as Romney asserted.[21] The exchange became pointed and recurring. Moderator Crowley corrected Romney and said the president did call the incident an "act of terror." The president asked her to repeat the correction more loudly. The first lady, Michelle Obama, broke the CPD audience rules for the debate and began to applaud the president, and the applause spread throughout the auditorium.[22]

PRESIDENTIAL DEBATE #3: OCTOBER 22, FOREIGN POLICY

In the final debate Romney and Obama focused on foreign policy. The moderator, Bob Schieffer, and the presidential-debate commission released the topics of the foreign-policy debate in advance. The most striking aspect of the final debate was the passive behavior of candidate Romney, who was surprisingly noncombative on several foreign-policy controversies. His most distinctive argument was likely his suggestion that Iranian leader Ahmadinejad should be tried for crimes of genocide. Romney seemed intent on continuing to bank a lead he felt he created in debate number one. He did not venture aggressive attacks on the president, and the polling afterward rather consistently suggested that President Obama won the debate.

OBSERVATIONS ON DEBATES HOSTED BY
THE PRESIDENTIAL DEBATE COMMISSION
FOR U.S. PRESIDENTIAL ELECTION 2012

These observations are based on data compiled on a chart shown in table 3.1:

1. More than fifty million people watched each of the four debates. These were among the most consistently watched debates in the history of televised debates. Nearly seventy million people watched the first debate—the third-largest viewing audience in history after the eighty million for Reagan/Carter and seventy-three million for Palin/Biden.
2. Romney and Ryan got 6 percent less speaking time but spoke almost 10 percent more during the debates. This means that both Ryan and Romney spoke more quickly than their Democratic opponents. Romney spoke about five hundred words more than Obama in each debate while Ryan tore up the tracks with one thousand words more than Biden. Ryan accomplished this despite being interrupted more than eighty times.
3. The Obama and Biden team interrupted their counterparts 150 percent more than did Romney and Ryan. Biden provided a bulk of interruptions with more than eighty. Obama/Biden interrupted Romney/Ryan 145 times while Romney/Ryan interrupted Obama/Biden 57 times during the four debates.
4. The moderators interrupted Romney and Ryan 125 percent more often than they interrupted Obama and Biden. Moderator interruptions for the two sides scored 151 to 79 respectively. In every debate, the moderator interrupted the Republican candidates more than the Democrats.
5. Moderators provided 10 percent of the speaking content in debates. Raddatz was the most involved moderator. She took 13 percent of the speech content in the debate. As noticed by most, Lehrer spoke the least—occupying 8.3 percent of the speech content.

6. Romney and Ryan interrupted the moderators 62 percent more frequently than their counterparts Obama and Biden. The most aggressive interruption pattern was in debate number one, where Romney interrupted Lehrer thirteen times. Romney and Ryan interrupted moderators forty times while Obama and Biden interrupted them twenty-six times.

7. Obama and Biden received almost ten more minutes of speech time during the course of the four debates. As noted earlier, despite having more time, they spoke less than their opponents. Romney set the speed record at 203 words per minute in debate number one. Biden spoke the slowest at 160 words per minute in his debate. Obama/Biden averaged 171 words per minute while Romney/Ryan average 196 words per minute. This means team Romney/Ryan spoke 15 percent faster than team Obama/Biden.

8. More than sixty thousand words were spoken during the four debates by the four candidates. Six thousand words were spoken by moderators trying to control the debates. The wordiest entry of the debate contest was 8,116 words, delivered by Romney in the last debate. Biden gave the most concise entry, with 6,631 words for his debate with Ryan.

9. The vice presidential debate was the least watched of the four debates. The first debate was the most watched, with sixty-seven million viewers. The final debate had an impressive 59.2 million viewers. These numbers do not include viewers on the Internet.

10. There were no moderators selected for these debates from Fox News. Fox News has the largest national viewing audience among news networks. Despite holding audiences two and three times larger than CNN and other networks such as ABC, Fox was not selected to provide moderators to any of the four debates. Fox is widely held to be the most conservative outlet among news organizations.

LEARNING FROM THE DATA

The public indicated protracted interest in the debate process that compared favorably with the lack of interest in the party conventions for the summer. The voter participation was observably diminished from 2008 with President Obama receiving a much lower vote count than he did in 2012 and candidate Romney surpassing the vote count of John McCain in 2008. At least four million fewer voters participated in election 2012. Debates are an important catalyst to the larger political process and should be seen in some part as a contribution to public participation and interest.

Despite the large audiences, improvements remain possible for the future of presidential debating. The most obvious is a need for greater fairness to both sides of the debate. Equal speech time is a glaring failing of the recent presidential debates in 2008 and 2012. In all four of the 2012 debates the Republican candidates got less time than the Democratic candidates. CNN suggested that this was due to president Obama's slow rate of delivery.[23] Such a defense is not acceptable to debate pedagogy and guides no known practice of debate activity. The general rhetorical sensation of combat and struggle between the candidates and the moderators was clearly distracting and arguably distorting to the overall communication process. Moderators occupied more than 10 percent of the overall speech time in the debates of 2012. For personalities that already wield too much influence on public opinion—according to public-opinion surveys—keeping this to a minimum would improve the civic quality of the debates.

RECOMMENDATIONS TO THE
PRESIDENTIAL DEBATE COMMISSION

Remove journalist moderators from the debates: From the inception of the televised presidential debate process in 1960, journalists play a prominent on-screen role interrogating candidates. Debates typically feature far less visible conduct. In most cases a debate judge is a largely silent and rather unseen component of the debate. Moving toward this more traditional pedagogy would reduce public debate about moderators and increase public focus on what candidates are saying and arguing. Presently moderators occupy almost 10 percent of the debate time (table 3.1).

Debate professionals should administer the debates: Debate professionals occupy a strangely peripheral relationship to the construction and conduct of presidential debates. Presently they primarily provide colorful backgrounds and opinions about strategy that may be employed in the debate and most importantly a judgment as to who won the debate. These functions do not promote debate as the core civic value necessary for good politics. Elevating debate professionals to the planning and conduct of debates will aid in reversing the general decline in political civility encouraged by the sound-bite culture presently driving presidential debate from the standpoint of television journalism. The question of journalist involvement in the debates is long standing and a matter of continued interest among those studying the debates from a communication perspective.[24] Using debate professionals as replacements to the journalist moderators would improve public perceptions of fairness and likely increase the content of arguments from candidates.

Host debates at presidential libraries: Debate sites are presently determined by a bidding process that allows universities to host the debates. There is no particular logic or rationale behind the choice of sites. Presidential libraries have served as candidate-debate sites for the presidential primaries, but they have not served this function for the general election. The presidential libraries are an important national repository of American civics, and they can provide a more compelling situational backdrop to the presidential-selection process. Choosing two Democratic and two Republican presidential libraries provides an intuitive balance to the process.

Enforce speech times, and maintain equality: This most glaring malfunction of the 2012 debates should be corrected. At minimum the errors need to be publicly acknowledged. Solutions are varied. Debaters could receive increments of extra time as the series of debates progress, in order to deter moderators from favoring one side so consistently as has been done with both candidate Obama in 2008 and President Obama in 2012. Microphones could be turned off when time expires, and visual transmission could be limited in the most severe cases. In any event, it is important to realize that hundreds and thousands of debates that take place every year from elementary schools to colleges and universities provide equal time to the opposing sides. To suggest that presidential candidates cannot do this is disingenuous.

No one should interrupt debates to give judgments or make decisions about contested points: The conduct of Candy Crowley should not be repeated. Debate moderators do not take the role of judges in a courtroom. The expressed purpose of debates is to place the contested opinions of the candidates in a free and fair public forum wherein the public is left to decide. Interrupting that forum and intervening to answer questions or allegations betrays the central civic function. Essentially a debate is over once a "moderator" departs from that explicit role and begins answering the controversies in the public argument. Here again literally thousands of debates happen every year with few if any interventions by outside judges or observers. Maintaining this observational clarity does not limit the speech or freedom of general commentary. Everyone is free to interpret the debates from their own individual vantage points. Of course the debaters will make accusations that seem urgent, but judgment of these must be left to the public observers of the debate—not moderators.

Give debaters more speech time: The primary exigency apparent in the debate for interruptions and exasperation from candidates is the short speech times provided to debaters. It is a positive trend that since 2004 candidate speech times have increased. The commission is aware of this concern. Moving toward traditional speech times of four minutes or more would make the presidential debates more conventional and less frustrating for participants. The journalistic paradigm brings an impatience to the process that stunts good debate. If more debates are needed to get more issues discussed, then let that be the practice rather than a rule that candidates must necessarily give too-brief answers to often long-winded questions posed by moderators.

It should be possible for 2016 to implement all or some of these reforms for at least one of the four debates. Further improvements to presidential debates will magnify the positive civic virtue that debate represents for American society and the world.

APPENDIX

Table 3.1. Debate Moderator Analysis

Debate-Moderator Analysis	Debate 1	Debate 2	Debate 3	Debate 4	Totals
Location	Denver	Kentucky	NY	Florida	
Format	moderator	moderator/ vp	town hall	moderator	
Moderator	Lehrer	Raddatz	Crowley	Schiefer	
Affiliation	PBS	ABC News	CNN	CBS	
Television-Viewing-Audience Size	67 million	51 million	65 million	59.2 million	
Date	October 3	October 11	October 16	October 22	

	Debate 1	Debate 2	Debate 3	Debate 4	Totals
Extra Time	+4:18 Obama	+1:22 Biden	+3:14 Obama	+:37 Obama	**9:31m**
Interruptions of Obama/Biden	6	30	43	28	**107**
Interruptions of Romney/Ryan	19	100	59	31	**209**
Speaking Time of Obama	0h 42m 40s	0h 41m 32s	0h 44m 4s	0h 41m 5s	**2h 49m 21s**
Speaking Time of Romney	0h 38m 14s	0h 40m 12s	0h 40m 50s	0h 41m 42s	**2h 40m 58s**
Last Word on Turns			8/3 +Obama		
Total Word Count Obama	7,294	6,631	7,506	7,556	**28,987**
Total Word Count Romney	7,802	7708	7,984	8,116	**31,610**
Words per Minute Obama	170.98	159.78	170.2	183.84	**171.20**
Words per Minute Romney	203.18	191.74	195.54	194.63	**196.27**
Number of Moderator Words	1,250	1,879	1,512	1,388	**6029**
Percent of Debate by Moderator	8.1%	12.8%	9.5%	8.6%	
Obama/Biden Interrupted Romney/Ryan	4	82	36	23	**145**
Romney/Ryan Interrupted Obama/Biden	1	15	28	13	**57**

Debate-Moderator Analysis	Debate 1	Debate 2	Debate 3	Debate 4	Totals
Romney/Ryan Interrupted Moderator	13	8	11	8	**40**
Obama/Biden Interrupted Moderator	7	9	9	1	**26**
Moderator Interrupted Obama/Biden	5	15	10	5	**35**
Moderator Interrupted Romney/Ryan	15	18	28	18	**79**
Cross Talk in Transcript	26	54	22	49	**151**

NOTES

1. Mitchell McKinney, "Debating Democracy: The History and Effects of the U.S. Presidential Debates," *Spectra* 48, no. 3 (September 2012).

2. "Historical TV Ratings for Presidential Debates: 1960–2008 Presidential Campaigns," About.com, accessed October 25, 2012, http://uspolitics.about.com/od/elections/l/bl_historical_tv_ratings_prez_debates.htm.

3. Lydia Saad, "Presidential Debates Rarely Game-Changers," Gallup, September 25, 2008, accessed October 25, 2012, www.gallup.com/poll/110674/Presidential-Debates-Rarely-GameChangers.aspx.

4. Leigh Holmwood, "Sarah Palin Helps Saturday Night Live to Best Ratings in 14 Years," *Guardian*, October 20, 2008, www.guardian.co.uk/media/2008/oct/20/ustelevision-tvratings.

5. Commission on Presidential Debates, "Our Mission," accessed January 3, 2012, www.debates.org/index.php?page=about-cpd.

6. McKinney, "Debating Democracy."

7. Saad, "Presidential Debates Rarely Game-Changers."

8. "ABC News/*Washington Post* Poll: Obama Leading Romney Ahead of First Debate," BNO News, October 1, 2012, http://bnonews.com/urgent/10046/abc-newswashington-post-poll-obama-leading-romney-ahead-of-first-debate/.

9. David Espo, "Clinton Boosts Obama in Rousing Convention Speech," Associated Press, September 6, 2012, http://news.yahoo.com/clinton-boosts-obama-rousing-convention-speech-032115498--election.html.

10. Tim Stanley, "Only a Spark of Magic Can Save Mitt Romney Now," *Telegraph*, October 2, 2012, www.telegraph.co.uk/news/worldnews/mitt-romney/9582135/Only-a-spark-of-magic-can-save-Mitt-Romney-now.html.

11. McKinney, "Debating Democracy."

12. Lymari Morales, "U.S. Distrust in Media Hits New Highs," Gallup, September 21, 2012, accessed October 5, 2012, www.gallup.com/poll/157589/distrust-media-hits-new-high.aspx.

13. Jeffrey Jones, "Romney Narrows Vote Gap after Historic Debate Win," Gallup, October 8, 2012, accessed January 6, 2012, www.gallup.com/poll/157907/romney-narrows-vote-gap-historic-debate-win.aspx.

14. "Romney's Strong Debate Performance Erases Obama's Lead," *Pew Research*, October 8, 2012, accessed October 15, 2012, www.people-press.org/2012/10/08/romneys-strong-debate-performance-erases-obamas-lead/2/.

15. Andrew Sullivan, "Live Blogging the First Presidential Debate," *Daily Beast*, October 8, 2012, accessed January 6, 2013, http://andrewsullivan.thedailybeast.com/2012/10/live-blogging-the-first-presidential-debate-2012.html.

16. Michael Taube, "TAUBE: Presidential Debate Moderator Mediocrity," *Washington Times*, October 18, 2012, 4, www.washingtontimes.com/news/2012/oct/16/taube-presidential-debate-moderator-mediocrity/.

17. Susan Krashinsky, "PBS Not Laughing at Obama's Big Bird Ad," *Globe and Mail*, October 10, 2012 A13.

18. Juan Williams, "How Twitter May Have Tipped the Election for Romney," Fox News, October 25, 2012, accessed January 4, 2013, www.foxnews.com/opinion/2012/10/25/how-twitter-may-have-tipped-election-for-romney/.

19. "The Bully vs. the Wonk," *Wall Street Journal*, October 12, 2012, accessed October 25, 2012, http://online.wsj.com/article/SB10000872396390443749204578051073494711456.html.

20. Paul Farhi, "CNN's Crowley Says She'll Have Active Role in Debate Despite Candidates' Efforts," *Washington Post*, October 16, 2012, C04.

21. Anneke E. Green, "GREEN: Obama's Incorrect 'Acts of Terror' Assertions," *Washington Times*, October 22, 2012, 3, www.washingtontimes.com/news/2012/oct/19/green-obamas-acts-terror-assertions/.

22. Katie Glueck, "Conservatives Call Out Michelle Obama's Clapping," *Politico*, October 17, 2012, www.politico.com/news/stories/1012/82537.html.

23. Geoffrey Dickens, "CNN Internal Memo: Obama Got More Debate Time Because He Speaks Slowly," NewsBusters, October 18, 2012, accessed October 25, 2012, http://newsbusters.org/blogs/geoffrey-dickens/2012/10/18/cnn-internal-memo-obama-got-more-debate-time-because-he-speaks-slo.

24. Robert Friedenberg, ed., *Rhetorical Studies of National Political Debates: 1960 to 1992*, 2nd ed. (Westport, Conn.: Greenwood Publishing, 1993).

4

"His to Lose": Strategic Keys to Challenging the Incumbent in 2012

Craig Allen Smith

For years President Obama's critics repeated the mantra, "No President has been reelected with unemployment this bad." Mitt Romney was so confident on election night that he prepared only a victory speech.[1] As returns came in, analyst Karl Rove dispute their accuracy on Fox News, prompting anchor Megyn Kelly to ask, "Is this just math that you do as a Republican to make yourself feel better, or is this real?"[2] Finger pointers quickly emerged, offering scapegoats ranging from Republican candidates who had voiced unpopular views about abortion to miscalculations of the whiteness of the electorate to Governor Christie's handling of Hurricane Sandy to Romney and his strategists. But it is exceedingly difficult to unseat an incumbent president, and their general expectations for 2012 were overly optimistic.

Presidential campaigns are rhetorical puzzles in which nominees strive to win pluralities in states sufficient to yield 270 electoral votes. This chapter contends that reelection campaigns are a unique variant of the puzzle in which incumbents win unless voters in states accounting for 270 electoral votes consider at least six of thirteen propositions to be false. This chapter will then apply that framework to 2012 to demonstrate that President Obama's defeat was never as probable as imagined in public discussion.

INCUMBENTS AND THEIR CHALLENGERS

The best place to begin a quest for the White House is in the White House. Countless people have run for president, but only thirty-three have been elected. Because five died in office, only twenty-eight could run for reelection: 10 percent (Polk, Pierce, and Hayes) were not renominated, 32 percent were renominated and lost, and 64 percent were reelected.[3]

Moreover reelection campaigns are rarely close. The seventeen presidents reelected before 2012 did not simply win, they triumphed by an average margin of 236 electoral votes and 16 percent of the popular vote. But the eight losers lost in comparable blowouts by average deficits of 232 electoral votes and 8.5 percent of the popular vote. The only close reelection contests were Wilson's in 1916 and Bush's in 2004.

Moreover merely occupying the White House boosts one's odds for continuation. Of the nine who succeeded to the presidency, four were not nominated, one was nominated and lost, and four were nominated and elected. But since the 1860s all five such presidents have been nominated and 80 percent have been elected; only Ford, who followed a resignation, failed to win.

The record suggests that candidates who solve the electoral puzzle once are more likely to solve it again than are those who have yet to solve it. In short, when a sitting president runs, the office is his to lose.[4]

THE REELECTION LANDSCAPE

Reelection is the incumbent's to lose, but several have. What variables have differentiated the winners from the losers? Political scientist Alan J. Lichtman provides guidance.

Lichtman's Keys to Reelection

Alan J. Lichtman's research led him to posit thirteen true/false "Keys to the White House" that will inform our study of reelection campaigns (see table 4.1).[5] Importantly, Lichtman writes, "when five or fewer statements are false, the incumbent party wins," so challengers need at least six false keys to beat an incumbent.[6]

It is tempting to regard Lichtman's keys as objective circumstantial statements merely to be verified. But observers of presidential-campaign communication recognize that perceptions matter, thus each key is a claim to be contested: What is an administration "success," and what is a "failure"? What is a "major" change in policy? In practice, strategists help candidates decide which keys to concede and which to contest, and among which citizens.

Contesting the Keys

How do candidates contest the thirteen keys? William Benoit's extensive research on campaign communication has quantified candidates' use of three essential speech acts: acclaims, attacks, and defenses.[7] Put simply, a candidate acclaims what he has done or supports, attacks what his opponent has done or supports, and defends his acclaims against the opponent's attacks. Benoit's research has identified empirical patterns in the distribution of attacks, acclaims, and defenses by a variety of candidates in a variety of campaign forms (such as ads and debates) and media.

Table 4.1. Lichtman's Keys to the White House

Key	Explanation
1. Incumbent-party mandate	The incumbent party gained congressional seats in the midterm elections.
2. Nomination contest	There is no serious contest for the incumbent-party nomination.
3. Incumbency	The sitting president is a nominee.
4. Third party	There is no significant "third-party" candidate.
5. Short-term economy	The economy is not in recession during the campaign.
6. Long-term economy	Real annual per capita economic growth during the term is at least equal to that of the two previous presidential terms.
7. Policy change	The incumbent made major changes in national policy.
8. Social unrest	There was no sustained social unrest during the term.
9. Scandal	The administration is untainted by scandal.
10. Foreign or military failure	The administration experienced no major failure.
11. Foreign or military success	The administration accomplished a major success.
12. Incumbent charisma	The incumbent is charismatic or a national hero.
13. Challenger charisma	The challenging candidate is not charismatic or a national hero.

Source: Alan J. Lichtman, *Predicting the Next President* (Lanham, Md.: Rowman & Littlefield, 2008), 3.

Unfortunately Benoit has yet to deal as extensively with the relationships among acclaims, attacks, and defenses. His work underplays Halford Ross Ryan's argument that defenses should be studied as part of a speech set (attacks-defenses).[8] It is reasonable to extend Ryan's logic to encompass acclaims-attacks as a second speech set, for acclaims that gain traction invite either concession or response. Thus acclaims, attacks, and defenses interconnect to create the campaign conversation.

In summary, reelection campaigns (1) require challengers to attack incumbents so as to convince voters that six (or more) of the keys are false and (2) require incumbents to acclaim and defend so as to convince voters that only five (or fewer) are false. But incumbents and challengers have different audiences.

Stages of Challenger and Incumbent Presidential Campaigns

Presidential campaigns evolve through four stages.[9] The *surfacing stage* runs from election night through the Iowa-precinct caucuses. Aspirants for nomination need to establish themselves as viable candidates for their party's nomination. This entails choices about running, campaign staff, fundraising, and policy stands. Progress toward viability can be measured by fundraising reports, media coverage, national polling, and a top-four finish in Iowa. But incumbent presidents have already surfaced and need only worry that intraparty opponents might surface.

The *nomination stage* encompasses the primaries and caucuses that commit state party delegates to vote for a candidate at the national convention. It runs from the first delegate contest (New Hampshire) through whatever state gives one candidate a majority of delegate commitments. The nomination stage consists of battles among the party faithful, and winning entails courting the support of the most feverish partisans. Nominations are therefore contested among each party's active participants, and they are ordinarily its more ardent and doctrinaire members. Moderation in the pursuit of an anti-incumbent nomination is no virtue, and extremism is rarely a vice. Meanwhile incumbents who avoid intraparty challenges get another free pass to renomination.

The fight for nomination requires a *consolidation stage*, which begins when the partisans have a presumptive nominee and culminates in the convention's nomination acceptance address. That candidate must begin immediately to mend fences with erstwhile adversaries lest the core party coalition splinter.

But incumbents without intraparty opposition begin with consolidation. In fact, incumbents' consolidation begins with their inaugural address and continues through their term with efforts to be perceived as president of "all the people." The president's election-year State of the Union address is his first major foray into the campaign-consolidation effort, and it occurs about the time that his challengers start to pummel each other in their primaries. The State of the Union is the incumbent's unique opportunity to consolidate the country behind his leadership and agenda and to have someone from the other party illustrate the disparity between an incumbent president and anyone else.

The *election stage* begins with the nominees' acceptance addresses and ends (although technically with the electoral college vote) on election night. The election stage is entirely about crystallizing the citizenry into three camps: (1) those who vote for the incumbent, (2) those who vote for the challenger, and (3) those who do not vote. The goal is to crystallize those groups of citizens and mobilize them into voters who deliver pluralities in states sufficient to cast 270 electoral-college votes for a candidate.

Unlike the nomination stage, the election stage is ordinarily decided by the center. The candidate who courted his party's extreme to win nomination suddenly must court moderates and undecided citizens to win electoral pluralities, all without alienating his party's true believers. Paradoxically the candidate attempting to unseat an incumbent must appeal to these two broad and divergent audiences for nomination and election while the incumbent gets to spend the whole year consolidating "all the people." Of course, it is conceivable that a candidate could win by mobilizing a strong partisan base. That was Karl Rove's 2004 strategy for the Bush reelection, but that is a risky strategy because neither party can lay claim to even 40 percent of the electorate, as the Pew typology of citizens shows.

The Pew Typology of Citizens

The Pew typology of American voters has tracked clusters of opinion in the electorate since the 1980s. The Pew typology is more useful to observers of campaign communication than are demographics because it clusters citizens who respond similarly to dichotomous questions about policy positions—the sorts of things that candidates acclaim, attack, and defend. This approach differs significantly from the traditional tracking of demographics.

While it may be nice to know that someone leads someone else among women, the demographic approach fails to tell us why—for what arguable reasons—those women are divided in their opinions. Candidates can speak more (or less) about positions that redistribute support, and they can enhance the salience of some identities rather than others, but trying to alter citizens' sex, age, or ethnicity is a futile strategy.

The Pew data show a variety of migrations in and out of party alignments since the 1980s, and they show rebranding or reconceptualizations of those groups. Candidates' rhetoric constitutes clusters of citizens around arguments and reconstitutes electoral coalitions from those clusters.[10]

The Electoral Tipping Point

As the candidates enter the final stage they need 270 electoral votes from state elections. That means that the outcome can best be projected by aggregating state-level polls rather than relying on national-percentage polls.

The Hotline began tracking state polls in 1984, and Electoral-vote.com has done so since 2004. In 2012 they both provided a daily "tipping-point" table of states that were "strongly" and "leaning" toward either candidate, those that were too close to call, and those that were tied based on the relation of the state poll's margin and its margin for error.

A tipping-point table ranks states downward from the greatest state-poll margin for one candidate and thus upward from the greatest state-poll margin for the other candidate. It includes columns that aggregate the projected electoral votes (upward and downward) such that one can easily see which state will provide the 270th vote or tipping point.

The tipping-point table shows what each candidate must accomplish to tip the election his way. One candidate need only carry states in which he already leads, whereas the other must carry all in which he leads and then take one or more states in which he trails by some margin. Strategically, the frontrunner must close the deal, whereas the trailer must first dislodge some states from the frontrunner and then win them.

Summarizing Lichtman's Keys

The reelection landscape consists of an incumbent and multiple challengers contesting the thirteen keys in various media. Challengers compete among their party's minority of the electorate for nomination, mend their fences, then pivot toward the less ideological and more moderate general electorate. The incumbent chooses between running as president of "all of the people" or as partisan-in-chief, seeking to establish at least eight of the contested keys as true in the eyes of voters in states providing 270 electoral votes.

A STRATEGIC READING OF CAMPAIGN 2012

The foregoing discussion of the situational requirements provides a framework for reading the 2012 presidential campaigns' strategic choices. We shall consider the landscape for the campaign in 2011 to understand the rhetorical problems facing the campaigns and the strategies appropriate for solving them during 2012 and the implications of the choices they made.

The Pew Landscape in mid-2011

Pew's May 2011 analysis identified a Republican-base coalition of "staunch conservatives" (9 percent of the electorate) and "Main Street Republicans" (11 percent) for a total of 20 percent of the electorate.[11] The nomination would therefore hinge on the candidates' ability to win primaries and caucuses in a Republican electorate that was 55 percent mainstream Republican and 45 percent Tea Party-ish. Yet all contenders were keenly aware that the Tea Party had mobilized primary voters to defeat incumbent mainstream Republicans in 2010. With the GOP thus polarized, the faction with one candidate would have a strategic advantage over the faction fragmented by multiple candidates. Nevertheless, the nominee who won and consolidated them all could then count only on 20 percent of the electorate.

Pew's Democratic coalition consisted of "solid liberals" (14 percent), "hard-pressed Democrats" (13 percent), and "new-coalition Democrats" (10 percent) for 37 percent of the electorate.[12] An unchallenged Democrat could begin immediately to consolidate that 37 percent while the Republicans were dividing their 20 percent. Then in November if only the base coalitions voted the Democrat would win the popular vote 37 percent to 20 percent (Pew does not yet consider their respondents' states of residence or electoral projections). But two other factors complicate that simplistic scenario.

The first is voter turnout. An energized minority can overpower an apathetic majority, and widespread disappointment in Obama suggested that he could not duplicate his 69.5 million–vote total of 2008. But would he need to? No one else had ever won that many votes. If Republicans managed to turn out all 20 percent of their base, Obama would only need 55 percent of his 37 percent base to beat them with 20.35 percent (if popular votes counted).

Of course Pew also identified clusters aligned with neither party, and these swing audiences could have proven decisive. "Disaffecteds" (11 percent) and libertarians (9 percent) were promising targets for Republicans and could expand their pool from 20 percent to 40 percent of the electorate. But "Postmoderns" (13 percent) had mostly supported Obama in 2008, expanding his pool to 50 percent.[13]

Thus Republicans seeking nomination in 2012 needed support from 20 percent of the electorate that was divided almost equally between "staunch conservatives" and "Main Street Republicans." But they needed to win in a way that would enable them to win and mobilize libertarians, disaffecteds, and more by November.

But the incumbent was free to choose between running as "president of everyone except the Republicans" (about 80 percent of the electorate) or as "chief Democrat" (about 37 percent of the electorate), leaving the three nonaligned clusters (23 percent) in play. That choice would hinge, in large measure, on the state of the thirteen keys.

The Lichtman Keys in 2011

Lichtman wrote that those challenging an incumbent need to cultivate false answers to at least six keys. So let us consider the state of those keys in the summer of 2011, deep into the surfacing stage and six months before Iowa and New Hampshire.

President Obama had six keys in good shape by the summer of 2011: he was an unopposed, charismatic, scandal-free incumbent whose team had killed Osama bin Ladin and experienced no notable foreign-policy failures. But his challengers had two false keys—the 2010 congressional victories and the long-term economic stagnation that Obama was unlikely to salvage before the general election (see table 4.2.).

Five keys remained unclear, such that Republicans needed to cultivate public impressions of the falseness of at least four of those five statements to win the necessary six. Thus the keys to the 2012 election would be:

1. Would anyone mount a significant "third-party" campaign?
2. Would the economy be in recession during the campaign?
3. Could President Obama demonstrate major changes in national policy?
4. Would there be widespread social unrest?
5. Would Republicans nominate a charismatic candidate?

Let us consider how these five keys were contested in 2012.

Contesting the Five Keys to 2012

Would Anyone Mount a Significant "Third-Party" Campaign?

Lichtman's work suggests that incumbents become vulnerable when a significant third-party campaign complicates the contest. But this presumes that party would draw votes from the incumbent (like Roosevelt in 1912, Ted Kennedy in 1980, and Ross Perot in 1992). But Democrats disappointed in Obama neither challenged his nomination nor advanced a third-party candidate.

Instead the most likely third-party candidate in 2012 was libertarian Ron Paul, whose opposition to aggressive foreign-policy stands undermined his appeal to mainstream Republicans. Had Paul run as the Libertarian candidate he might have

Table 4.2. Lichtman's Keys in Summer 2011

Key	Explanation	Summer 2011 Status
1. Incumbent-party mandate	The incumbent party gained congressional seats in the midterm elections.	FALSE #1: Democrats suffered severe losses in 2010 midterms.
2. Nomination contest	There is no serious contest for the incumbent party nomination.	TRUE #1
3. Incumbency	The sitting president is a nominee.	TRUE #2
4. Third party	There is no significant "third-party" candidate.	UNCLEAR #1: Would Ron Paul run a third-party campaign?
5. Short-term economy	The economy is not in recession during the campaign.	UNCLEAR #2: Would real GDP decline for two consecutive quarters by the October 2012 report?
6. Long-term economy	Real annual per capita economic growth during the term is at least equal to that of the two previous presidential terms.	FALSE #2: Highly unlikely that negative real annual per capita economic growth would exceed the Bush record of 1.10 by the October 2012 report.
7. Policy change	The incumbent made major changes in national policy.	UNCLEAR #3: Would the stimulus plan work? Would the health-care law survive the court challenge? Would Congress pass the jobs bill?
8. Social unrest	There was no sustained social unrest during the term.	UNCLEAR #4: Tea Party unrest had led to 2010 victories. But would their unrest continue or other unrest emerge?
9. Scandal	The administration is untainted by scandal.	TRUE #3
10. Foreign or military failure	The administration experienced no major failure.	TRUE #4
11. Foreign or military success	The administration accomplished a major success.	TRUE #5: The killing of Osama bin Ladin

Key	Explanation	Summer 2011 Status
12. Incumbent charisma	The incumbent is charismatic or a national hero.	TRUE #6: Obama had a reputation for charisma, even though he had rarely displayed it as president.
13. Challenger charisma	The challenging candidate is not charismatic or a national hero.	UNCLEAR #5: Unlike John McCain, no challengers were heroes. Whether the emerging nominee would be charismatic could not yet be known.

Source: Alan J. Lichtman, *Predicting the Next President* (Lanham, Md.: Rowman & Littlefield, 2008), 3, modified by author.

combined his Tea Party–oriented economic plans with support for gay rights, disentanglement from foreign involvement, and legalization of marijuana to attract votes from citizens aligned with neither party. But because Gary Johnson secured the Libertarian nomination early on, Paul would have been running against both the Republican and Libertarian nominees.

In short, a third-party Paul campaign would have falsified a key but not in any way that would have significantly enhanced the prospects for Obama's defeat. In any case, Republicans needed to falsify the other four unclear keys.

Would the Economy Be in Recession during the Campaign?

Economists define *recession* as two consecutive quarters of declining real per capita gross national product (GNP). Real gross domestic product (GDP) hit its low point in late 2009 and began to rebound in 2010.[14] Technically Obama's challengers needed that rebound to end and become a six-month decline. Thus every economic report was highly anticipated, but the rebound—however modest—continued.

But few citizens are prone to analyzing economic data. More important for voting purposes is the general impression that "the economy is in recession during the campaign." In fact Lichtman's second edition of the keys shifted the focus from "the last major turn of the economy" to whether "the *overwhelming public perception* is one of the economy in recession" (emphasis added).[15] This invited two lines of argument from the challengers.

The first line of argument dealt with the meaning of *recession*. Republican voices worked overtime to transform "recession" from a technical economic term into an ideograph. Ideographs are "figures of thought" that invoke ideologies by linking them to other conversations (much as a hyperlink transports us from one Web source to another).[16] As Mary Stuckey observed, "communities of meaning are created through the development of shared agreement on the meaning(s) of ideographs at any given point in time."[17] The ideograph <recession> captured diverse public impressions of widespread economic hardship familiar to many Americans since the 2008 meltdown and associated them with the incumbent. To the extent that voters still felt they were in "hard times" the <recession> continued, per capita GNP notwithstanding.

The second line of argument was that President Obama's economic policies had done too little to move the country out of the <recession>. They argued that any of the Republicans' economic policies would have stimulated more growth and thus more job creation and therefore moved the country more quickly and decisively out of <recession>.

To defend this key, President Obama needed voters to perceive <recession> as a problem from the recent past caused by Bush-era Republican policies and to associate Obama's policies with "hope and change" from <recession>. The economy was improving, slowly, he argued, and his policies deserved credit. Patience and resolve would be more important than the Republican policies that, he insisted, had caused the 2008 recession in the first place. This key would be contested throughout the campaign in terms of (1) whose policies are to blame for hard times and (2) whose policies are likely to end them.

Could President Obama Demonstrate Major Changes in National Policy?

By "major changes" Lichtman means dramatic departures from established policies and groundbreaking innovations recognized as such at the time; he does not require that those changes be popular.[18] In this regard the incumbent could certainly point to the auto industry rescue/bailout of 2009 and The Affordable Care Act of 2010. This key therefore presented the incumbent with a rhetorical quandary: should he acclaim and defend these widely unpopular changes as major, or should he defend them as moderate and traditional?

Republicans faced a comparable quandary. Attacking Obama's unpopular policies mobilized primary supporters but risked conceding the key's emphasis on significance that suggests reelection. But attacking the significance of his policies would disappoint anti-Obama citizens seeking an advocate and ready to donate and volunteer.[19]

Would There Be Widespread Social Unrest?

The Tea Party revolt of 2009 and 2010 had the appearance of widespread social unrest. It culminated in the 2010 victories of several Tea Party candidates in Republican primaries and congressional elections. This suggested to many observers that the political "center" had moved to the right. But it was also possible that the Tea Party victories had instead moved the alternatives to Obama to the right, leaving to him more of the political center. After all, the Tea Party candidates had unseated moderate Republicans, not liberal or moderate Democrats.

As presidential candidates began to surface they divided Tea Party supporters. Ron Paul had appeal, as did Michele Bachmann and Herman Cain. But the harder they tried to win staunch conservatives the more they fragmented them and crystallized the party regulars behind Romney. As the primaries unfolded the question arose, Where is the Tea Party's clout? The answer was, Divided.

On the other end of the spectrum there emerged the Occupy protests of 2011. Like the Tea Partiers, the Occupiers disliked government support of Wall Street, but they looked and behaved quite differently. Some pundits considered the Occupiers pro-Obama, but that was not entirely clear. In any case, outdoor occupations became less popular by winter, and the protests failed to gel into a concerted social movement.

By 2012—when challengers could have used widespread unrest to encourage a false key—both the Tea Party and the Occupy protests were fading from view. Republicans, by nature, seem disinclined to stir widespread social unrest (as opposed to media rants), and, consequently, they allowed citizens to infer that this key should go to the incumbent.

Would Republicans Nominate a Charismatic Candidate?

The Republican hopefuls included some interesting characters. Perhaps the most charismatic was New Jersey governor Chris Christie. Influential conservative Ann Coulter told CPAC, "if we don't run Chris Christie, Romney will be the nominee and we'll lose."[20] But Christie declined to run. That left former Speaker Newt Gingrich and Ron Paul among the most charismatic of the group. Michele Bachmann and Herman Cain could also attracted personal attention, and Texas Governor Rick Perry offered some unusual behaviors that went viral. The least charismatic candidates were perhaps Jon Huntsman, Rick Santorum, and Mitt Romney.

The Republican problem here was that the more charismatic candidates surfaced poorly and the less charismatic candidates surfaced well. Romney raised $32 million early, more than Perry and Paul combined and more than the other seven Republicans combined. Gingrich led the pack with 35 percent name recognition, but Romney was second at 22 percent, and none of the others cracked 12 percent. Perry, Romney, and Gingrich accounted for comparable Google hits by January of 2012, but little of the Gingrich and Perry news was good. That left Iowa.

The key to surfacing is a top-four finish in the Iowa precinct caucuses while having the resources to compete for delegates in the primaries. Rick Santorum finished first in the Iowa-precinct caucuses (although we did not know that right away) while ranking ninth in fundraising and sixth in name recognition and news coverage. Basically, he won Iowa because he never campaigned anywhere else. Meanwhile Romney campaigned everywhere else, used his money to run ads in Iowa, and then campaigned in Iowa's larger districts. Santorum campaigned as if winning Iowa mattered to the nation, whereas Romney campaigned nationally and used his visibility to finish a very close second in Iowa.

An incumbent can be beaten by a charismatic candidate, but it takes more than charisma to surface and win delegates. Because Romney surfaced effectively he could better compete for delegates in the primaries. But that left the Republicans without a candidate known for his charisma, and so this key went to the incumbent.

Summarizing the 2012 Landscape

Republicans entered 2012 needing to win at least four of the five unclear keys. But there was no significant third-party campaign, the social unrest of 2010 and 2011 had seemed to disappear, and the primaries had left them without a charismatic nominee. All three of these historically important keys were, in 2012, traps for Republicans.

Trap 1: Republicans needed a significant third-party effort, but the only possibility would have split the anti-Obama vote.

Trap 2: Republicans needed widespread social unrest (like the Tea Party and Occupy protests) that most Republicans find unpleasant.

Trap 3: Republicans needed a charismatic candidate, but the charismatic candidates had weak organizations and fundraising, and their strongest candidate for nomination was not charismatic.

Lichtman's keys suggest that a Paul campaign, widespread Tea Party and Occupy protests, and the nomination of a more charismatic candidate would have helped defeat the incumbent; but none of those keys was comfortable territory for Republicans in 2012. Thus the landscape severely disadvantaged those trying to unseat the incumbent.

That left the anti-Obama forces with only two unclear keys to victory. One was to turn the technical definition of recession into the sense of <recession> as a lack of economic growth, and this they continued to do.

The other strategy was to demonstrate that President Obama had accomplished no major changes in national policy. But this, too, was a trap.

Trap #4: Every Republican attack on Obama's record implied the significance of his accomplishments, and significance rather than popularity of change is Lichtman's key.

By 2012 the Republicans were in real trouble that they apparently failed to grasp. Needing to win six or more keys they could count on only two with five up for grabs. But those five keys entailed four traps, such that winning the historically important keys would have split the anti-Obama voters, encouraged unrest, undermined their most effective campaigner, and treated Obama's unpopular accomplishments as significant. Moreover, even if the Republicans had persuaded citizens to answer the recession and accomplishment keys false, they still would have created only four false keys—two short of the number necessary to defeat an incumbent.

Obama's Strategic Choices

If the keys disadvantaged Republicans, they hardly ensured an Obama victory. With the keys in their favor, Clinton in '96, Reagan in '84, Eisenhower in '56, and Roosevelt in '36, '40, and '44 buried their challengers and gained substantial congressional seats; Nixon in '72 trounced George McGovern but made only modest congressional support, and Wilson in '16 and Bush in '04 won close elections. Incumbents' strategic choices matter.

Strategy #1: Avoid an Intraparty Challenge

Most important to Obama was the prevention of any Democratic opposition to his renomination. If he were to avoid being the next Carter in '80 or Bush in '92, Obama would have to avoid the kinds of intraparty challenge that Ted Kennedy and Pat Buchanan had waged against those candidates. By succeeding Obama not only saved campaign funds but campaign arguments.

Strategy #2: Run as the President Rather Than a Partisan

This strategy suggests that the incumbent present himself not as partisan-in-chief but as president of all the people. Obama could do so precisely because his Democratic flank was unchallenged, and he did so in two early speeches.

On December 8, 2011, in Osawatomie, Kansas—the site of a famous speech by Theodore Roosevelt—President Obama focused on the middle class. "This is the defining issue of our time," he said. "This is a make-or-break moment for the middle class and for all those who are fighting to get into the middle class. Because what's at stake is whether this will be a country where working people can earn enough to raise a family, build a modest savings, own a home, secure their retirement."[21] Speaking in heavily Republican Kansas, Obama closed by quoting Republican Progressive Teddy Roosevelt: "'The fundamental rule of our national life,' he said, 'the rule which underlies all others, is that, on the whole, and in the long run, we shall go up or down together.'"[22]

The second speech, seven weeks later, was Obama's 2012 State of the Union address. Again he spoke as the incumbent president of all Americans. He acclaimed his administration's successes and acknowledged continuing problems. Again he stressed "the basic American promise that if you worked hard, you could do well enough to raise a family, own a home, send your kids to college, and put a little away for retirement."[23] But he also spoke as a determined leader, seeking cooperation but unwilling to yield: "As long as I'm president, I will work with anyone in this chamber to build on this momentum. But I intend to fight obstruction with action, and I will oppose any effort to return to the very same policies that brought on this economic crisis in the first place."[24] His speech combined the Osawatomie middle-class theme with an emphasis on the political center. CBS News reported that 91 percent of Americans agreed with the positions articulated in the speech.[25]

Incumbents unchallenged for nomination who mobilize the political center have frequently won landslide victories. But it must be tempting, as primary contenders relentlessly attack, to move toward one's base. Indeed, that was Karl Rove's 2004 strategy for Bush's reelection that would be the closest in eight decades. Obama eventually yielded to that temptation.

As Romney moved toward nomination the Obama campaign made several questionable choices. First, they shifted their strategic balance from acclaiming and defending to attacking Romney. As the frontrunner in the primaries Romney drew virulent attacks from his competitors, especially Gingrich. Romney's core acclaim (some would say his only acclaim) was that his business experience made him the one person to fix the economy and generate jobs.

Because acclaims invite attacks Gingrich attacked Romney's business record, calling him "a heartless capitalist, a 'corporate raider,' who made his money off other people's misfortunes."[26] It may be unusual for one Republican to attack another for making money. But the immediate audience for the Gingrich attacks was the populist Right antagonized by the government/Wall Street alliance, and they comprised about half of those active in the Republican primaries. Strategically the attacks represented an effort to fragment the Republican coalition into its constituent Pew clusters by separating Romney and the enterprisers from social conservatives, staunch conservatives, and libertarians.[27]

Obama's advisors embraced Gingrich's attacks on Romney and made them their own. They used the intraparty attacks to further isolate him from the rest of the electorate, an eventuality apparent to many who study campaigns.[28] They congratulated themselves for defining Romney before he could define himself, although Gingrich did so first. Yet even as their attacks may have helped some nonaligned voters to consider Romney an unappealing alternative, they undermined Obama's opportunity to unify the country behind a politically centrist middle-class incumbency.

Strategy #3: Acclaim Your Policy Successes, and Blame Shortcomings on Congressional Opponents

The Obama campaign employed this strategy but less effectively than they might have done. In 1948 an unpopular President Truman ran against the "good-for-nothing" Congress.[29] Although he won reelection, his working relations with Congress grew even worse. But Obama already had fierce Republican opposition in Congress, and it was exacerbated by Tea Party pressure on moderate Republicans. In 2012 President Obama could have campaigned aggressively for Democratic House and Senate candidates who would have improved his legislative leverage. Instead, like Nixon's Reelect the President campaign of 1972, he waged a more personal campaign and gained only a few seats in Congress.

Strategy #4: Mobilize Your Citizens, and Turn Them into Voters

Support is nice, but votes are decisive. The Obama campaign had effectively mobilized voters in 2008, and their operations in key states like Ohio never stopped working. Their impressive operation employed analytics to assess every citizen's likely vote. But for 2012 they tweaked their algorithm for likelihood of voting and support for Obama to include each person's susceptibility to the campaign's persuasive efforts.[30] They then focused on turning out Obama supporters otherwise unlikely to vote and turning out likely voters still undecided.

The massive Obama get-out-the-vote (GOTV) operation required a tremendous number of volunteers, and those most likely to volunteer are to be found among the partisan base rather than among moderates or undecided or apathetic citizens. That was the audience susceptible to Obama's partisan-in-chief appeals, and volunteers were that strategy's payoff. But once Obama decided to shift toward arguments mobilizing his base for volunteers, he might well have doubled down and campaigned aggressively for Democratic House and Senate candidates.

Yet by strategizing to mobilize volunteers for the GOTV effort in swing states Obama, like his predecessor Bush, campaigned for a simple electoral-college victory. In so doing he relinquished opportunities to transform his governing prospects for the second term.

A centrist-incumbent campaign might have led to an overwhelming popular-vote win (recall the 91 percent approval of his State of the Union) and a clear mandate for the second term (like Reagan and Clinton's reelections). But electoral votes count, and Obama therefore focused on winning them by capturing swing states.

The Tale of the Tipping Point

The Electoral-vote.com data for the tipping point shows that President Obama began 2012 with more than 270 likely electoral votes. Although his projections dipped below 270 once Mitt Romney secured the nomination, he nevertheless maintained a sizeable electoral-vote margin over Romney throughout the year, even excluding states that were statistically tied.[31] Unlike John McCain in 2008, Romney never caught or led Obama in projected electoral votes.

The final tipping-point table showed, to no one's surprise, that both candidates needed to win Ohio to decide the election. But the more constructive approach to the table is to consider the state poll margins surrounding the tipping point. These showed that Obama would need to carry all of his likely states plus three of the five states he led by 3 percent. Romney's 270 required him to carry every state he led, one that was tied, those where he trailed Obama by 1 to 2 percent, and then win at least two states where he trailed Obama by 3 percent. Thus the final tipping-point projections showed Obama receiving 303 electoral votes to Romney's 220 (the final tally would be 332–206). Meanwhile, CNN's final national popular-vote poll reported a statistical tie: Romney 49 percent to Obama 48 percent.[32] The difference between national polls and aggregated state polls can be both dramatic and important.

CONCLUSIONS

Imagine Team Obama pondering the historical pattern of incumbent campaigns. They had a 90 percent chance of renomination and a 64 percent chance of winning by 230 electoral votes and a double-digit popular-vote margin. But they also had a 38 percent chance of popular repudiation, a 230 electoral-vote disaster, and therefore a successor committed to overturning his accomplishments. Optimistic Republicans saw Obama as their Hoover, Carter, or Bush I and ripe for defeat.

This chapter has argued that Obama's defeat was never as likely as his critics believed. While it is true that no incumbent had ever before been reelected in so weak an economy, Lichtman's research shows that this economic key is an insufficient predictor for failure or success. To defeat Obama his critics could have benefited from several of the following: (1) a foreign-policy failure, (2) a decline in real GNP, (3) widespread social unrest, and (4) a scandal, but who really wants to encourage such things? They could also have used (5) a Democratic challenge, (6) a liberal third-party campaign, and (7) a charismatic nominee, but those are difficult to cultivate. Moreover, they were trying to unseat the candidate who in his first election had received more popular votes than any presidential candidate in history.

This chapter also suggests that President Obama did not win reelection because of his team's wise strategic choices. His popular-vote margin of 3 percent was the fourth smallest of the fifteen comparable candidates (after Bush in '04, Cleveland in 1892, and Wilson in '16), and his 126 electoral-vote margin, surprising as it was to Rove and Romney, ranks thirteenth of eighteen.[33] Put differently, Grover Cleveland (himself a former president) came closer than Romney to ousting the incumbent in 1892, Charles Hughes fared better against Wilson, and John Kerry did better against Bush. In short, Romney's anti-incumbent campaign did very well, and he lost.

The incumbent won but could have run a stronger campaign. In light of the landscape Obama might well have (1) continued to unify the 80 percent of the non-Republican electorate he had at his State of the Union, (2) acclaimed his agenda, and (3) campaigned for House and Senate candidates to enhance his second-term prospects.

Some readers will object that this chapter overlooks important considerations, as any chapter must. Republicans did underestimate, and thus estranged, Latino voters. Romney's "47 percent gaffe" to prospective donors went viral and alienated many prospective voters. Obama bombed in the first debate and created an opportunity for Romney. The killing of our ambassador in Benghazi had the potential to become a foreign policy failure.

But this chapter suggests the importance of considering those moments in the context of the contested keys, the Pew typology, and the tipping-point table. Viewed in that context, the 2012 election was the incumbent president's to lose, and he held on—to the relief of his supporters and the frustration of his critics.

Why, then, did the news media and both campaigns characterize the 2012 campaign as a likely Republican win? First, both parties needed the race to appear close if they were to attract donations, volunteers, and voters. Second, the news organizations needed their audiences to consider the outcome unclear to cultivate viewers' and readers' appetites for news and opinions. With the major stakeholders all having a vested interest in a perception of the outcome as razor thin, critical distance and sober historical reflection fell out of fashion. Clearly Romney and Rove came to believe their press releases. Imagine (if you can) Obama, his critics, and the press all saying, "History suggests that the keys to election favor the incumbent, who has a 90 percent chance of nomination and a 64 percent chance for reelection regardless of his opposition's campaign." Billions of dollars in contributions, millions of dollars in advertising revenue, thousands of volunteer hours, and hundreds of hours of talk shows would have been sucked into the void, perhaps in exchange for a better understanding of the difficulty of unseating an incumbent president.

NOTES

1. *Washington Post* staff, "Romney Prepared Victory Speech for Election, but Delivered Concession Speech Instead," *Washington Post*, November 17, 2012, accessed January 5, 2013, http://articles.washingtonpost.com/2012-11-07/politics/35504045_1_mitt-romney -romney-plane-romney-first.

2. Noreen Malone, "Megyn Kelly Can Save Fox News," *New Republic*, November 9, 2012, accessed January 5, 2013, www.tnr.com/article/109941/megyn-kelly-can-save-fox-news#.

3. Calculations and discussions of past election results are derived from data available at *Dave Leip's Atlas of U.S. Presidential Elections*, accessed November 2012–January 5, 2013, http://uselectionatlas.org.

4. Because much has been written about challenger and incumbent campaign styles we must pause to differentiate the present chapter from that line of analysis. Trent, Friedenberg, and Denton established that any candidate can choose between archetypal challenger and incumbent styles regardless of their actual status. Without discounting the importance of challenger and incumbent styles this chapter considers the other side of the coin. It contends that actual incumbency matters apart from the choice of campaign style. Judith S. Trent, Robert V. Friedenberg, and Robert E. Denton, Jr., *Political Campaign Communication: Principles and Practices*, 7th ed. (Lanham, Md.: Rowman & Littlefield, 2011), 83–115.

5. Alan J. Lichtman, *Predicting the Next President* (Lanham, Md.: Rowman & Littlefield, 2008).

6. Lichtman, *Predicting the Next President*, 3.

7. See for example William L. Benoit, *Seeing Spots: A Functional Analysis of Presidential Television Advertisements, 1952–1996* (Westport, Conn.: Praeger, 1999); and William L. Benoit, Joseph R. Blaney, and P. M. Pier, *Campaign '96: A Functional Analysis of Acclaiming, Attacking and Defending* (Westport, Conn.: Praeger, 1998).

8. "*Kategoria* and *Apologia*: On Their Rhetorical Criticism as a Speech Set," *Quarterly Journal of Speech* 68 (1982): 254–61. Ryan's article was the foundation for an anthology of rhetorical attack/defense analyses for which Benoit wrote the chapter on Ted Kennedy's Chappaquiddick speech. See Halford Ross Ryan, ed., *Oratorical Encounters: Selected Studies and Sources of Twentieth-Century Political Accusations and Apologies* (Westport, Conn.: Greenwood Press, 1988).

9. Craig Allen Smith, *Presidential Campaign Communication: The Quest for the White House* (Cambridge: Polity, 2010).

10. Samuel Kernell calls these clusters *protocoalitions* in *Going Public: New Strategies of Presidential Leadership*, 2nd ed. (Washington, D.C.: CQ Press, 1993), 13–14, 23–24. On constitutive rhetoric see Maurice Charland, "Constitutive Rhetoric: The Case of the *Peuple Québécois*," *Quarterly Journal of Speech* 73 (1987): 133–50; and Charles J. Stewart, Craig Allen

Smith, and Robert E. Denton, Jr., "Constituting Social Movement Organizations," *Persuasion and Social Movements*, 6th ed. (Long Grove, Ill.: Waveland, 2012), 173–212.

11. Pew Research, "Beyond Red vs. Blue: The Political Typology," Pew Research, May 4, 2011, accessed May 10, 2011, www.people-press.org/2011/05/04/beyond-red-vs-blue-the -political-typology.

12. Pew Research, "Beyond Red vs. Blue."

13. Pew Research, "Beyond Red vs. Blue."

14. The World Bank, "GDP per Capita (Current US$)," *World Bank*, accessed January 7, 2013, http://data.worldbank.org/indicator/NY.GDP.PCAP.CD?order=wbapi_data_ value_2009+wbapi_data_value&sort=asc.

15. Lichtman, *Predicting the Next President*, 33.

16. Michael Calvin McGee, "The 'Ideograph': A Link between Rhetoric and Ideology," *Quarterly Journal of Speech* 66 (1980): 1–16.

17. Mary E. Stuckey, *Jimmy Carter, Human Rights, and the National Agenda* (College Station: Texas A&M University Press, 2008), 75–76.

18. Lichtman, *Predicting the Next President*, 37.

19. Further complicating this key was Senate Minority Leader Mitch McConnell's comment that "the single most important thing we want to achieve is for President Obama to be a one-term president." By 2012 popular wisdom held that McConnell had said this shortly after the inauguration whereas he actually said it in an October 23, 2010, *National Journal* interview about the midterm elections. McConnell also said, "I don't want the president to fail; I want him to change. . . . If he's willing to meet us halfway on some of the biggest issues, it's not inappropriate for us to do business with him." Glenn Kessler, "When Did McConnell Say He Wanted to Make Obama a 'One-Term President'?" *Washington Post: The Fact Checker*, September 25, 2012, accessed December 10, 2012, www.washingtonpost.com/blogs/ fact-checker/post/when-did-mcconnell-say-he-wanted-to-make-obama-a-one-term-presiden t/2012/09/24/79fd5cd8-0696-11e2-afff-d6c7f20a83bf_blog.html. The first portion of his interview went viral, and the rest was largely forgotten. Supporters of the incumbent used the comment to argue that Congressional Republicans were more interested in defeating Obama than helping the country with respect to votes on Obama's jobs bill and the debt ceiling. The only way for Republicans to refute that characterization would have been to point out McConnell's desire to work together, and that was not good anti-incumbent rhetoric. Consequently this key also would be contested throughout the campaign.

20. Shane D'Aprile, "Coulter: Nominate Christie, Because Romney Will Lose," *Ballot Box: The Hill's Campaign Blog*, February 12, 2011, accessed December 10, 2012, http://thehill.com/ blogs/ballot-box/presidential-races/143697-coulter-nominate-christie-because-romney-will-lose.

21. Barack Obama, "Remarks by the President on the Economy in Osawatomie, Kansas," White House, December 6, 2011, accessed December 13, 2012, www.whitehouse.gov/the -press-office/2011/12/06/remarks-president-economy-osawatomie-kansas.

22. Obama, "Remarks by the President on the Economy in Osawatomie, Kansas."

23. Barack Obama, "Remarks by the President in State of the Union Address," White House, January 25, 2012, accessed September 14, 2012, www.whitehouse.gov/photos-and -video/video/2012/01/25/2012-state-union-address-enhanced-version#transcript.

24. Obama, "Remarks by the President in State of the Union Address."

25. Lucy Madison, "High Marks for Obama's State of the Union Speech," CBS News, January 26, 2012, accessed September 14, 2012, www.cbsnews.com/8301-503544_162 -20029581-503544.html.

26. Julian Zelizer, "Gingrich's Attacks Now Could Help Obama Later," CNN Election Center, January 16, 2012, accessed January 7, 2013, www.cnn.com/2012/01/16/opinion/zelizer-romney-weakness/index.html.

27. Pew data demonstrate the party coalitions are constructed from various opinion clusters. See Pew, "Beyond Red vs. Blue," and their previous typology of the same title, "Beyond Red vs. Blue," May 10, 2005, www.people-press.org/2005/05/10/beyond-red-vs-blue.

28. See for example Zelizer, "Gingrich's Attacks."

29. See for example David Pietrusza, *1948: Harry Truman's Improbable Victory and the Year that Transformed America* (New York: Union Square Press, 2011), 279–90.

30. Sasha Issenberg, "Why Obama Is Better at Getting Out the Vote," *Slate*, November 5, 2012, accessed December 10, 2012, www.slate.com/articles/news_and_politics/victory_lab/2012/11/obama_s_get_out_the_vote_effort_why_it_s_better_than_romney_s.2.html.

31. See "Electoral College Graphs," Electoral-vote.com, http://electoral-vote.com/evp2012/Pres/ec_graph-2012.html.

32. Paul Steinhauser, "Inside the polls: Voters Evenly Divided on Most Questions," CNN, November 6, 2012, accessed December 10, 2012, www.cnn.com/2012/11/05/politics/inside-the-polls.

33. *Dave Leip's Atlas of U. S. Presidential Elections*, http://uselectionatlas.org. The difference in comparisons is due to the fact that popular votes for Washington, Madison, and Monroe were not recorded.

5

Political Advertising in the 2012 U.S. Presidential Election

John C. Tedesco and Scott W. Dunn

The 2012 U.S. presidential election signifies the first time the two major political-party candidates and their supporters exceeded the $1 billion mark in political-advertising expenditures.[1] In an era when most voters have access to a extensive array of broadcast-television and -radio political-news programs via cable or subscription services, abundant partisan and nonpartisan blogs, and an ever more expansive range of Internet, social-media, and microblog (e.g., Twitter) political resources, political advertising continues to serve an important purpose for campaigns. In fact, candidates continue to spend upward of 75 percent of their campaign finances on the production and placement of advertisements. Expenditures from third-party groups, many of which were formed expressly for advertising, are likely to exceed 75 percent of their campaign dollars. Thus advertisements remain a crucial consideration for presidential campaigns.

In the modern media age, political campaigns use sophisticated marketing techniques to employ segmented and specialized advertising-message strategies tailored to the characteristics of particular viewing audiences. Although we do not explore the subtleties of segmentation strategies of candidates to advertise specific messages in targeted battle areas, we do explore the number and scope of political ads developed by the candidates and third-party groups during the 2012 election. This chapter offers a descriptive analysis of the major themes that emerged in advertisements sponsored by the two major-party campaigns and by outside groups supporting the two candidates.

CAMPAIGN CONTEXT

The 2012 presidential campaign occurred in the midst of a sluggish economic recovery with a public that was deeply divided in its views of the sitting president.[2]

Governor Romney sought to convince voters to blame President Obama for the country's economic woes but ultimately failed to paint himself as a viable alternative, with polls consistently showing that voters found Romney to be out of touch with the needs of ordinary Americans.[3] Voters widely perceived the campaign as being more negative and less focused on issues than past campaigns.[4]

The 2012 presidential campaign shattered records for spending on advertising, especially by third-party groups unaffiliated with the candidates or their political parties. For the first time, the two major-party campaigns and their supporters spent more than $1 billion on advertising, with $580 million and $470 million spent to support Obama and Romney, respectively.[5] This total is significantly more than the $700 million spent supporting the major-party candidates in the 2008 presidential campaign or the $620 million spent in 2004.[6] Much of that spending came from corporations set up to independently spend large amounts of money supporting candidates, colloquially known as *Super PACs*, established in the wake of the United States Supreme Court's decision in *Citizens United v. Federal Election Commission*. The court's controversial ruling essentially extended to corporations our constitutionally protected individual free-speech rights, allowing them an unprecedented voice in our political process and removing many of the campaign restrictions on corporations.

The newly formed Super PAC organizations spent nearly $642 million during the 2012 presidential-election campaign, much of it on advertising, with a large percentage of that spending coming from the conservative groups American Crossroads ($176 million) and Restore Our Future ($143 million) and the liberal group Priorities USA ($66 million).[7] Although the potential for corruption in the campaign-finance system has been a long-standing concern, the emergence of Super PACs intensified those concerns for many observers. In particular, commentators expressed concern that the existence of Super PACs increased opportunities for wealthy donors to disproportionately influence the political system and that Super PAC advertisements were overwhelmingly negative.[8]

LITERATURE REVIEW

Political advertising remains a significant feature of election campaigns despite the ever-expanding political-information sources available to voters. Evidence of advertising's importance to campaigns is clear when advertising expenditures are considered. The huge leap from $240 million spent by presidential candidates and political parties in 2000[9] to more than $1 billion by candidates, parties, and groups in 2012[10] should convince most observers of the value candidates and political organizations place on this leading form of candidate-controlled political communication. Ads remain valuable to campaigns since they continue to serve potentially vital campaign purposes of attracting and converting undecided, or loosely aligned, voters and reinforcing and mobilizing the campaign's base, or partisan, voters.[11] The extensive body of research on political advertising largely examines ad contents or their effects. Since this study explores political-advertising content, the literature review will focus on significant content features addressed by prior research.

Perhaps most important about political advertising is its ability to reach a large viewing audience of voters, or potential voters, who typically do not consume political messages. Since ads are not "programmed," television viewers tuning in to the evening news or their favorite television programs are exposed to advertisements through their routine viewing patterns.[12]

Negative advertising is much maligned by the voters.[13] Nevertheless, political campaigns continue to rely heavily on negative advertising. In fact, research demonstrates increases in the negative content within political advertisements from our more recent presidential elections.[14] Unfortunately for viewers who express disapproval of negative political attack ads, increased use of negative appeals in ads may be wise. Research on negative advertising has demonstrated fairly consistently across campaign contexts that negative ads increase cognitive understanding of candidates and issues[15] while also demonstrating an ability to diminish evaluations of the opponent or the target of the negative ads.[16] The sponsor of the ad, or the person waging the attack, is also an important consideration in negative political-advertising research. For decades researchers had supported the notion that negative ads created a backlash or boomerang for the sponsor, resulting in diminished evaluations for the candidate going on the offensive.[17] However, research on negative-advertising backlash has been thrown into question by more recent research[18] that suggests independent or third-party attack ads function much in the same way as candidate-sponsored negative ads. In fact, effects from negative political advertisements are reportedly four times more powerful than effects of positive ads, particularly when evaluations of candidates are being made.[19]

Yet additional research on negative-ad effects indicates that the type of negative appeal results in different effects. Research demonstrates that attacks on an opponent's issue positions are considered more effective than personal attacks.[20] Advertisements that blend attacks on the opponent with candidate-positive statements, typically referred to as comparative ads, also have the power to diminish the potential backlash of purely negative ads.[21]

Whether a political advertisement focuses on candidate issues or candidate image is also an important distinction in political-advertising research. Image advertisements result in increased knowledge about the candidate's personal qualities,[22] while issue advertisements increase knowledge about the candidate's issue agenda and important issues of the campaign.[23] Research on the use of Aristotelian appeals is also important to political advertising. Whether the advertising content attempts to persuade viewers through logical, emotional, or credibility appeals results in mixed effects depending on the sponsor and the individual characteristics of the viewer. But a blending of appeals helps to assure that a candidate's strategies will resonate with voters as research suggests that voters are not uniformly influenced by appeal type.

Although effects studies do not seem to isolate and evaluate specific incumbent or challenger[24] strategies used in political ads, research measuring candidates' use of these appeal types varies significantly. Research on the use of incumbent and challenger strategies demonstrates a mix of approaches. Some candidates have relied solely on one strategy or the other, depending on their status, while others have ignored the traditional techniques and employed incumbent and challenger strategies regardless of their status.[25]

The purpose of this chapter is to assess the strategies used by the candidates and their supporters. Results will be presented and discussed in relation to the political-advertising literature and the election outcome with the goal of understanding the specific strategies used by the campaigns. The chapter will conclude with a discussion about future research possibilities for political-advertising studies.

THE 2012 PRESIDENTIAL-CAMPAIGN ADVERTISEMENTS

Data on political-advertising expenditures during the 2012 presidential-campaign cycle tell only part of the story that will define this advertising campaign in history. Research from the Campaign Media Analysis Group, a division of Kantar Media,[26] confirms that Republicans outspent Democrats in TV advertising during the general election.[27] Results of their analysis indicate that pro-Republican groups produced more advertisements than pro-Democratic groups. Advertising totals show that Romney's campaign was responsible for 93 of the 259 (36 percent) advertisements aired by Romney and the thirty-seven unique pro-Republican groups compared to Obama's 142 of the total 215 (66 percent) advertisements produced by Obama's campaign or one of the twenty-one pro-Democratic sources sponsoring presidential ads in his support. Thus 474 unique presidential-campaign advertisements were aired, which shatters the advertisement totals from prior presidential campaigns and establishes the 2012 presidential election as the one with the most presidential advertisements in history.[28] In fact, data suggests that the candidates, national-party committees, and third-party groups aired nearly 40 percent more ads than in 2008 and 2004.[29]

Although Romney may have benefitted from the large number of advertisements produced on his behalf by the thirty-seven unique pro-Republican advertisement sponsors, his campaign had direct control over only 36 percent of the advertisements produced. While Obama did not benefit as much as Romney from the number of advertisements supporting his reelection campaign, the fact that he had message control in 66 percent of the advertising messages was likely an advantage in terms of message consistency and coherence.[30]

Among the leading pro-Republican groups to advertise on Romney's behalf were Restore Our Future PAC, American Crossroads, Crossroads GPS, Americans for Prosperity, Republican National Committee (RNC), American Future Fund, Americans for Job Security, National Rifle Association (NRA), Concerned Women of America Legislative Action Fund, Thomas Peterffy, American Energy Alliance, and Secure America Now. Although Priorities USA Action was the most powerful Super PAC supporting Obama's campaign, the campaign also received support from several large labor unions like the Service Employees International Union (SEIU) and American Federation of State, County and Municipal Employees (AFSCME).

Identifying each unique advertisement sponsored by either presidential campaign or one of the sponsoring issue groups was not an easy task. Thus the researchers relied on support from political resource centers. The Political Communication Lab at Stanford University provided links to 383 television advertisements it collected for the 2012 general-election campaign, which included a handful of Spanish-language ads. Although there were several other Web resources for political advertising, this was the most comprehensive source available to researchers.[31] The analysis here reflects a careful review of available advertisements. Advertisements were viewed by the researchers multiple times to identify not only major themes in the advertisements but also unique and distinguishing features of advertisements.

The dominant themes in the advertisements were established after a careful viewing of the ads. The overwhelmingly negative tone, issues like the economy and health care, and misinformation dominate much of the political-advertising landscape from 2012. The analysis that follows addresses these major themes and discusses implications for the 2012 election and beyond.

ANALYSIS AND DISCUSSION

Analysis from Kantar Media and the Campaign Media Analysis group's assessment of issue mentions in political ads during the presidential election shows that economic topics (jobs, taxes, government spending, and financial services) dominated issues in the presidential ads. Health care and energy followed behind economic issues, with education, foreign policy, and social services rounding out the list of more prevalent issues in political spots.[32] Due to the limited space for this chapter and the large number of political ads and the broad range of issues, we focus on the major themes of the political ads.

Ads and the Issues

Economy

The political landscape was complex in 2012, to say the least. The nation was still reeling from the effects of one of the worst economic crises in its history, high unemployment, increasing debt and a downgraded credit rating, and a battle over taxes and the way forward and out of the economic troubles. Couple the economic problems with an uncertain health-care environment, especially regarding the Affordable Care Act and concern for how changes in health-care administration would alter Medicare, public concern over energy independence and energy costs, and the continued strife in the Middle East, and the context for an advertising war was set.

With regard to the economy, Obama's ads attempted to emphasize that the nation was shedding the effects of the worst recession since the Great Depression and that indicators of the recovery were improving. Romney, as the challenger, hit hard on the continued economic problems, the slow pace of recovery, and the continued high unemployment.

The economy and related issues (e.g., jobs, taxes, budget deficit, and government spending) were the most dominant issues to appear in the presidential-candidate ads.[33] To a lesser degree, concern about financial reform and the need for regulation was an issue that received attention in advertisements sponsored by Obama or other Democratic groups. In an analysis of issue content in ads from April to October of 2012, results show that 76 percent of negative references to Bain Capital appeared in Obama's advertisements, with the Democratic groups referencing it to a lesser degree.[34] In a particularly effective advertisement aimed at bolstering Romney's image as a compassionate leader, Restore Our Future produced a positive ad featuring Robert Gay, a former Bain Capital executive, providing a testimonial about Romney's decision to close the Bain offices and offer support in the search to find Gay's missing daughter. "Saved," which was this Super PAC's most-aired political spot, is an engaging and emotional ad that includes the following narration from a visibly emotional Gay:

> My fourteen-year-old daughter had disappeared in New York City for three days. No one could find her. My business partner stepped forward to take charge. He closed the company and brought almost all of our employees to New York. He says, "I don't care how long it takes, we're going to find her." He set up a command center and searched through the night. The man who helped save my daughter was Mitt Romney. Mitt's done a lot of things that people say are nearly impossible, but for me the most important thing he's ever done is to help save my daughter.[35]

This advertisement subtly resembles the Progress for America ad "Ashley's Story" from the 2004 presidential election. That advertisement was a positive advertisement that cut through the negative advertising environment to demonstrate the compassionate side of George W. Bush. Ashley, a girl who'd lost her mother in the September 11 terrorist attacks, is comforted by Bush after he learns of her emotional story. The advertisement features Bush giving Ashley a big hug, which serves to portray his compassionate side, demonstrate his human and fatherly qualities, and offer a positive message unburdened by complex issues in the ad.[36] Simply, it was a feel-good advertisement, much like what Restore Our Future was attempting to accomplish in "Saved."

While Restore Our Future's ad cut through the negativity in the campaign with this favorable ad, it was not characteristic of third-party advertisements that campaign season. In fact, a Priorities USA ad also featured a testimonial about Romney. In "Heads or Tails" Priorities USA was not as kind to Romney's character. A former employee of an organization purchased by Bain narrates:

> With Romney and Bain Capital, the objective was to make money. Whether the companies they came in and worked with made money or not was irrelevant. He promised us the same things he's promising the United States. He'll give you the same thing he gave us: nothing. He'll take it all.[37]

"Saved" and "Heads or Tails" also demonstrate a way the issues of the campaign were debated through political ads.

The campaigns battled for dominance in interpretation of the state of the economy as well. Many of the advertisements also featured an interplay of sorts between Obama's controversial $800 million bailout, its failure to create as many jobs as expected, and the fact that many Americans remain buried by the economic crisis. One Romney advertisement, "Helping the Middle Class," used footage from his successful first presidential debate to emphasize that Americans had been "crushed" by Obama's failed policies during the recession and its recovery and that many families earn less now than when Obama first took office. Romney concluded the ad by emphasizing that his tax plan would "bring down rates to get more people working."[38] "Putting Jobs First" is another Romney advertisement that attempted to use footage from his successful debate performance to emphasize his stance on the economy. He argued,

> We've got twenty-three million people out of work or stopped looking for work. They're suffering in this country. The president would prefer raising taxes. . . . The problem with raising taxes is that it slows down the rate of growth. I'm not going to raise taxes on anyone, because when the economy is growing like this, when we're in recession, you shouldn't raise taxes on anyone.

The advertisement's final appeal captures Romney's debate statement, "My priority is putting people back to work in America."[39]

"Main Street" centers on jobs and manufacturing and is another ad that features testimony from citizens. However, this ad represents an example of the recovery Obama wanted voters to see, even if it was not typical of what they were observing in their areas. Employees from a manufacturing plant are used in the ad to emphasize that under Obama manufacturing had increased so much at their shop that an entire second shift of employees was hired to increase production. A male employee commented, "When you look at the president's plan, I don't think there can be any question that we're on the right course for today's economy."[40]

Advertisements about the economy, jobs, taxes, and the recession also featured China and trade issues prominently. In fact, it is possible that the factory was the most prominent image in the advertisements, other than the two candidates.[41] The Republican ads pointed the finger at China with accusations of currency manipulation and implications that Obama did not do enough to force China's hand to make changes. The Democrats, rather, tended to focus on problems with American companies shipping operations oversees to low-wage employees, which was a significant source of reduced manufacturing jobs in the United States.[42]

Romney's ads were particularly hard-hitting against China and Obama's policies toward and treatment of China. The ad "Stand Up to China" included the following:

> Fewer Americans are working today than when President Obama took office. It doesn't have to be this way. If Obama would stand up to China. China is stealing American ideas and technology. Everything from computers to fighter jets. Seven times Obama

could have taken action. Seven times he said no. His policies cost us two million jobs. Obama had years to stand up to China. We can't afford four more.[43]

Not only were Romney's attacks on China concerning—especially regarding how he said he would negotiate with China after such allegations were he elected president—but reviews were also mixed as to whether Romney's proposal would even work or merely boomerang and result in a significant trade war between the two countries. FactCheck.org raised significant challenges to the allegations Romney made in "Stand Up to China."[44] It argued that the trade tariffs Obama sought to impose on China were upheld by the World Trade Organization and that U.S. exports to China increased 45 percent during Obama's first term, which seem to counter the allegations waged by Romney.

Health

Not surprisingly, health care and health-care reform featured prominently in the 2012 presidential-campaign ads. The deep divide on the issue of health-care reform, the long, intense, and often bitter battle for passage of the Affordable Care Act, the lawsuit against the federal government from several states' attorneys general, and the continued uncertainty about what health-care reform would mean for many citizens made health care an important issue in 2012. With all the confusion surrounding the Affordable Care Act, and the "death panel" fear appeals that had been so pervasive prior to the passage of the bill, it is no surprise that fear appeals were used to perpetuate concern over health-care changes. Kathleen Jamieson, a political-communication expert with the University of Pennsylvania's Annenberg Center and director of the FlackCheck.org project,[45] emphasized that "deceptive dramatization" was a strategy employed by both sides in the health-care debate, especially during the early general-election ads.[46] "It is easy to deceive on the issue because the knowledge base of the electorate when it comes to the complexities of health care is relatively low," Jamieson argued.[47]

But the complexities of the health-care debate were sidelined somewhat by the controversies surrounding a videotape from a Romney fundraiser that shows Romney, in his own words, saying 47 percent of the population have a victim mentality and are convinced they deserve government rescue. Obama's ad, "My Job,"[48] attacks Romney by using footage from the fundraiser:

> There are 47 percent of the people who will vote for the president no matter what . . . who are dependent upon government, who believe that they are victims, who believe that government has a responsibility to care for them, who believe that they are entitled to health care, to food, to housing, to you-name-it.

The ad ends with Romney stating, "And so my job is not to worry about those people. I'll never convince them they should take personal responsibility and care for their lives."

Romney's words proved problematic for his campaign and gave Obama, and the pro-Democrat Super PACs, a gift to use in attacking Romney's ability to represent the entire population if elected president. Romney's words were used against him in several additional television spots and radio spots by Priorities USA and AFSCME, particularly in the battleground states of Ohio and Virginia.[49] Some pundits argue that the strategy to use Romney's own words against him in an attack ad created some of the most effective spots of the election.[50]

Health-care reform was center stage in the campaign when the controversy erupted over the health-care mandate that companies and organizations supply, without copay, insurance coverage for birth control. Romney used this policy to attack Obama's values. The ad "Be Not Afraid" argues that "President Obama used his health-care plan to declare war on religion, forcing religious institutions to go against their faith."[51] Characterizing the health-care reform as a war on religion may have been a stretch, but it nevertheless stirred emotions on both sides of the aisle and created additional complexities to support for the health-care changes. In both cases, Obama and Romney muddied the health-care debate by focusing on each others' values.

Energy

Narration of 2012's political advertising would not be complete without discussion of the energy-related advertisements, which were a favorite topic for the third-party groups. Americans for Prosperity—a conservative Super PAC supported in part by oil-industry billionaire David Koch and his brother William—and Crossroads GPS were two such organizations that played a significant role in attacking Obama's energy policy. More specifically, the advertisements advocated for increased fossil-fuel exploration and production while criticizing Obama's spending on failed solar- and wind-energy endeavors. Solyndra, a company that received more than a half a billion dollars from the Obama administration in 2009 and was forced to file for bankruptcy, was a favorite target for the conservative groups and was used as evidence that Obama's solar- and wind-energy initiatives were failing.[52]

Additional groups, such as the American Energy Alliance, capitalized on the high price of gasoline as proof that Obama's energy policies had failed. Political pundits, throughout much of the early part of the general-election campaign, discussed the problems a $4-a-gallon price tag on gasoline could create for Obama's reelection, emphasizing the average American's struggle to absorb the continued economic burden of high gas prices.

One particular ad, "Wasteful Spending" from Americans for Prosperity, hit the airwaves in late April and played a significant role in shaping the attack on the president's failed energy policies:

> Washington promised to create American jobs if we passed their stimulus. But that's
> not what happened. Fact: Billions of taxpayer dollars spent on green energy went to

jobs in foreign countries. The Obama administration admitted the truth that $2.3 billion dollars of tax credits went overseas, while millions of Americans can't find a job. $1.2 billion dollars to a solar company that's building a plant in Mexico. Half a billion to an electric-car company that created hundreds of jobs in Finland. And tens of millions of dollars to build traffic lights in China. President Obama wasted 34 billion dollars on risky investments. The result: Failure! American taxpayers are paying to send their own jobs to foreign countries. Tell President Obama American tax dollars should help American taxpayers.[53]

In fact, the importance of energy in 2012 is evidenced through analysis of ads from the candidates, parties, Super PACs, and energy-industry and trade-association PACs prior to the start of the intense advertising period (typically Labor Day to Election Day).[54] The *New York Times* reported that 138 presidential-campaign ads, airing up to early September 2012, addressed energy issues.[55] Estimates on campaign spending showed a significant imbalance, with spending on clean coal and increases in oil and gas drilling exceeding $153 million compared to an estimated $41 million in support of clean-energy initiatives and defense of Obama's energy policies.[56] "Energy themes have played an outsized role in the 2012 campaign season,"[57] but the *Citizens United* ruling changed the political landscape and enabled wealthy individuals and groups with vested interest in the energy issue to play a meaningful role in shaping the energy debate.

Types of Attack Ads

The 2012 campaign continued the trend of increased negativity in presidential-campaign advertising. Ads supporting both campaigns were predominantly negative, but the specific types of attacks varied depending on the candidate and the sponsoring organization. Romney and his supporters largely focused their attacks on Obama's performance during his first term in the White House, while Obama and his supporters primarily attacked Romney for his positions on issues and the consistency of his issue positions. These strategies both make sense considering the election context. Like most challengers running against an incumbent president, Romney's goal was to turn the election into a referendum on the president's first term and to convince voters to reject his bid for a second term. Obama's goal was to convince voters that Romney's candidacy did not provide a viable alternative, and his campaign seemed to pursue this goal largely by emphasizing Romney's perceived inconsistency on issues over the course of his career as a businessman and politician.

The ad "A Better Future: Virginia; Energy" provides a representative illustration of Romney's strategy. The ad begins with a clip from Romney's acceptance address at the Republican National Convention in which he states, "This president can ask us to be patient. This president can tell us it was someone else's fault. But this president cannot tell that you're better off today than when he took office." Following this clip, a narrator connects the clip with the concerns of Virginia voters, stating, "Here in Virginia, we're not better off under President Obama. His war on coal, gas, and oil is crushing energy and manufacturing jobs." The narrator then switches to a positive message contrasting Romney's policies with Obama's.[58] The same clip from Romney's acceptance speech was paired with statements on different issues in various states around the country as Romney attempted to build on the critique of Obama's first term that he'd offered in his acceptance speech and throughout his campaign.[59]

Other Romney ads attacked Obama's record as president with statistics illustrating the effects of Obama's "failing" policies. An ad titled "Failing America's Workers" contrasted the loss of American manufacturing jobs with the increase in Chinese manufacturing during Obama's first term.[60] A similar ad titled "Failing America's Families" contrasted falling personal income with the rising national debt. In all of these ads and throughout the campaign Romney echoed Ronald Reagan's famous question from the 1980 presidential campaign—"Are you better off than you were four years ago?" His ads attempt to answer that question with a resounding no. These ads uniformly focused on economic issues, suggesting that the Romney campaign and the outside groups supporting it believed that the outcome of the election largely hung on voter's attitudes toward Obama's handling of the economy.

Obama's strategy of attacking Romney's lack of consistency on his issue positions was evident in many of the president's ads, including "The Problem,"[61] where he criticized Romney's apparent reversal on China policy. Another example is "Not One of Us," an ad that responds to an earlier Romney ad in which the Republican candidate called himself "a friend of coal country." The Obama ad attacks Romney's claim using a clip of a 2003 speech in which Romney pointed at a coal plant and said, "I will not create jobs or hold jobs that kill people, and that plant, that plant kills people."[62] Like many of the issue-based attacks used in Obama's ads, this one was not a direct attack on Romney's position but rather on his inconsistency on the issue. Indeed, it is not clear from this ad which of Romney's positions Obama opposes, only that Romney's inconsistency should be a problem for voters.

Ads from each side frequently used anonymous announcers and surrogates to attack their opponent and rarely featured the candidate himself attacking his opponent. Surrogates included former president Bill Clinton's appearances in Obama's ads[63] and actor Clint Eastwood in support of Romney,[64] as well as ordinary people featured in "plain folks" appeals. A widely discussed Obama ad titled "Mandatory" featured a voiceover explaining that a group of coal miners seen at a Romney rally in an earlier ad had been coerced by their employers to attend the rally. The ad also featured the use of surrogate David Blomquist, the radio host who'd initially broken the story that the miners had been forced to attend the rally.[65] Although Blomquist had had no intention of acting as an Obama surrogate,[66] the Obama campaign used his radio report to supplement their voiceover in order to provide a variety of voices attacking Romney.

The Obama campaign particularly made use of ads that used Romney's own words to attack him, usually in connection with a more direct attack from an unidentified announcer. For example, the Obama campaign ad "The Problem," mentioned above, began with a clip of Romney saying that "the Chinese are smiling all the way to the bank, taking our jobs and taking a lot of our future, and I'm not willing to let that happen," followed by a voiceover accusing Romney of outsourcing jobs to countries like China during his time at Bain Capital. The voiceover concluded, "Mitt Romney's not the solution, he's the problem."[67] Another previously mentioned Obama ad exclusively used Romney's words, specifically his infamous "47 percent" comments, juxtaposed with images of ordinary Americans.[68] The use of Romney's words in Obama's campaign ads reinforced the the impression that Romney was inconsistent on issues and out of touch with ordinary Americans. Romney's words made this argument more forcefully than Obama or his surrogates could have, as hearing Romney speak in his own voice reduced viewer skepticism about what Romney had actually said. Although using the opponent's own words against him is not a new strategy, Obama seemed to rely on this approach frequently in the 2012 campaign.

Even when addressing specific issues, the campaigns used their negative ads to call their opponents' credibility into question. For example, Obama's campaign combined a logical issue-based appeal with a credibility appeal when responding to Romney's allegation that Obama was eliminating work requirements for welfare recipients. The reply ad, "Blatant," argued that, "in fact, Obama's getting states to move 20 percent more people from welfare to work," refuting the substantive charge previously leveled by Romney.[69] However, the overall focus of the ad was not on the welfare issue itself but on the questions that Romney's allegedly false claims raise about his credibility.

The pro-Romney group Checks and Balances for Economic Growth took a similar approach in an ad responding to the previously mentioned Obama ad alleging that coal miners had been forced by their employer to attend a Romney rally. In this ad, after a narrator explains that a group of coal miners had issued a letter characterizing Obama's claims as "absolute lies," one of the miners asks, "Why would you lie about the five hundred working miners who have signed this letter?"[70] Again in this case, the ad is barely about the issue of coal and more about Obama's honesty and personal integrity.

Campaigns Ads Compared to Super PAC Ads

The ads run by outside groups in the 2012 campaign suggest that pundits were right to be concerned that the influx of money from such groups would lead to more personal attacks in presidential advertising. These ads overwhelmingly featured attacks on opponents, usually coming from ordinary people acting as surrogates. It is not surprising that the candidates themselves do not appear in ads sponsored by outside groups, since these groups are legally obligated to avoid coordinating their efforts with the candidates. However, the use of surrogates appears to be a strategic decision that differs from the use of anonymous announcers preferred by the official campaigns.

Examples of the use of surrogates in pro-Romney ads include Super PAC ads featuring a wounded Iraq War veteran who'd met Romney while recovering at Walter

Reed Army Medical Center[71] and Romney's former business partner, Robert Gay, whose missing daughter had been rescued in part thanks to Romney's efforts.[72] The Super PAC ads echoed the Romney campaign ads' attacks on Obama's past performance in office, giving less emphasis to attacks on issue positions; unlike the official campaign ads, however, these Super PAC ads attacked Obama's personal characteristics. In fact, many of the Super PAC ads were multi-taskers, presenting multiple appeals simultaneously. One representative ad, "New Normal," made the following appeal against Obama's reelection:

> Welcome to the new normal, where over 8 percent unemployment is "doing fine" and millions of Americans have simply given up, where our children will grow up under the weight of crushing debt in a world where America is no longer the leader and we're told we're going forward even as we fall further behind. This is the new normal. This is President Obama's economy. Demand better.[73]

In the span of thirty seconds, this ad addresses the issues of unemployment, the national debt, and the United States' leadership position in the world. Simultaneously, the ad uses images of Obama overlaid with his statement that "the private sector is doing fine,"[74] thus combining the issue-based attack with a personal attack that called into question Obama's ability to understand the reality of the nation's economic situation. The ad also uses emotive language to connect the issue appeal with concerns about future generations having to pay off "crushing debt," thus completing the trifecta of logical-, emotional-, and credibility-based appeals.

The pro-Obama Super PAC Priorities USA similarly used its ads to present vicious attacks on Romney's personal credibility. Most notable was the ad "Understands," in which a laid-off worker named Joe Soptic relates the story of his wife dying of cancer after he and his family lost their health insurance, allegedly because of layoffs initiated by Romney's company, Bain Capital.[75] Although the ad stops well short of actually saying that Romney caused Soptic's wife to die, the implicit connection is hard to ignore. This ad follows a similar strategy as the Obama campaign's official ads, calling into question Romney's credibility and suggesting that he is out of touch with the needs of ordinary Americans. However, by implicitly connecting Romney's actions as a businessman with this tragic story, this ad reaches a level of personal attack that the official Obama campaign ads had never approached.

The examples cited here suggest that independent groups feel freer to engage more directly in personal attacks because they are less concerned about the backlash that can sometimes harm a campaign voters think is going too negative. Since the Super PACs are not officially affiliated with the candidates, perhaps they feel that any backlash against their ads will not negatively affect their preferred candidate's chances. And while the campaigns clearly have no problem including attacks in their ads, they may feel that there is less risk of a backlash when they attack an opponent for his or her issue positions or past performance than when the attacks are more personal in nature, so they leave the stronger personal attacks to the outside groups.

Accuracy in 2012 Campaign Ads

One trend in recent elections is the rise of fact-checking organizations like Fact-Check.org and PolitiFact. These organizations had plenty of work in this election cycle keeping up with all of the dubious claims that appeared in ads from the official campaigns and outside groups.[76] For example, Obama's ad alleging that coal miners had been forced to attend a Romney rally caused a backlash among coal miners who'd willingly attended the rally (which became the subject of its own ad), as previously discussed. Although none of the major fact-checking organizations found evidence that the initial claims were false, it appears that the coerced miners represented, at most, a small percentage of the miners who'd attended the rally. Throughout the campaign, voters had to navigate a virtual minefield of half-truths, creatively employed statistics, and out-of-context attributions.

One ad that emerged late in the campaign and achieved notoriety for its false claims was the Romney ad "Who Will Do More?" alleging that Obama had "sold Chrysler to Italians who are going to build Jeeps in China."[77] Even before the ad ran, Chrysler executives had dismissed the claims that Jeep production would move to China, stating that the plan was to open additional Jeep plants, not move existing facilities.[78] The ensuing attention from fact-checking organizations and a response ad from the Obama campaign[79] seems to have mitigated any benefit Romney might have otherwise gotten from the last-minute attempt to win votes in states like Ohio that rely economically on the automobile industry.[80]

Romney's campaign also defied the fact checkers in "Right Choice," which accused Obama of eliminating work requirements for welfare recipients.[81] Although the Obama campaign made some changes to give states more flexibility in implementing welfare-to-work requirements, major fact-checking organizations agreed that the ad's assertion that Obama's policy "guts welfare" was inaccurate.[82] In response to the reaction this ad generated, Romney pollster Neil Newhouse famously told ABC News, "We're not going to let our campaign be dictated by fact checkers."[83] This quotation suggests that the campaigns began to feel constrained by the visibility of the fact-checking organizations.

President Obama similarly bent the truth in an ad accusing Romney of supporting a ban on all abortions, including cases in which pregnancies resulted from rape or incest. The ad centered on a response at a Republican-primary debate, where moderator Anderson Cooper had asked Romney if he would sign a bill "banning all abortions" were *Roe v. Wade* overturned. As seen in the ad, Romney responded, "I'd be delighted to sign that bill."[84] While Romney's response about banning "all abortions" may have implied support for banning abortions in cases of rape and incest when viewed in isolation, Romney had repeatedly said that he supported rape and incest exceptions before and after that debate.[85] Using this one response to imply that Romney held a more extreme position on abortion than he really did earned the Obama campaign a "pants-on-fire" rating from PolitiFact.[86]

The fact checkers also faulted the Obama campaign for a key strategy they used to paint Romney as out of touch. Throughout the campaign Obama cited Romney's history of outsourcing jobs during his time at Bain Capital, including an ad that called Romney a "corporate raider"[87] and another claiming that "Romney's companies were pioneers in shipping U.S. jobs overseas."[88] As fact-checking organizations pointed out, the sources cited in these ads actually reported on a few isolated cases of outsourcing under Bain's watch, most of which occurred after Romney had left the company.[89] Although these sources suggested Romney's indirect involvement in some cases of outsourcing, his fringe involvement doesn't seem to have justified the broad claims made by these Obama ads.

CONCLUSION

Unfortunately for those citizens turned off by negative campaign advertisements, or political ads in general, the 2012 presidential election broke records for advertising expenditures and for the number of ads produced by candidates, parties, and third-party groups. Fears that the presidential election would be the most negative on record—due mostly to the influx of advertisements from Super PACs following the *Citizens United* ruling—proved to be true. Perhaps more problematic was the fact that advertisements "stretching" the truth, or completely ignoring it, were also pervasive. The undecided voter, for whom political ads are largely focused, would have had a difficult time navigating the political landscape and verifying the claims made by the advertising sponsors. In some battleground locations, it would have seemed impossible for media or civic organizations to fact check all the ads aired in their market, which complicated the campaign for those who'd hoped to make an informed decision based on accurate information. In this regard, uncoordinated advertising could be problematic for democracy.

Another fear stemming from *Citizens United* was that a select group of wealthy Americans could potentially have a sizable influence on the election dialogue. Particularly in the area of energy, the Koch brothers received a lot of attention for their sizable financial investment in political ads. However, 2012 is another example of an election where the candidate with the most money, and the most external support, does not always win: Romney's campaign and the pro-Republican sources supporting him spent more on advertising than Obama and the pro-Democratic groups. Here message control and message targeting seemed to play a larger role than did the amount of advertising. Romney had more groups supporting him, true, but they were also not governed by the official Romney campaign message, which means that his message was more likely to have been overshadowed somewhat by the varied messages from the many pro-Romney groups, especially considering that these groups represented more than 60 percent of advertisements aired. Obama, although supported by fewer independent groups, was more in control of the advertising message. In the future, scholars may wish to focus on just various sponsor ads to learn of the effects and influence of such ads on the campaigns they support.

The intense negativity of the campaign may have played against Romney as well. Although it was important for Romney to challenge Obama's reelection messages and point to problems with his presidency, research shows that 89 percent of Romney's general-election ads and 92 percent of all pro-Republican-group general-election ads included some form of attack.[90] Perhaps if Romney had spent more time constructing a positive message to reinforce his base, for example, and less of his advertising on the offensive he would be president today.[91] The Romney campaign's failure to create a positive image of their candidate and to coordinate messages in the face of Super PAC dominance may have been a source of election demise for Romney. Romney's campaign also hit very hard on the economy issues, perhaps to the detriment of other issues where the president was vulnerable.

Yet another feature of the advertising strategy observed in 2012 was Obama's early advertising efforts and his marketing and segmentation strategy. Obama's campaign strategist David Axelrod acknowledged the campaign's tactic of advertising early, from May to August, to capitalize on lower advertising rates, avoid the cluttered advertising environment in the final weeks of the campaign, and create impressions early.[92] Obama's campaign also spent more in key battleground media markets, making his message seem more tailored to audiences. It is possible that such a strategy made an important difference in the election outcome.

Despite the wide array of media sources available to voters, political advertising continues to be a vital tool for candidates. Advertising has always been about rallying partisans and recruiting the few undecided voters, and it has been a critical tool for moving the few voters who make up the margin in close elections. The 2012 presidential election was a very close race, which may have placed more emphasis on political advertising than in many previous presidential elections. This was the first election to witness political advertising under the changed political landscape brought about by *Citizens United*. It will be interesting to see whether Campaign 2012 results in calls for changes to campaign finance, again, and the role of political advertising in future elections.

NOTES

1. "2012 Presidential Campaign Finance Explorer," *Washington Post*, December 7, 2012, www.washingtonpost.com/wp-srv/special/politics/campaign-finance/.

2. Jeffrey M. Jones, "Americans' Views of Obama More Polarized as Election Nears," Gallup, October 12, 2012, www.gallup.com/poll/158018/americans-views-obama-polarized -election-nears.aspx.

3. Andrew Kohut, "Misreading Election 2012," *Wall Street Journal*, November 13, 2012, accessed January 17, 2013, http://online.wsj.com/article/SB10001424127887323894704578113231375465160.html.

4. "Low Marks for the 2012 Election: Voters Pessimistic about Partisan Cooperation," Pew Research Center for the People and the Press, November 15, 2012, accessed January 17, 2013, www.people-press.org/2012/11/15/low-marks-for-the-2012-election/.

5. "2012 Presidential Campaign Finance Explorer," *Washington Post.*

6. Lynda Lee Kaid, "Videostyle in the 2008 Presidential Advertising," in *The 2008 Presidential Campaign: A Communication Perspective*, ed. Robert E. Denton, Jr. (Lanham, Md.: Rowman & Littlefield, 2009), 210.

7. "Outside Spending," Center for Responsive Politics, accessed January 18, 2013, www .opensecrets.org/outsidespending/index.php.

8. John Nichols and Robert W. McChesney, "The Assault of the Super PACs," *The Nation*, February 6, 2012, www.thenation.com/article/165733/after-citizens-united-attack-super-pacs, 11–17.

9. Patrick Devlin, "Contrasts in Presidential Campaign Commercials of 2000," *American Behavioral Scientist* 44, no. 12 (2001): 2338–69.

10. Kaid, "Videostyle in the 2008 Presidential Advertising."

11. John C. Tedesco and Lynda Lee Kaid, "Style and Effects of the Bush and Gore Spots," in *The Millennium Election*, ed. Lynda Lee Kaid, John C. Tedesco, Dianne G. Bystrom, and Mitchell S. McKinney (Lanham, Md.: Rowman & Littlefield, 2003), 5.

12. Charles K. Atkin, Lawrence Bowen, Oguz B. Nayman, and Kenneth G. Sheinkopf, "Quality versus Quantity in Televised Political Ads," *Public Opinion Quarterly* 37 (1973): 209–24.

13. Michael M. Franz, Paul F. Freedman, Kenneth M. Goldstein, and Travis M. Ridout, *Campaign Advertising and American Democracy* (Philadelphia: Temple University Press, 2008); Lynda Lee Kaid, "Political Advertising," in *Handbook of Political Communication Research*, ed. Lynda Lee Kaid (Mahwah, N.J.: Lawrence Erlbaum, 2004), 155–202.

14. Lynda Lee Kaid, Mitchell S. McKinney, and John C. Tedesco, "Applied Political Communication Research," in *Handbook of Applied Communication Research*, ed. Lawrence Frey and Kenneth Cissna (Mahwah, N.J.: Routledge, 2009), 453–80.

15. Craig Brians and M. W. Wattenberg, "Campaign Issue Knowledge and Salience: Comparing Reception from TV Commercials, TV News, and Newspapers," *American Journal of Political Science* 40 (1996): 172–93.

16. Spencer Tinkham and Ruth Ann Weaver-Lariscy, "A Diagnostic Approach to Assessing the Impact of Negative Political Television Commercials," *Journal of Broadcasting and Electronic Media* 37 (1993): 377–99.

17. Gina Garramone, "Voter Responses to Negative Political Ads," *Journalism Quarterly* 61 (1984): 250–59.

18. Michael Pfau, R. Lance Holbert, Erin A. Szabo, and Kelly Kaminski, "Issue-Advocacy versus Candidate Advertising: Effects of Candidate Preferences and Democratic Process," *Journal of Communication* 52 (2002): 301–15.

19. Amy Jasperson and David P. Fan, "An Aggregate Examination of the Backlash Effect in Political Advertising: The Case of the 1996 U.S. Senate Race in Minnesota," *Journal of Advertising* 31, no. 1 (2002): 1–12.

20. Kenneth L. Fridkin and Patrick J. Kenney, "Do Negative Messages Work? The Impact of Negativity on Citizens' Evaluations of Candidates," *American Politics Research* 32 (2004): 570–605.

21. Patrick Meirick, "Cognitive Responses to Negative and Comparative Political Advertising," *Journal of Advertising* 31, no. 1 (2002): 49–62.

22. Valerie A. Sulfaro, "Political Advertisements and Decision-Making Shortcuts in the 2000 Election," *Contemporary Argumentation and Debate* 22 (2001): 80–99.

23. Guy J. Golan, Spiro K. Kiousis, and Misti L. McDaniel, "Second-Level Agenda-Setting and Political Advertising," *Journalism Studies* 8 (2007): 432–43.

24. Judith S. Trent, Robert V. Friedenberg, and Robert E. Denton Jr., *Political Campaign Communication: Principles and Practices* (Lanham, Md.: Rowman & Littlefield): 103–4.

25. Lynda Lee Kaid and Anne Johnston, *Videostyle in Presidential Campaigns* (Westport, Conn.: Greenwood Publishing Group, 2001).

26. Campaign Media Analysis Group is one of several companies under the Kantar Media conglomerate. The Kantar group offers a range of analysis and strategy services for its clients through its media and consumer research of traditional-, digital-, and social-media monitoring.

27. Elizabeth Wilner, "Romney and Republicans Outspent Obama, but Couldn't Out-Advertise Him," *Ad Age*, November 9, 2012, http://adage.com/article/campaign-trail/romney -outspent-obama-advertise/238241/.

28. Laura Baum, "Presidential Ad War Tops 1M Airings," Wesleyan Media Project, November 2, 2012, http://mediaproject/wesleyan.edu/2012/1/02/presidential-ad-war-tops-1m-airings/.

29. Baum, "Presidential Ad War Tops 1M Airings."

30. Wilner, "Romney and Republicans Outspent Obama."

31. Political Communication Lab, "Campaign 2012: Presidential Election Ads: Obama vs. Romney," Stanford University, http://pcl.stanford.edu/campaigns/2012/.

32. Wilner, "Romney and Republicans Outspent Obama."

33. Elizabeth Wilner, "What's Hot and What's Not in 2012 Presidential Advertising," *Ad Age*, October 4, 2012, http://adage.com/article/campaign-trail/presidential-advertising-score -card/237594.

34. Wilner, "What's Hot and What's Not in 2012 Presidential Advertising."

35. Restore Our Future, "Saved," YouTube, uploaded February 23, 2012, www.youtube .com/watch?v=j5WI1FrUNzA.

36. Progress for America 2004, "Ashley's Story," YouTube, uploaded May 2, 2006, accessed February 20, 2012, www.youtube.com/watch?v=LWA052-Bl48.

37. Priorities USA Action, "Heads or Tails," YouTube, uploaded May 15, 2012, accessed February 20, 2013, www.youtube.com/watch?v=fncJZXrzG8k.

38. Romney for President, "Helping the Middle Class," YouTube, uploaded October 10, 2012, accessed February 20, 2013, www.youtube.com/watch?v=7iBCEAdO0Tc.

39. Romney for President, "Putting Jobs First," YouTube, uploaded October 10, 2012, accessed February 20, 2013, www.youtube.com/watch?v=6OD5Uyca36M.

40. Obama for America., "Main Street," YouTube, October 15, 2012, accessed February 20, 2013, www.youtube.com/watch?v=i-RCZU0gXS8.

41. Matt Visilogambros, "Jobs, Trade Dominated Presidential Advertising in 2012," *National Journal*, November 13, 2012, www.nationaljournal.com/2012-presidential-campaign/ jobs-trade-dominated-presidential-advertising-in-2012-2011113.

42. Visilogambros, "Jobs, Trade Dominated Presidential Advertising in 2012."

43. Romney for President, "Stand Up to China," YouTube, uploaded 24, 2012, accessed February 20, 2013, www.youtube.com/watch?v=TRViUQntMfs.

44. Eugene Kiely, "Romney Ad on China Mangles Facts," FactCheck.org, September 25, 2012, www.factcheck.org/2012/09/romney-ad-on-china-mangles-facts/.

45. www.factcheck.org.

46. Ricardo Alonso-Zaldivar, "Health Care Horror Stirred by Political Ads," *Huffington Post*, May 29, 2012, www.huffingtonpost.com/2012/05/29/health-care-ads-_n_1552221.html.

47. Alonso-Zaldivar, "Health Care Horror Stirred by Political Ads."

48. Obama for America, "My Job," YouTube, uploaded September 27, 2012, accessed February 17, 2013, www.youtube.com/watch?v=B9xCCaseop4.

49. Sabrina Siddiqui, "Obama Campaign's New Ad Attacks Romney's 47 Percent Idea 'In His Own Words,'" September 27, 2012, *Huffington Post*, www.huffingtonpost.com/2012/09/27/obama-47-percent_n_1919157.html.

50. Siddiqui, "Obama Campaign's New Ad Attacks Romney's 47 Percent Idea."

51. Republican National Committee, "Be Not Afraid," YouTube, uploaded August 9, 2012, accessed February 20, 2013, www.youtube.com/watch?v=IMv28sYQzCY.

52. Andrew Restuccia and Andres Feijoo, "Koch-Backed Group Takes Aim at Obama Green-Energy Policies with $6.1M Ad Buy," *E2 Wire*, April 26, 2012, http://thehill.com/blogs/e2-wire/e2-wire/224055-koch-backed-group-take-aim-at-obama-on-energy-with-61-million-ad-buy.

53. Americans for Prosperity, "Wasteful Spending," YouTube, uploaded April 26, 2012, accessed February 14, 2013, www.youtube.com/watch?v=lUQdP6y0ArM.

54. Eric Lipton and Clifford Krauss, "Fossil Fuel Industry Ads Dominate TV Campaign," *New York Times*, September 13, 2012, www.nytimes.com/2012/09/14/us/politics/fossil-fuel-industry-opens-wallet-to-defeat-obama-html.

55. Lipton and Krauss, "Fossil Fuel Industry Ads Dominate TV Campaign."

56. Lipton and Krauss, "Fossil Fuel Industry Ads Dominate TV Campaign."

57. Lipton and Krauss, "Fossil Fuel Industry Ads Dominate TV Campaign."

58. Romney for President, "A Better Future: Virginia; Energy," YouTube, uploaded September 7 2012, accessed February 3, 2013, www.youtube.com/watch?v=ICKXdV_-m2w.

59. Richard K. Barry, "Behind the Ad: Romney Still Wants to Blame Obama for Not Fixing Bush's Mess Fast Enough," *Reaction*, September 10, 2012, http://the-reaction.blogspot.com/2012/09/behind-ad-romney-still-wants-to-blame.html.

60. Romney for President, "Failing America's Workers," YouTube, uploaded September 13, 2012, accessed February 18, 2013, www.youtube.com/watch?v=58pq658byzI.

61. Obama for America, "The Problem," YouTube, uploaded July 7, 2012, accessed February 3, 2013, www.youtube.com/watch?v=o0tZK_qHHCc.

62. Obama for America, "Not One of Us," YouTube, uploaded September 23, 2012, accessed February 3, 2013, www.youtube.com/watch?v=TXudE_NKe00.

63. Obama for America, "Clear Choice for America," YouTube, uploaded August 25, 2012, accessed February 17, 2013, www.youtube.com/watch?v=NG2jDaaY48U.

64. American Crossroads, "At Stake," YouTube, uploaded October 24, 2012, accessed February 17, 2013, www.youtube.com/watch?v=5i09PWEtc_w.

65. Obama for America, "Mandatory," YouTube, uploaded October 2, 2012, accessed February 17, 2013, www.youtube.com/watch?v=-GBGIFdahSo.

66. Erica Martinson, "It's Miner against Miner in Ohio Coal War Ads," *Politico*, October 17, 2012, www.politico.com/news/stories/1012/82542.html.

67. Obama for America, "The Problem."

68. Obama for America, "My Job."

69. Obama for America, "Blatant," YouTube, uploaded August 10, 2012, www.youtube.com/watch?feature=player_embedded&v=sWTPRrMW6Dk; and see "Obama TV Ad: Romney Welfare Attack 'Blatantly False,'" RealClearPolitics Video, August 10 2012, accessed February 3, 2013, www.realclearpolitics.com/video/2012/08/10/obama_tv_ad_romney_welfare_attack_blatantly_false.html.

70. Checks and Balances for Economic Growth, "Why Would You Lie?," YouTube, uploaded October 14, 2012, accessed February 17, 2013, www.youtube.com/watch?v=9oE1O38-IIE.

71. Restore Our Future, "Genuinely Cares," YouTube, uploaded October 23, 2012, accessed February 4, 2013, www.youtube.com/watch?v=twDwAzRfJu0.

72. Restore Our Future, "Saved."

73. Restore Our Future, "New Normal," YouTube, uploaded October 4, 2012, accessed February 4, 2013, www.youtube.com/watch?feature=player_embedded&v=65ZrTjBsc7I.

74. "Obama: 'The Private Sector Is Doing Fine,'" RealClearPolitics, June 8, 2012, accessed February 4, 2013, www.realclearpolitics.com/video/2012/06/08/obama_the_private_sector_is _doing_fine.html.

75. Priorities USA Action, "Understands," YouTube, uploaded August 7, 2012, accessed February 18, 2013, www.youtube.com/watch?v=Nj70XqOxptU.

76. Lori Robertson, "Whoppers of 2012, Final Edition," FactCheck.org, October 31, 2012, www.factcheck.org/2012/10/whoppers-of-2012-final-edition/.

77. Romney for President, "Who Will Do More?," YouTube, uploaded October 28, 2012, accessed February 18, 2013, www.youtube.com/watch?v=VQ8P04q6jqE.

78. Gualberto Ranieri, "Jeep in China," Chrysler.com, October 25, 2012, http://blog .chryslerllc.com/blog.do?id=1932&p=entry.

79. Obama for America, "Collapse," YouTube, uploaded October 29, 2012, accessed February 18, 2013, www.youtube.com/watch?v=7iE5wBfM1LQ.

80. Abby D. Phillip, "How Mitt Romney's Auto Ad Triggered a Political Showdown," ABC News, November 1, 2012, http://abcnews.go.com/Politics/mitt-romneys-ohio-auto-ad -triggered-political-showdown/story?id=17617082.

81. The Republican National Committee, "Right Choice," YouTube, uploaded August 7, 2012, accessed February 18, 2013, www.youtube.com/watch?v=0F4LtTlktm0.

82. "Does Obama's Plan 'Gut Welfare'?," FactCheck.org, August 9, 2012, www.factcheck .org/2012/08/does-obamas-plan-gut-welfare-reform/.

83. Gregory Simmons, "Romney Power Team Dissects 2012 Together in Tampa," ABC News, August 28, 2012, http://abcnews.go.com/blogs/politics/2012/08/romney-power-team -dissects-2012-together-in-tampa/.

84. Obama for America, "Seen," YouTube, uploaded October 18, 2012, accessed February 18, 2013, www.youtube.com/watch?v=fhppCd4cWUk.

85. Robert Farley, "Twisting Romney's Abortion Stance," FactCheck.org, July 9, 2012, http://factcheck.org/2012/07/twisting-romneys-abortion-stance/.

86. "Obama Ad Says Romney Opposed Abortion, Even in Cases of Rape and Incest," PolitiFact, July 24, 2012, accessed February 18, 2013, www.politifact.com/truth-o-meter/ statements/2012/jul/25/barack-obama/romney-abortion-rape-incest/.

87. Obama for America, "Come and Go," YouTube, uploaded June 20, 2012, accessed February 18, 2013, www.youtube.com/watch?v=bVaw5cTjxmk.

88. Obama for America, "Revealed," YouTube, uploaded June 26, 2012, accessed February 18, 2013, www.youtube.com/watch?v=Oi0qLHHWBbc.

89. Robert Farley and Eugene Kiely, "Obama's 'Outsourcer' Overreach," FactCheck.org, June 29, 2012, http://factcheck.org/2012/06/obamas-outsourcer-overreach/.

90. Wilner, "Romney and Republicans Outspent Obama."

91. Wilner, "Romney and Republicans Outspent Obama."

92. Nate Silver, "Were Obama's Early Ads Really a Game Changer?" *FiveThirtyEight* and *New York Times*, December 29, 2012, http://fivethirtyeight.blogs.nytimes.com/2012/12/29/ were-obamas-early-ads-really-the-game-changer/?pagewanted=print.

6

"Death by Taxes": A Postmortem on Romney's Tax-Return Apologia

Joseph M. Valenzano III and Jason A. Edwards

The postmortem on presidential elections in the United States often begins shortly following the concession speech. In the case of former Massachusetts governor Mitt Romney, the Republican candidate in 2012 against incumbent President Barack Obama, the autopsy found several glaring deficiencies and problems with the candidate, as well as a shrewd strategy by his opponent. One of the more interesting aspects of the 2012 campaign was that the election became about the Republican challenger and not about the first term of the president. Just two days after the election the *Wall Street Journal* noted that Obama "said little during his campaign about his first term and even less about his plans for a second. Instead, his strategy was to portray Mitt Romney as a plutocrat."[1] In fact, Team Obama used the summer of 2012 to turn Romney's greatest strength into an albatross that helped prevent him from unseating the sitting president.

In a campaign defined by the economy and job losses, Romney constructed his image as the candidate with the business acumen to solve the nation's fiscal woes. Beginning in the Republican primaries Romney stressed his experience as chief executive officer for the private equity-investment firm Bain Capital. At Bain Romney invested in, and successfully helped turn around, a number of different businesses that he claimed created over one hundred thousand jobs. Moreover, he stressed his turn-around of the 2002 Winter Olympics in Salt Lake City, Utah. When Romney took over as president and CEO of the games, the organization was in danger of bankruptcy and reeling from allegations of corruption. Romney was largely credited with stabilizing the games, which ended with a significant financial surplus. Romney used these experiences during the 2012 campaign to create and manage his image as the candidate who knew how to create jobs, balance a budget, and accelerate the economic recovery.

Despite Romney's attempts to portray himself as a wise business leader, his opponents turned this supposed business acumen back on him in a number of attacks in the Republican primaries and the general-election campaign. Early in the 2012 Republican-primary debates, Romney's counterparts consistently attacked him for his "vulture capitalism."[2] Former speaker of the House Newt Gingrich engaged in some of the most audacious attacks against Mitt Romney with his production of the campaign film *King of Bain*, in which Romney and Bain Capital were portrayed not as saviors of struggling businesses but destroyers wreaking economic havoc and raking in profit at others' expense. During the general-election campaign, accusations of Romney's economic malfeasance returned, as in an early summer attack ad featuring a man named Joe Soptic, who seemingly blamed Romney for his wife's death from cancer because Bain Capital had closed the plant where the man worked, thus depriving him and his family of health insurance. Although repudiated by multiple media outlets as a false, misleading, and unethical advertisement, the story still contributed to a negative image of Romney with the public.[3] Additionally the Obama campaign bought $1.2 million worth of ads in Ohio alone, charging Romney with outsourcing American jobs while with Bain and hiding money in foreign tax shelters.[4] In September Romney's now-infamous "47 percent" comment, recorded at a private fundraiser without authorization, helped reinforce the narrative that he was an "out-of-touch greedy millionaire."[5] The attacks against Romney, both from his fellow Republicans during the primary season and later by President Obama during the general-election campaign, redefined his personal wealth and private business acumen, twisting them into more of a liability than an asset. And try as he might, he could not shake the negative image, which cost him dearly at the polls in November.

In this chapter we examine how Governor Romney attempted to counter these redefinitions of his image. Specifically we focus on how Mitt Romney handled the issue of his tax returns as a microcosm of his larger strategy for shaping and reshaping his appearance as a business leader. Ironically it was Mitt Romney's father, former Republican presidential candidate George Romney, who established the tradition of releasing multiple years of tax returns. Mitt Romney did manage the issue fairly well during the Republican primaries but responded poorly when the attacks mattered most, during the summer and fall of the general election. We argue that his responses during the January campaign allowed him to seemingly take ownership of the issue and diffuse the matter as a larger primary campaign issue but that in the summer months he relied on surrogates to defend him on the subject, making it seem like he did not deem it an important enough topic to discuss.

In the next section we begin by briefly describing the theory of image repair, the primary lens through which we examine Governor Romney's responses. Then we focus our analysis on how the governor dealt with the tax-return issue during the primary campaign and the general election. Finally we draw conclusions about Romney's rhetorical strategy in defending himself from attacks on his wealth and private-sector success and discuss how his approach offers unique insight into political apologia.

IMAGE-REPAIR THEORY

Defending oneself against accusations during a presidential campaign is hardly anything new. In fact, all campaigns engage in discourse where they promote themselves, attack their opponents, and defend themselves against attacks.[6] Image-repair research, which focuses on defense discourse in the campaign, has become one of the most studied areas of communication literature. The research is drawn from, among others, the rhetorical works of Kenneth Burke,[7] literature from sociology on accounts research,[8] and apologia research.[9]

In a number of different essays, communication theorist William Benoit combined and refined the available research to develop the theory of image repair,[10] in which he asserted that creating and maintaining one's image is primarily communicative activity.[11] Moreover if that image has been damaged in some way then a response, an attempt at image repair, is essential. In composing his theory, Benoit offered a typology of five general approaches with multiple substrategies from which political candidates might choose to defend themselves from the slings and arrows of a campaign.

The first general strategy is denial, which can come in two forms. *Simple denial* is where the speaker clearly states no wrong act was committed. The second form, *shifting the blame* (also known as *victimage*), concedes that the action occurred but then shifts responsibility onto another party. Both of these strategies allow a speaker to deny wrongdoing.

The second broad category is evading responsibility, which contains four specific rhetorical postures. *Provocation* occurs when the speaker claims the offense was in response to the negative actions of another; in essence, the speaker was provoked, and therefore responsibility lies with the instigator. The speaker employs *defeasibility* by arguing that events outside of their control caused the action. In attempts to evade responsibility a speaker also might argue that the wrongful act was *accidental*, and thus not their fault. Finally, a speaker sometimes claims *good intentions* for the offensive act ought to mitigate responsibility. And, ultimately, all four of these strategies represent attempts to avoid responsibility for the offensive act, thus repairing, at least in part, the damage done to an image.

Benoit's third category in this taxonomy, reducing offensiveness, contains the most substrategies for image repair. *Bolstering* entails extoling one's virtuous and good qualities in an attempt to engender positive feelings for oneself while simultaneously making the action seem less offensive. Or an accused person can argue the violation was not as offensive as it was made out to be, thus *minimizing* its damage. A speaker may *differentiate* the offensiveness of an act by comparing it to another, far more aberrant and distasteful, action. Or rhetors can attempt *transcendence*, placing the action in a broader, more positive light. The accused may turn the tables and *attack the accuser*'s credibility and motives so as to make the accuser's offense seem even viler than the one committed by the speaker. The sixth and final method of reducing offensiveness is *compensation*, wherein the speaker attempts to reimburse the victims of the offense, although this does not necessarily come with an admission of guilt.

The fourth category of image-repair strategies available to speakers is corrective action, and like denial it comes in two forms. In the first form the accused offers to *repair* any damage that resulted from the offending action. Sometimes this involves charitable giving, volunteering, or even seeking professional assistance. In the event that the action's damage cannot be reversed, the speaker may enumerate plans to *prevent the recurrence* of the offending act. Both of these strategies show a willingness to materially participate in the repair of an image, but, again, neither is necessarily accompanied by an admission of guilt.

The admission of guilt, or *mortification*, is the final image-restoration category explicated by Benoit, where a speaker takes full responsibility for their actions and apologizes to those damaged by the offense. Often admissions of guilt are accompanied by other strategies from the other categories and when done well by a speaker can quickly repair an image.

As we will now demonstrate, Mitt Romney deployed several of these strategies when confronted about releasing his tax returns. Like other politicians who have been attacked over a long period of time about a single issue, Romney's image repair and rhetorical defense contained several different tactics that resulted in differing levels of success and failure. We begin by discussing the first stage in the attacks concerning the release of his tax returns, which took place during the Republican primary season, specifically during three January 2012 debates. We then shift our attention to the second stage of the attacks, when during the summer President Obama's campaign assaulted the very same issue. We demonstrate that during the primary Romney's image-repair strategies were largely successful but that they failed during the general campaign for, primarily, one significant reason.

THE REPUBLICAN PRIMARIES:
MITT ROMNEY DEFENDS HIMSELF (SORT OF)

Modern candidates for president from both parties traditionally release their tax returns to the public. As noted earlier, this practice began with Mitt Romney's own father, George, in the 1968 presidential campaign. He released twelve years of tax returns all at once, reportedly saying that "one year could be a fluke," while neither his fellow Republican challenger, Nixon, nor the Democratic candidate, Hubert Humphrey, released any. Although George Romney's actions set a precedent for future candidates to release their own returns, no standard was established for how many a person should release, nor is there any legal requirement to do so.

While often the tax-return-release expectation is used as a political weapon, at other times it is meant to provide a window into the financial lives of wealthier candidates. In 2008 then-candidate Barack Obama released seven years of tax returns in an effort to get frontrunner Hillary Clinton to do the same. In that same election Republican candidate Senator John McCain released two years of returns. The most ever provided to the public was by Senator Bob Dole in 1996, when he released thirty years of tax returns. Bowing to this public scrutiny has become more important for wealthier candidates, although in 2004 Senator John Kerry did not release the returns of his wife, heiress to the Heinz fortune—something Mitt Romney pointed out during his own campaign eight years later.[12]

January 19, 2012: Birth of the Tax-Return Issue

Mitt Romney's personal fortune has made him one of the wealthiest candidates to ever run for office. This, combined with the fact that he is the son of the man who began the tradition of releasing tax returns, firmly trained the spotlight on the release of his own returns. The issue was first brought into the public eye during the primaries when an audience member at the January 19, 2012, South Carolina Republican Presidential Primary Debate asked the candidates when they would release their tax returns.[13] Newt Gingrich immediately quipped, "an hour ago."[14] Moderator John King turned his attention to Ron Paul, who stated he would not release his tax returns. Then King directed the question to Mitt Romney, who responded,

> When my taxes are complete for this year, and I know that if I'm the nominee the president's going to insist that I show what my income was this last year and so forth . . . I know what's going to come. Every time the Democrats are out there trying their very best to—to try and attack people because they've been successful. And—and I have been successful. But let me tell you, the—challenge in America is not people who've been successful. The challenge in America, and President Obama doesn't want to talk about this, is you've got a president who's played ninety rounds of golf while there are twenty-five million Americans out of work. . . . That's the problem in America, not the attacks they make on people who've been successful.[15]

Herein Romney interwove strategies of preemptive defense and attacks on his accusers. Susan Sarapin argued that preemptive defense should be added to the typology of image-repair tactics. Further, she noted that a preemptive defense is launched when the rhetoric anticipates and answers a particular attack from an opponent before the attack is provided.[16] Governor Romney anticipated that President Obama and the Democrats would use his financial success against him, as he knew full well "what's going to come." However, Romney turned this defensive tactic into an offensive one. He implied that he knew exactly how to combat the attacks President Obama would make but then went one step further, attacking President Obama's inability to get the economy moving again. Romney thus implied that he was the candidate who could meet and defeat President Obama in the general election using an economic argument.

Despite this answer, John King noted that criticism of Romney regarding his tax returns did not come just from Democrats but from "some of your rivals up here. Speaker Gingrich has said you owe them to the people of South Carolina before they vote. Governor Perry made that point as well before he left the race. Why not should the people of South Carolina before this election see last year's return?"[17] The governor explained:

> Because I want to make sure that I beat President Obama. And every time we release things drip by drip, the Democrats go out with another array of attacks. . . . If I'm the nominee, I'll put these out at one time so we have one discussion of all of this. I—I obviously pay all full taxes. I'm honest in my dealings with people. People understand that. My taxes are carefully managed, and I pay a lot of taxes . . . and when I have our—our taxes ready for this year, I'll release them.[18]

Here Romney combined preemptive defense with the tactic of bolstering. The former Massachusetts governor recognized his personal wealth was a weakness and would be subject to vociferous attacks by Democrats. However, the governor demonstrated he had a clear strategy to limit those attacks by having "one discussion" of his wealth instead of letting the issue linger, "drip by drip." Romney suggested to the Republican electorate that he could easily survive "one discussion" of his tax returns and personal wealth. Once he weathered that storm he could focus on the economy, an issue "President Obama doesn't want to talk about," where Romney felt assured of a win because of "success" in the private sector. At the same time, Romney bolstered his campaign credentials by assuring the viewing audience that he was an "honest" person, whose taxes were "carefully managed," who paid "all full taxes" in accordance with the law. By emphasizing his honesty, coupled with the fact he had a clear strategy for dealing with any potential weakness his personal wealth exposed, he minimized the impact his tax returns and personal wealth would have on the primary and general election.

January 23: On the Eve of Releasing Returns

What Governor Romney did not anticipate was the amount of flak he would receive from his Republican opponents, particularly Newt Gingrich. Four days later at the next primary debate at the University of South Florida the issue of Romney's returns again came up when moderator Brian Williams stated that Romney had "set [things] in motion for tomorrow when you release one year's tax returns and your estimates for 2011 . . . Can you tell us tonight what's in there that's going to get people talking? What in there that's going to be controversial? What's in there that you may find yourself defending?"[19] Romney answered,

> No surprise, Brian. The most extensive disclosure that I made was the financial-disclosure requirements under the law. . . . The real question is not how much are my taxes but the taxes of the American people. The real question people are going to ask is, Who's going to help the American people at a time when folks are having real tough times?"[20]

Romney then proceeded to outline his plans to lower taxes on individuals and corporations while reshaping the tax code to make America more competitive. Brian Williams followed up by asking, "so, across the country tomorrow, when people learn the details of the tax return you release . . . nothing will stick out, nothing will emerge that will be talked about by this time tomorrow night?" The governor rejoined:

> Oh, I'm sure people will talk about it. I mean, you'll see my income, how much taxes I've paid, how much I've paid to charity. You'll see how complicated taxes can be. But—but I pay all the taxes that are legally required, not a dollar more. . . . And will there be discussion? Sure. Will it be an article? Yeah? But is it entirely legal and fair? Absolutely. I'm proud of the fact that I pay a lot of taxes."[21]

Note how Romney interwove strategies of denial, transcendence, and minimization. He denied there would be any surprises in his tax returns and immediately attempted to transcend the issue by focusing on the larger problem of taxes and the economy. Throughout the Republican primaries this was his consistent strategy. As we saw earlier, in the South Carolina debate he'd anticipated attacks made against him but then attempted to turn the question to the larger issue of the economy where he could emphasize his plans to fix the country's problems. Ultimately his strategy minimized and circumscribed the grounds on which his opponents could attack him. By effectively answering actual and potential arguments, Romney could focus his attention on his vision for the country, which then allowed him to appear as if he were above the fray.

Romney continued that strategy in a later exchange regarding his personal wealth. Brian Williams asked the governor about his father's model of releasing twelve years' worth of returns. Romney replied,

> I agree with my dad on a lot of things, but we also disagree. And—and going out with twelve years of returns is not something I'm going to do. I'm putting out two years, which is more than anyone else on this stage. I think that it'll satisfy the interest of the American people to see that I pay my taxes, where I give my charitable contributions to, and I think that's the right number.

Williams followed up, asking, "More broadly, Governor, just as an aside, have you been surprised at the degree to which your wealth has become an issue?" Romney answered,

> Yeah, I knew that was going to come from the Obama team. I understand that. We see that on the Left. I was surprised to see people in the Republican Party pick up the weapons of the Left and start using them to attack free enterprise. I think those weapons will be used against us. . . . I will not apologize for having been successful. I did not inherit what my wife and I have, nor did she. What we have—what—what I was able to build, I built the old-fashioned way, by earning it, by working hard. And I was proud of the fact that we helped create businesses that grew, that employed people.[22]

Here Romney clearly referenced the attacks made by his Republican opponents, particularly Newt Gingrich, regarding his time at Bain Capital. His answer suggests an apology for Republicans in general, that in attacking his tenure at Bain Capital Republicans had lowered themselves to the levels of Democrats. Romney expected "free enterprise" to be attacked by the "Left," but in "using the weapons of the Left" Republicans were debasing themselves just to win in an election cycle. Romney and his wife did not "inherit" their wealth but built it "the old-fashioned way, by earning it, by working hard" in helping to create businesses. This hard-work, pull-yourself-up-by-your-bootstraps way of making a living is the quintessential American Dream, where people of all stripes are given an opportunity to make their own way in the United States. That is the Republican Party credo, the credo of the United States, and thus attacks against Romney, Romney suggested, only debase that credo. Accordingly, Romney's success in free enterprise bolstered his claim to be the only Republican who could beat President Obama. Immediately after the debate Mitt Romney released his tax returns for 2010 and an estimate for 2011.

January 26: Gingrich versus Romney (Round III)

Despite the release of the forms, the issue reappeared at the primary debate in Jacksonville, Florida. CNN's Wolf Blitzer, the moderator, opened up the issue by asking Newt Gingrich whether he was satisfied with the information the Romney campaign had released. Gingrich attacked Blitzer for the question, explaining his remarks were fine for an "interview on a TV show, but this is a national debate where you have a chance to get the four of us to talk about a whole range of issues." After a back-and-forth between Blitzer and Gingrich, Romney interjected that it would "be nice if people made accusations somewhere else that they weren't willing to defend here,"[23] thus reigniting the argument between the two candidates that had smoldered the previous two weeks of the primary season. Gingrich then said, "Okay. Alright. Given that standard, Mitt, I did say I thought it was unusual. And I don't know of any American president who has had a Swiss bank account. I'd be glad for you to explain that sort of thing." Romney retorted, "Okay, I will. I will. I'll say it again." Here, Romney entered into a lengthy explanation, as he had done earlier in the debate, about his investment strategies. He emphasized that his investments were "in a blind trust. That was so that I would avoid any conflicts of interest." He further noted:

> Speaker, you've indicated that somehow I don't earn that money. I have earned the money that I have. I didn't inherit it. I take risks. I make investments. Those investments lead to jobs being created in America. I'm proud of being successful. I'm proud of being in the free-enterprise system that creates jobs for other people. I'm not going to run from that. I'm proud of the taxes I pay. My taxes, plus my charitable contributions, this year, 2011, will be about 40 percent. So, look, let's put behind this idea of attacking me because of my investments or my money, and let's get Republicans to say, You know what? What you've accomplished in your life shouldn't be seen as a detriment; it should be seen as an asset to help America.[24]

Romney used bolstering to defend himself as he did in the previous debate. The governor extolled his own ability to take "risks," make "investments," and be in the "free-enterprise system that creates jobs for other people." Moreover, he said, he'd spent a good deal of his own money contributing to the coffers of the U.S. Treasury and to treasuries that help people. His answer implied that out of all of his opponents *he* was the real Republican, the quintessential American success story, a success achievable by any individual with access to the opportunity to do so, an opportunity he argued was being snuffed out by the Obama presidency. And any attacks made by Gingrich and Santorum against Romney's personal wealth and success, he believed, debased the Republican and American credo. Consequently, naysayers disqualified themselves from being Republican standard-bearers. In defending himself from the attacks targeting his tax returns and personal wealth—because of his success and because of his economic vision for America—Romney underwrote his ability to win the Republican nomination and appeared to inoculate himself, or at least illuminate his defense against the attacks Democrats would certainly launch against him later that summer, given the chance.

THE GENERAL ELECTION:
ROMNEY LETS OTHERS DEFEND HIM

In July the issue of Romney's wealth and tax returns predictably reentered the national conversation and dogged Romney through the rest of the campaign, in large part because of his failed efforts at apologia during this period. Over the next four months of the general election Romney's tax returns persisted in the headlines. In July Romney relied exclusively on surrogates to defend his decision on releasing his tax returns. In August he delivered his only public interview on the issue but continued to use surrogates to defend his decision, dispatching his wife, Ann, to give an interview shortly after his own. Despite these efforts, the Obama campaign continued to press the issue, and on August 23 Romney released a statement explaining why he chose to hold back most of his returns. In September Romney finally released two full years of tax returns, while surrogates continued to defend him on the talk-show circuit. Finally, in October, at the second presidential debate at Hofstra University, President Obama and Governor Romney have a brief exchange regarding each other's financial portfolios. But let's return first to July, when Romney began to rely on the surrogate-defense strategy when challenged about his tax returns.

July: Return of the Tax Returns

As the summer heated up, Governor Romney received scathing criticism from President Obama and his campaign surrogates regarding their belief that he'd failed to disclose his tax returns to the public. By the end of July pressure had skyrocketed, with

Senate Majority Leader Harry Reid accusing Romney of not paying his taxes for ten years, albeit without proof.[25] As these accusations echoed the attacks from Newt Gingrich during the primary campaign the previous winter, prominent Republicans and conservative columnists also began calling for Romney to release more returns. Unlike the earlier episodes during the primary debates, Romney failed to respond directly to the criticisms in almost every instance, preferring to rely on surrogates for his defense. Among those coming to his assistance that July were House Speaker John Boehner and former primary challengers and critics Newt Gingrich and Rick Santorum.[26]

Romney's persistent silence during this blistering opening round of general-campaign-season criticism evidenced a switch in tactic—and a unique form of apologia. His traditional defense in the primaries meant he'd responded directly to his accusers. But in using surrogates he'd abandoned the traditional apologia—even apologia by association.[27]

The attacks against Romney during this month emanated from both Democrats and prominent Republican columnists. From July 8 to 14 prominent Republicans like former Mississippi Governor Haley Barbour, former Republican National Committee Chair Michael Steele, and conservative columnists Bill Kristol and George Will all called for Romney to release more returns, claiming that if he did not it was because he was hiding something. Both Kristol and Will acknowledged the temporary hit Romney would take in so doing but predicted (accurately) that the long-term damage of withholding the returns would be worse. On ABC's *This Week* Will stated that "the costs of not releasing the returns are clear. . . . Therefore he must have calculated there are higher costs in releasing them."[28]

In response to this wave of criticism Romney relied on statements from House Speaker Boehner and former rivals Newt Gingrich and Rick Santorum. At a press conference with future vice presidential candidate Paul Ryan, Boehner leapt to Romney's defense when Ryan failed to aggressively respond to a question about the candidate's tax returns:

> Listen, listen. Americans are asking, Where are the jobs? They're not asking where in the hell the tax returns are. . . . This is another sideshow intended to draw the American people's attention away from the real issue, and the real issue is that the president's economic policies have failed. They've actually made things worse. And as a result he can't run on his record. He's got to run on something else. And so, whether it's the tax returns, whether it's Bain Capital, you'll see every distraction known to man because the president can't run on his record.[29]

Gingrich, who'd so needled the candidate on this very issue only months earlier, tried to suggest that the American people didn't care much about tax returns: "I've tried to raise the issue, but, frankly, I think the results of the primary also indicated that the American voters are pretty comfortable that this is a guy who has had good accountants, good lawyers, he has obeyed the law."[30] Santorum, for his part, argued to CNN that Romney was the subject of an unfair expectation, especially given what he claimed was a lack of transparency by the White House.[31]

Each of these three men used strategies that Romney himself had employed during the primaries. Boehner's lengthy rejoinder attacked the accuser while minimizing, arguing that the American people did not even consider the tax returns to be an issue. Santorum also minimized the tax return issue through differentiation, comparing it to what he saw as the more distasteful and reprehensible concealment of the Obama White House. Gingrich bolstered Romney by reminding the public that he'd raised the tax return topic in the primaries but believed the American people didn't care about it and understood Romney's virtues, that he had "good accountants, good lawyers, he obeyed the law." Therefore, the three stand-ins suggested, Romney did no wrong. Yet as the debate roiled, the accused remained silent. And this made it appear as if Romney, not thinking the issue important to address, farmed it off to surrogates. But the strategy was unsuccessful, and the controversy did not die down.

On July 31, 2012, Harry Reid continued to pile on the Romney tax-release issue, claiming that the reason Romney did not want to release more returns was because he hadn't paid any taxes in the last decade:

> He didn't pay taxes for ten years! Now, do I know that that's true? Well, I'm not certain. But obviously he can't release those tax returns. How would it look? You guys have said his wealth is $250 million. . . . Not a chance in the world. It's a lot more than that. I mean, you do pretty well if you don't pay taxes for ten years when you're making millions and millions of dollars.[32]

Still producing no evidence to back his claim, Reid's accusation based upon a supposed conversation with a Bain investor resonated with the public because of Romney's repeated failure to release several years' worth of returns and because he had not commented publicly on the issue in months. After Reid's attack, Romney finally weighed in.

In an interview with Fox Radio, Governor Romney unequivocally denied the claims levied by Reid. He called the Senate Majority leader's statement "totally and completely wrong" and accused the White House of putting Reid up to it. Romney called it "untrue, dishonest, and accurate" and called on Reid to release his sources, saying it was "probably the White House."[33] Here Romney first denied the accusation and then attacked the accuser, Reid being a stand-in for the Obama campaign. Effectively, Romney had attacked the surrogate after denying his claims. This exchange proved a mere prelude to an even more difficult month for the Romney campaign.

The Dog Days of August

As the calendar turned to August Romney continued to be dogged by the tax-return issue. He remained stalwart on his position, refusing to release more returns, and on August 9, 2012, gave his only interview on the matter to *Bloomberg Businessweek*.[34] But this proved too little, too late, insufficiently quelling the criticism, with a CNN/ORC poll taken shortly after indicating that 63 percent of Americans believed that Romney should release more returns.[35] On August 16 Ann Romney publicly defended his decision to not release more returns.[36] The next day the Obama campaign pressed the advantage, calling for Romney to release five years of returns.[37] On August 23 Romney explained he did not want to release the returns to protect his church.[38]

In the *Bloomberg Businessweek* interview Romney had almost escaped without having to address the issue, but the last question from interviewer Josh Tyrangiel framed his returns in the context of a business:

> TYRANGIEL: Let's frame the issue around your tax returns in a slightly different way. If you're an investor and you're looking at a company and that company says that its great strength is wise management and fiscal know-how, wouldn't you want to see the previous, say, five years' worth of its financials?

> ROMNEY: I'm not a business. We have a process in this country, which was established by law, which provides for the transparency which candidates are required to meet. I have met with that requirement with full financial disclosure of all my investments but in addition have provided and will provide a full two years of tax returns. This happens to be exactly the same as with John McCain when he ran for office four years ago. And the Obama team had no difficulty with that circumstance. The difference between then and now is that President Obama has a failed economic record and is trying to find any issue he can to deflect from the failure of his record. Thanks, guys. Goodbye.[39]

In the first part of Romney's response he denied any wrongdoing. He then argued his releases were the same as Senator John McCain's, the 2008 Republican nominee. He finally differentiated the tax-return issue from the failed economic record of the president, which he implicitly claimed was far worse and what people should pay more attention to. But the attacks on his returns and wealth continued.

So on August 16 Romney dispatched his wife, perhaps his most powerful and popular surrogate, to discuss his tax returns. In an exchange with NBC reporter Natalie Morales, Ann Romney used several different image-repair strategies to defend against claims of lack of transparency. She first shifted the blame of the tax-release issue to the press and Obama campaign, insisting that "the more we release, the more we get attacked, the more we get questions, the more we get pushed. We have done what's legally required, and there's going to be no more tax releases given."[40] Here she blamed others for making a major issue out of nothing, suggesting that public focus had been on their finances not because of their lack of transparency (they had already released the information) but because their opponents had perpetually focused on it and would never be satisfied with any amount of disclosure. Ann Romney also said that her husband's document releases when governor of Massachusetts were "huge." Finally, she employed transcendence, casting their tax burden in a broader, more positive light by "adding" their charitable contributions to the total they contribute to society: "The other thing you have to understand is that Mitt is honest; his integrity is, is just golden. We pay our taxes. . . . Beyond paying our taxes, we also give 10 percent of our income to charity."[41] Here she portrayed her husband and their charitable contributions in a much more positive light, making taxes only one small part of a larger contributory equation. Unfortunately, even Ann Romney's ardent defense could not derail public demands that they release more returns, as the very next day the Obama campaign challenged Romney to release five years of returns, which he flatly refused to do.

In an effort to put the subject to rest once and for all, Romney issued one more statement on the tax returns on August 23, telling *Parade* in an interview scheduled for release that Sunday that the reason he did not want to release more returns was to protect his church. "One of the downsides of releasing one's financial information," Romney told the magazine, is that this is now all public but we had never intended our contributions to be known. It's a very personal thing between ourselves and our commitment to our God and to our church."[42] Here Romney employed transcendence in much the same way his wife had a week earlier, saying the disclosure was to protect his church and his faith. This move to a transcendence strategy from the earlier efforts to attack the accuser illustrates how the narrative of his tax returns had shifted his personal success from a strength to a liability.

September and October: The Home Stretch

In September, reeling from continued attacks, the Romney campaign attempted to move the conversation away from the candidates' finances. On the 21st he finally conceded to release two full years' worth of returns—adding his full 2011 returns to the 2010 documents he'd released that January,[43] demonstrating efforts at mortification and corrective action. This release was met with more attacks from Left-leaning organizations, like *Mother Jones*,[44] and also initiated a televised duel of sorts between President Obama's political strategist David Axelrod and chair of the Republican National Committee, Reince Priebus, and other surrogates.[45] This exchange between campaign surrogates would mark the last major discussion of Romney's taxes during the campaign.

Romney's attempt at corrective action had fallen short of what the Obama campaign and the general public had been calling for. Two years' worth of returns was a far cry from the twelve his father had released and still left him open to questions regarding his finances. Despite the fact that Romney did exactly what he'd been saying he was going to do since January, his action did little to reverse the damage nine months of public debate and inquiry into his financial background and success had wrought. His Democratic accusers sought to use the tax-return issue to elevate their indictment of his economic policies. Specifically, on ABC's *This Week with George Stephanopoulos* and *Fox News Sunday* David Axelrod and Robert Gibbs, Obama campaign surrogates, argued that the issue was not that Romney hadn't revealed his own taxes but that he did not reveal what he would do to the taxes of all Americans. In response, Romney campaign surrogate Reince Priebus called the attacks "bogus" and stated that the Romneys had "given way over 30 percent of their income to charity,"[46] an image-repair defense hinged both on denial and transcendence. Romney, however, remained quiet on the issue in September. In fact, there would be only one more passing reference to the tax-return issue during the remainder of the campaign.

This occurred in a tense exchange between Romney and Obama at the second presidential debate at Hofstra University when Romney was asked about his wealth and in response tried to turn the issue back on the president, asking Obama if he had looked at his own pension. Obama replied, "You know, I—I don't look at my pension. It's not as big as yours, so it doesn't take as long."[47] This statement served as a veiled reminder of the successful negative narrative created around Romney's wealth and repeated unwillingness throughout the entire year to release more than two years of tax returns.

The issue of Romney's wealth, which he'd once hoped would enhance his presidential bona fides, instead dogged him throughout the entire campaign. His handling of Republican demands during the primaries to release his returns was seemingly successful in that the topic faded after the January 23 debate. However, it proved to only have gone into hibernation, returning in force all throughout the summer months, through September. Romney was never able to effectively move the focus from his tax returns and thus damaged his chances at unseating the president. And so in the following we discuss the implications of this episode within the 2012 campaign and what it means for candidates and what it contributes to our understanding of image-repair theory.

CONCLUSION

To be sure, there was no one mortal wound that doomed the Romney presidential bid in 2012. But the image management surrounding the tax-return issue amounted to serious self-inflicted damage to his campaign. Our examination of both that damage and his efforts at mitigation provides insight into his campaign's failure to unseat a president presiding over a poor economic climate, the nature and importance of certain periods of time during a campaign, and how politicians choose to defend against attacks from their opponents. While we do not contend that had Romney handled his tax return release with more rhetorical panache he would be president, we do believe it may have fundamentally altered the course of the election and allowed him to campaign on his greatest strength instead of having that strength become his most glaring weakness. This episode during the 2012 campaign also raises some interesting questions for communication scholars.

In examining the two stages of the campaign, the primary- and general-election cycles, there appears to be one significant change in tactics by Romney: the use of surrogates. During the primary campaign when Newt Gingrich repeatedly challenged Romney to release his returns Romney deftly managed the crisis by directly confronting the issue in word and action, verbally parrying Gingrich's criticisms and actually releasing a part of his tax returns. During the summer, after he'd secured the nomination, Romney primarily relied on surrogates to defend his record, including Gingrich and Santorum, two rivals who had only recently chastened him over the very same issue. His choice of surrogates in this instance was somewhat puzzling as both Santorum and Gingrich—especially Gingrich—dented their own credibility in defending the man over the very issue for which they'd just excoriated him. This defense tactic also allowed surrogates for the Obama administration to continue to harp on Romney's wealth and taxes throughout the summer. His momentary attempts to wade into the debate during August did not put the issue to rest but merely highlighted a change in his rationale for not releasing the returns, indicating a lack of preparedness—as he'd claimed during the primaries—to defend against Democratic attacks on his success. As his tax record gained full attention throughout the summer, his greatest strength, being an economic wunderkind from his days at Bain, became a major liability, and somehow, by the end of the summer, he'd become to the American people a corporate plutocrat who took advantage of tax loopholes to hide his actual earnings.

There are two significant takeaways from this. The first relates to the use of surrogates. There is a paucity of research on surrogates during a campaign, particularly when it comes to their effective use and which surrogates carry the most gravitas. Romney's experience seems to indicate that presidential candidates are more effective at responding directly to criticism than are their surrogates. And although Ann Romney was popular among the American public, the timing of defense seemed to come too late in the game to staunch the bleeding and fell well after Romney's other surrogates had ineffectively responded to demands for more returns. Further investigation into the ethos and timing of surrogate messages might help us understand this strategy of surrogate apologia in greater detail.

The second major insight we gain from the Romney experience in 2012 relates to the importance of the summer in a presidential campaign. It is a commonly held notion that the summers between the primaries and general elections can make or break campaigns, despite the seeming lack of activity. But the attacks on Romney's tax returns—and his ensuing failure to adequately respond and eliminate the issue—grew to a crescendo during this period, mounted even before the candidate had been officially nominated. Romney lost the summer and as a result created too large of a gap between himself and the presidency to overcome in the fall. Further scholarship might also explore what made the attacks by the Obama campaign and its allies so effective.

As taxing as the issue was, Romney's shift in rhetorical approaches between the primaries and the general election left him open to a death by a thousand cuts during the summer of 2012. Future candidates would do well to learn from this and be more direct and immediate in their handling of controversial issues. It might have made a difference for Governor Romney.

NOTES

1. "Hope over Experience: A Divided Country Gives Obama a Second Chance," *Wall Street Journal*, November 8, 2012, accessed December 22, 2012, http://online.wsj.com/article/SB10001424052970204349404578102971575770036.html.

2. Felicia Somnez, "Rick Perry Doubles Down on 'Vulture Capitalist' Criticism of Mitt Romney," *Washington Post*, January 11, 2012, www.washingtonpost.com/blogs/post-politics/post/rick-perry-doubles-down-on-vulture-capitalist-criticism-of-mitt-romney/2012/01/11/gIQAziWqqP_blog.html.

3. Guy Benson, "CNN Slams 'Outrageous' Anti-Romney 'Cancer' Ad, Team Obama Refuses to Condemn," Townhall.com, August 8, 2012, accessed December 22, 2012, http://townhall.com/tipsheet/guybenson/2012/08/08/cnn_that_obama_superpac_cancer_ad_is_outrageous_and_full_of_falsehoods.

4. Lisa Lerer, "Romney Lost Race in Summer after Obama Redefined Résumé," *Bloomberg*, November 7, 2012, accessed December 22, 2012, www.bloomberg.com/news/2012-11-07/romney-lost-race-in-summer-after-obama-redefines-resume.html.

5. "Full Transcript of the Mitt Romney Secret Video," *Mother Jones*, September 19, 2012, accessed December 22, 2012, www.motherjones.com/politics/2012/09/full-transcript-mitt-romney-secret-video.

6. William L. Benoit, *Communication in Political Campaigns* (New York: Peter Lang, 2007).

7. Kenneth Burke, *The Rhetoric of Religion* (Berkeley: University of California Press, 1961).

8. Marvin B. Scott and Stanford Lyman, "Accounts," *American Sociological Review* 33 (1968): 46–62.

9. B. L. Ware and Wil A. Linkugel, "They Spoke in Defense of Themselves: On the Generic Criticism of Apologia," *Quarterly Journal of Speech* 59 (1973): 273–83.

10. See William L. Benoit, "Richard M. Nixon's Rhetorical Strategies in His Public Statements on Watergate," *Southern Speech Communication Journal* 47 (1982): 192–211; William L. Benoit, Paul Gulifor, and Daniel A. Panici, "President Reagan's Defensive Discourse on Iran-Contra," *Communication Studies* 42 (1991): 272–94.

11. William L. Benoit, *Accounts, Excuses, and Apologies: A Theory of Image Restoration Discourse* (Albany: State University of New York Press, 1995).

12. For a more detailed history of the tax returns of presidential candidates, see The Tax History Project, or visit Robert Farley, Lucas Isakowitz, Nathan Emmons, and Jesse Dubois, "Romney and the Tax Return Precedent," FactCheck.org, July 19, 2012, accessed December 22, 2012, http://factcheck.org/2012/07/romney-and-the-tax-return-precedent/.

13. "Full Transcript of the CNN Southern Republican Debate 2000–2200 EST," CNN, January 19, 2012, http://transcripts.cnn.com/transcripts/1201/19/se.05.html.

14. "Full Transcript of the CNN Southern Republican Debate."

15. "Full Transcript of the CNN Southern Republican Debate."

16. Susan Sarapin, "Obama's Pastor Disaster and Apologia by Proxy: A Change in Structure for Image Restoration," a paper presented at the National Communication Association Conference, Chicago, 2009. Preemptive defense is similar to proleptical argumentation. Prolepsis is where a rhetor anticipates an argument ahead of time and answers it. See Douglas Walton, "Proleptical Argumentation," *Argumentation and Advocacy* 43 (2008): 143–54; Jason A. Edwards and Liza-Anne Cabral, "Managing an Economic Crisis: President Bill Clinton and the Mexican Peso Crisis," *Relevant Rhetoric* 3 (2012), accessed January 3, 2013, http://relevantrhetoric.com/wp-content/uploads/Managing-an-Economic-Crisis.pdf.

17. "Full Transcript of the CNN Southern Republican Debate."

18. "Full Transcript of the CNN Southern Republican Debate."

19. "Republican Debate Transcript, Tampa, Florida, January 2012," *Council on Foreign Relations*, January 23, 2012, accessed December 12, 2012, www.cfr.org/us-election-2012/republican-debate-transcript-tampa-florida-january-2012/p27180.

20. "Republican Debate Transcript, Tampa, Florida, January 2012."

21. "Republican Debate Transcript, Tampa, Florida, January 2012."

22. "Republican Debate Transcript, Tampa, Florida, January 2012."

23. "Full Transcript of CNN Florida Republican Presidential Debate," CNN, January 26, 2012, accessed December 12, 2012, http://archives.cnn.com/transcripts/1201/26/se.05.html.

24. "Full Transcript of CNN Florida Republican Presidential Debate."

25. Sam Stein and Ryan Grim, "Harry Reid: Bain Investor Told Me That Mitt Romney 'Didn't Pay Any Taxes for Ten Years,'" *Huffington Post*, July 31, 2012, accessed December 22, 2012, www.huffingtonpost.com/2012/07/31/harry-reid-romney-taxes_n_1724027.html.

26. For stories on each of their defenses of Romney's decisions, see Russell Berman, "Speaker Boehner Defends Romney on Tax Returns, Calls Issue a 'Sideshow,'" *The Hill*, July 18, 2012, accessed December 22, 2012, http://thehill.com/homenews/house/238635-boehner-defends-romney-on-tax-returns-calls-issue-a-sideshow; Ewa Kochanska, "Gingrich Defends Romney on Tax Returns, Israel/Palestine Comments," *Examiner*, July 30, 2012, accessed December 22, 2012, www.examiner.com/article/gingrich-defends-romney-on-tax-returns-israel-palestine-comments; Dana Davidsen, "Santorum Defends Romney's Trip, Expects Convention Speaking Slot," CNN, July 31, 2012, accessed December 22, 2012, http://politicalticker.blogs.cnn.com/2012/07/31/santorum-defends-romneys-trip-expects-convention-speaking-slot/.

27. Kasie Mitchell Roberson and Stacey L. Connaughton, "On the Presidential Campaign Trail: Apologia of Association," *Public Relations Review* 36 (2010): 181–83.

28. Pema Levy, "Conservative Pundits Wonder if Romney's Hiding Something in Unreleased Tax Returns," *Talking Points Memo*, July 15, 2012, accessed January 7, 2012, http://2012.talkingpointsmemo.com/2012/07/conservative-romney-taxes-returns-hiding-something.php.

29. Berman, "Speaker Boehner Defends Romney."

30. Kochanska, "Gingrich Defends Romney."

31. Davidsen, "Santorum Defends Romney's Trip."

32. Stein and Grim, "Harry Reid."

33. Rachel Weiner, "Romney Responds to Reid: 'Put Up or Shut Up,'" *Washington Post*, August 2, 2012, accessed January 7, 2012, www.washingtonpost.com/blogs/the-fix/post/romney-responds-to-reid-put-up-or-shut-up/2012/08/02/gJQAj9MlSX_blog.html.

34. Josh Tyrangiel, "Exclusive Romney Interview: On Humility and Tax Returns," *Businessweek*, August 9, 2012, accessed January 7, 2012, www.businessweek.com/articles/2012-08-09/exclusive-romney-interview-on-humility-and-tax-returns#p3.

35. As cited in Jon Walker, "Americans Overwhelmingly Think Romney Should Release More Tax Returns," Firedoglake.com, August 10, 2012, accessed December 22, 2012, http://elections.firedoglake.com/2012/08/10/americans-overwhelmingly-think-romney-should-release-more-tax-returns/.

36. Robin Abcarian, "Ann Romney Fiercely Defends Decision to Withhold More Tax Returns," *Los Angeles Times*, August 16, 2012, accessed December 22, 2012, http://articles.latimes.com/2012/aug/16/news/la-pn-ann-romney-tax-return-defense-20120816.

37. Sabrina Siddiqui, "Obama Campaign Wants Romney to Release 5 Years of Tax Returns," *Huffington Post*, August 17, 2012, accessed December 22, 2012, www.huffingtonpost.com/2012/08/17/obama-romney-tax-returns_n_1796291.html.

38. Thomas Burr, "Romney Says His Mormon Tithing Shouldn't Be Public," *Salt Lake City Tribune*, August 23, 2012, accessed December 22, 2012, www.sltrib.com/sltrib/politics/54744938-90/romney-says-church-tithing.html.csp.

39. Tyrangiel, "Exclusive Romney Interview."

40. Abcarian, "Ann Romney Fiercely Defends Decision."

41. Abcarian, "Ann Romney Fiercely Defends Decision."

42. Burr, "Romney Says His Mormon Tithing."

43. Megan McArdle, "Romney Drops His Tax Returns," *Daily Beast*, September 21, 2012, accessed December 22, 2012, www.thedailybeast.com/articles/2012/09/21/romney-drops-his-tax-returns.html.

44. Nick Baumann and Adam Serwer, "Nine Things to Know about Mitt Romney's Tax Returns," *Mother Jones*, September 21, 2012, accessed December 22, 2012, www.motherjones.com/mojo/2012/09/mitt-romney-tax-returns.

45. Sean Sullivan, "Mitt Romney Not Being 'Straight' about Personal Taxes or Tax Plan for Americans, Democrats Say," *Washington Post*, September 23, 2012, accessed December 22, 2012, www.washingtonpost.com/blogs/the-fix/wp/2012/09/23/mitt-romney-not-being-straight-about-personal-taxes-or-tax-plan-for-americans-democrats-say/.

46. Sullivan, "Mitt Romney Not Being 'Straight.'"

47. "Final Transcript: President Barack Obama and Former Gov. Mitt Romney Participate in a Candidates Debate, Hofstra University, Hempstead, New York," Hofstra.edu, October 16, 2012, accessed December 22, 2012, www.hofstra.edu/pdf/debate/debate_transcript_2012.pdf.

7

Presidential Campaigns as Cultural Events: The Convergence of Politics and Popular Culture in Election 2012

Jeffrey P. Jones

A term with great currency in media studies these days is *convergence*, which signifies the coming together—economically, technologically, socially, and culturally—of what were once distinct media- or cultural-related phenomena into a new experiential or phenomenological whole. Media corporations that were once distinct in function—for instance, television, film, and print media—have converged into economic conglomerates that maintain great fluidity among their film, television, recording, and print divisions. Similarly, in a digital world the ability for citizens to engage phenomena across platforms—watch a debate on television, post Twitter responses as it happens, create satirical Photoshopped memes, and read live-updated blogs about it while the debate is occurring—demonstrates a convergence of once-distinct or -segregated participatory behaviors. Perhaps more than any other scholar Henry Jenkins has theorized this "convergence culture," including his articulation of how convergence collapses popular culture and politics as distinct realms of action.[1]

In examining the role that popular culture played in the 2012 presidential election, what seems most notable is how indistinct popular culture turned out to be from the myriad campaign and electoral events that are divided and subdivided in this volume. The 2012 election demonstrated just how convergent contemporary politics and popular culture truly are. Certainly any analysis is, by definition, the process of separating elements for inspection and scrutiny, and I won't question the merits of doing so within this book. But what seems distinctive about the 2012 election is how popular culture was an integral part of each and every campaign moment and event. From the primaries, conventions, and debates to campaign and Super PAC advertising, campaigning faux pas, or simply politically relevant media genres or platforms (i.e., news or social media), each found reverberations, amplifications, or articulations within broader cultural behaviors and mediated venues. Thus it may not make much sense to continue thinking of these traditional measures of campaign "activities" as distinct communication events that exist independent of a range of cultural influences and affectations that then ripple out for analysis or comment by media organizations (such as the news). Rather, the presidential campaign in the digital era has become a cultural event, one in which activities such as debates and commercials are simply contributing agents to the extended performance of a lengthy civic ritual that is made meaningful by an array of industrial and personal engagements taking place within daily cultural life. In a 24/7 media–saturated world, there is little separation between action and reaction, whether by candidates, campaigns, media creators, or citizens. In particular, Internet-based communication and citizen exchange through social media has transformed public engagement with the presidential campaign, making the campaign much more of a long-running, daily cultural event rather than a series of sporadic newsworthy events or encounters (local or mediated) with politicians.

This is not to argue that there are no events or moments arising from popular-cultural industries that are specifically designed for entertainment purposes, each with the potential to affect the election (if only in occupying media attention and discursive space). Indeed, such occurrences were quite prevalent in the two previous presidential elections. Michael Moore's 2004 documentary critique of George W. Bush's run-up to the Iraq War in *Fahrenheit 9/11* and *Saturday Night Live*'s parodies of Sarah Palin in 2008 are the most notable examples.[2] In 2012 as well, there were certainly numerous attempts by actors within popular culture to exploit the campaign as content for entertainment, recognition, or profit-driven goals, as well as by political actors who saw the language of popular culture as a vehicle for attempting to affect the campaign. Yet such popular cultural "events" were less successful in attracting the enormous outpouring of press and public attention in 2012 as the two previous campaigns.[3]

What was much more the case was how traditional campaign events, activities, and rituals were so integrated with popular culture. The discussion here assesses the ways in which the campaign was thoroughly infused with, connected to, or amplified by broader cultural engagements in mainstream media, niche media, and social media.

REPUBLICAN-PRIMARY DEBATES AS A REALITY TV SHOW

Over the last decade low-cost reality TV programming has come to dominate prime-time programming across cable and broadcast networks in the United States. One of the most popular of the reality TV subgenres is competition shows, where program participants compete with each other for some valued spot—a singing contract on *American Idol*, a high-level management job on *The Apprentice*, a million dollars on *Survivor*, a hand in marriage on *The Bachelor*. Viewers are invited, through expert casting and editing, to become subjectively involved with the "characters," picking which ones to like and which to loathe and who—in some instances—to vote for via

Internet or telephone voting. Thus the prevalence of such shows on television means that Americans are quite familiar with and fond of the genre and its conventions.

Given this dominant cultural practice, it is not, then, a stretch to see how the Republican-primary process could be seen as just such a reality TV show that aired within the 2011–2012 television season. This observation is not original, having been offered by several reporters, including the *New York Times*'s media reporter Brian Stelter.[4] Several factors contribute to the analogy. First was the fact that the Republicans held a total of twenty debates—one every nine days, on average, from early September 2011 to the end of January 2012 (see table 7.1).[5] If the debates felt like a television series, that is because they appeared with similar frequency and seasonal length as many contemporary television productions.

Second, the competition between candidates created a familiar feel to that of many reality-show competitions. Since the presumptive party nominee, Mitt Romney, was not the favored candidate of many conservative and right-wing voters (the same voters who tend to dominate the primary process), these voters displayed serious interest—as measured by opinion polls—in at least five of the non-Romney challengers, searching for what we might call the "anti-Romney candidate." Given the particular eccentricities or political liabilities of many of the contenders, none proved capable of sufficiently emerging as a viable option to a Romney nomination. Through the debates, what transpired was a scenario in which each candidate—Michele Bachmann, Rick Perry, Herman Cain, Newt Gingrich, and Rick Santorum—became a popular anti-Romney favorite at some juncture. Thus it was as if each week someone else was being "voted off the island" (to paraphrase a line from *Survivor*).

Third, many of the candidates simply were not viable as national contenders to unseat a sitting president due to their far-right ideological leanings or their tendency to say ridiculous things. Herman Cain, for instance, established his foreign-policy credentials by noting in one interview, "When they ask me who's the president of Ubeki-beki-beki-beki-stan-stan, I'm going to say, you know, I don't know. Do you know? And then I'm going to say, How's that going to create one job?"[6] Santorum made one of many headlines for his rhetorical flourishes when he noted in a speech before a college audience, "Earlier in my political career, I had the opportunity to read [President John Kennedy's speech on the importance of the separation of church and state], and I almost threw up."[7] The debates, then, became an opportunity—as with many reality TV shows—to marvel in the spectacular things the contestants/candidates might say. In short, these candidates proved highly entertaining. During the November 12, 2011, debate, for instance, Bachmann offered this about Communist China: "If you look at China, they don't have food stamps. They don't have the modern welfare state, and China's growing. . . . And so what I would do is look at the programs that LBJ gave us with the Great Society, and they'd be gone."[8] And during the October 11, 2011, debate, she argued, "When you take [Cain's] 9-9-9 plan and turn it upside down, the devil is in the details."[9]

As with reality shows like *The Real Housewives of New Jersey* (one among an array of shows featuring personal confrontations for dramatic appeal), we saw in the

Table 7.1. Republican Party Debates and Television Viewership, 2011–2012

Debate Date	Television Sponsor/ Election Primary	Perceived Frontrunner[1]	Poll Leader(s)[1]	Viewership[2]	Avg. Network Primetime Viewership[2]	Increase (decrease) Viewership
5/5/11	Fox News	Mitt Romney	Romney–16.5%	3,258,000	1,856,000	75%
6/13/11	CNN	Mitt Romney	Romney–21.6%	3,162,000	655,000	382%
8/11/11	Fox News	Rick Perry	Romney–20.4%, Perry–15.4%	5,050,000	1,856,000	172%
9/7/11	NBC/MSNBC	Rick Perry	Perry–29%	5,411,000	773,000	600%
9/12/11	CNN	Rick Perry	Perry–31.8%	3,613,000	655,000	451%
9/22/11	Fox News/Google	Rick Perry	Perry–28.4%	6,107,000	1,856,000	229%
10/11/11	Bloomberg	Herman Cain	Romney–21.7, Cain–16.3%	1,300,000 (est.)	N/A	N/A
10/18/11	CNN	Herman Cain	Romney–23.9%, Cain–23.4%	5,468,000	655,000	734%
11/9/11	CNBC	Herman Cain	Cain–25.2%, Romney–23.3%	3,332,000	N/A	N/A
11/12/11	CBS	Herman Cain	Romney–22.5%, Cain–22%	5,480,000	11,748,000	54% (decrease)
11/22/11	CNN	Newt Gingrich	Gingrich–23.2%, Romney–21%	3,599,000	655,000	449%
12/10/11	ABC News/Yahoo! News	Newt Gingrich	Gingrich–33.3%	7,631,000	8,360,000	9% (decrease)
12/15/11	Fox News/Iowa	Newt Gingrich	Gingrich–33.2%	6,713,000	1,856,000	261%
1/7/12	ABC News/New Hampshire	Mitt Romney	Romney–27.2%	6,271,000	8,360,000	25% (decrease)
1/8/12	MSNBC/Meet the Press	Mitt Romney	Romney–29.3%	4,151,000	1,856,000	123%
1/16/12	Fox News/South Carolina	Mitt Romney	Romney–31.2%	5,475,000	655,000	735%
1/19/12	CNN/South Carolina	Mitt Romney	Romney–31.6%	5,022,000	773,000	549%
1/23/12	NBC/Florida	Mitt Romney/ Newt Gingrich	Romney–29.5%, Gingrich–23%	7,125,000	7,384,000	4% (decrease)
1/26/12	CNN	Newt Gingrich	Gingrich–31%	5,400,000	655,000	724%
2/22/12	CNN/Arizona	Rick Santorum	Santorum–33.7%	4,700,000	655,000	617%

Sources: 1—RealClearPolitics; 2—Nielsen Ratings Company.

debates endless bickering and ad hominem attacks between contestants. During the December 10, 2011, debate Mitt Romney famously challenged Rick Perry to a $10,000 bet in a dispute over similarities between Romney's version of health care while serving as governor of Massachusetts and the national version that was passed by Obama (and loathed by conservative voters). In the February 22, 2012, debate the following exchange occurred between CNN moderator John King and candidates Paul and Santorum.

> JOHN KING: Congressman Paul, you've questioned the conservative—fiscal-conservative credentials of all these gentlemen but particularly this week, Senator Santorum. You have a new television ad that labels him a fake. Why?
>
> RON PAUL: Because he's a fake.
>
> RICK SANTORUM: I'm real, John. I'm real.[10]

Not to be outdone, the audience itself became part of the action when in two debates—September 7 and September 22—audience members clapped at the mention of the execution of 234 death row inmates and shouted approval at Ron Paul's willingness to let young people die because they don't have health insurance, respectively.

What is more, many of the candidates seemed straight out of central casting in their looks and comportment—Bachmann, the attractive, wild-eyed, and nasal-toned Minnesotan; Perry, the low-IQ, good-looking Texas cowboy with a drawl; Cain, the South Carolinian "playa" businessman with no political experience; Paul, who seems like the stranger who wandered into a backyard Texas barbecue; Gingrich, the vicious and low-blow-throwing fat guy from Georgia; Santorum, the pious, gay-bashing Christian from Pennsylvania; and Romney, the straight-laced Mormon from Utah who would repeatedly say just about anything to be liked. All in all, they were a colorful and eclectic mix of characters who worked well according the entertainment values of television. In sum, these factors aligned to produce a slate of competitors who were willing to put on a show, and the cable and broadcast news networks jumped at the opportunity to exploit it.

As we can see in table 7.1 (above), the debates proved to be a ratings hit for the networks. Four years earlier the Republican primary debates had drawn about three million viewers. But on numerous occasions in the 2012 election cycle the debates drew between five and seven million viewers. For cable networks such as CNN and CNBC, these were enormous ratings gains, drawing between five and ten times the average viewership in primetime, with millions more watching through online streaming. The networks all invested heavily in production, renting larger arenas, crafting new theme music, and employing new technology and expanded commentary staff. These specially programmed debates served as tentpoles for the networks, showcasing their talent, lending prestige to their brand, attracting viewership for candidate interviews, and increasing click-throughs online.[11] In short, the debates became an easily packagable "program" or series that could contribute to the cable networks' brand images as politics channels.

As I have argued elsewhere, brand has supplanted traditional journalistic practices as the central and driving force in constituting cable news. The theme around which news brands are built today is primarily politics. The advent of 24-hour cable news channels meant that, despite the notoriously expensive costs associated with the production of news, the networks would need to find inexpensive means of filling airtime, such as a heavy reliance on talk and commentary. They would also need to produce programming with more variety, stylistic flair, and audience appeal beyond a reliance on the traditional means of packaging events and public affairs information if they hoped to attract and sustain viewers. A reliance on "breaking news" and "rolling news" does little to distinguish the channels, since all three can cover events in a like manner. What cable channels need is an identity, a hook on which to build performances that offer some means of distinction. That identity is largely achieved through politics.[12]

In sum, between the needs of the candidates and the needs of the cable news networks, what resulted was a series of programs that heavily resembled that found on other television channels in the form of reality TV—this one just happened to employ people seeking to be president of the United States. The campaign became a cultural event as audiences were invited to employ the interpretive schema developed through viewing reality TV, recognizing the style, flow, and expectations the genre routinely presents, and reveling in the entertainment value of the characters found there. And as the numbers attest, the audience seemed to find the programming to their liking, at least more so than in previous elections.

THE COLBERT REPORT'S SUPER PAC SEGMENTS

The Colbert Report, Comedy Central's parody of cable pundit shows, starring Stephen Colbert, is known for various forays into real-world electoral politics beyond simply mocking bloviated talk-show hosts on the television screen.[13] Following the 2010 Supreme Court's *Citizens United* ruling that allowed for unlimited financial contributions from unions and corporations in elections (as long as the funds did not go directly to candidates or coordinated with their campaigns), Colbert decided that he wanted to create his own Super PAC, a special form of political-action committee that the ruling essentially allowed for. As Colbert noted, these new organizations "have created an unprecedented, unaccountable, untraceable cash tsunami that will infect every corner of the next election. . . . And I feel like an idiot for not having one."[14] To do so, Colbert hired former FEC commissioner and Washington lawyer Trevor Potter to guide him through the process and routinely invited Potter on the show to explain to him and his audience how they would go about doing so. Although the means for going about setting up a Super PAC was new and seemingly complicated, Potter would, in each four- to five-minute segment, explain how simple the process actually was. With Potter's help, Colbert set up his own Super PAC called Americans for a Better Tomorrow, Tomorrow, and began receiving donations from viewers.

In the September 29, 2011, episode, for instance, Colbert pointed to the names of people (scrolling at the bottom of the screen) who had contributed to his Super PAC but expressed his frustration that corporations hadn't started giving him big sums of money. Potter explained that these corporations would be nervous about having to publically disclose their contributions but that there was a way around that. As Potter noted, by creating an IRS designated group called a 501(c)4, contributions would no longer have to be disclosed. Potter then proceeded to hand Colbert the paperwork necessary to set up a Delaware shell corporation and noted that the papers didn't have to be filed with the IRS until May 2013. A surprised Colbert then exclaimed, "So I can get money for my (c)4, use that for political purposes, and nobody knows anything about it 'til six months after the election?" Potter replied, "That's right, and even then they won't know who your donors are," to which Colbert slyly and smugly responds, "That's my kind of campaign-finance restriction."[15]

As the segment proceeded, Colbert learned what he can do with the money, including purchasing political ads to attack or promote candidates as he wished. But Colbert inquired further:

STEPHEN COLBERT: So can I take this (c)4 money and donate it to my Super PAC?

TREVOR POTTER: You can.

COLBERT: Wait. Super PACs are transparent, and the (c)4 is secret. So I can take secret donations from my (c)4 and give it to my supposedly transparent Super PAC.

POTTER: And it will say *given by your (c)4*.

COLBERT: What is the difference between that and money laundering?

POTTER: It's hard to say.[16]

Colbert's Super PAC eventually ran several advertisements in various media markets nationally, most quite humorous but with questionable direction and end-goal purpose beyond having something to show eventually on his program.[17] What made these segments significant, though—they eventually won a Peabody Award recognizing their civic importance—is how they explained what was occurring in contemporary politics as a result of *Citizens United* and its interpretation by the Federal Election Commission. This includes explanations of what Republican functionary Karl Rove was doing with his own American Crossroads Super PAC and his Crossroads GPS 501(c)4, which, after the formation of the (c)4, raised $5.1 million in one month. As Amber Day notes, the segments also had the effect of increased reporting on Super PACS, as numerous journalists took note and reported what Colbert was doing, as well as further explained to readers what Super PACS were and how they worked.[18] Thus the significance of the segments was their role as public pedagogy, teaching the viewing public how this "brave new world" (as Colbert called it) of campaign-finance law worked and calling attention to the nefarious nature and questionable ethics of it all.

Indeed, after the campaign was over, Colbert hosted Potter an additional time to figure out what to do with the leftover $800,000 in the Super PAC.

STEPHEN COLBERT: So let me see if I can make clear what's happening. I've got a 501(c)4 called Colbert Super PAC SHH. I take the money from the Super PAC. I pass it through [as Colbert passes a check through an open-ended manila envelope] the 501(c)4 into a second unnamed 501(c)4 [as Colbert now places the check in a lock box]. I place all the money inside that second 501(c)4, and through the magic of your lawyering and the present federal tax code, after I close this and lock it, that money is gone forever [as Colbert reveals a now-opened magic box with a disappeared check], and nobody knows what happens to it?

TREVOR POTTER: You'll know, but nobody else will.

. . . .

COLBERT: So what do I have to tell the IRS about what happened with this money?

POTTER: Nothing.

COLBERT: Well, Trevor, thanks for nothing.[19]

2016: OBAMA'S AMERICA,
THE REPUBLICANS' *FAHRENHEIT 9/11*

There is little doubt that Michael Moore's documentary *Fahrenheit 9/11* was an enormously important political statement in the 2004 presidential election. Not only did the movie go on to become the top-grossing documentary of all time ($119 million at the box office alone), but as I have detailed elsewhere, the themes articulated in that movie were subsequently used by Democratic presidential nominee John Kerry in his attacks on candidate George W. Bush after the movie's release.[20] The movie also became a place for liberals to see and hear arguments about Bush and the run-up to the Iraq War that simply were difficult to find in broader public discourse at the time, especially television news.

During the 2012 election campaign conservative writer Dinesh D'Souza, author of *The Roots of Obama's Rage*[21] and *Obama's America: Unmaking the American Dream*,[22] joined with producer Gerald R. Molen (Academy Award winner for *Schindler's List*) and codirector John Sullivan in an attempt to craft a similarly damning documentary, this time aimed at Democratic incumbent Barack Obama. D'Souza hoped his film might have similar impact on public attention and political discussion, if not also sway the election outright or draw similarly significant profits. The film was released on July 13, 2012, at only one theatre in Houston. The film was picked up by distributor Lionsgate Films and subsequently exhibited on 1,091 screens by August 26, bringing in $9 million, then jumping to 1,747 screens one week later (raising the sum to $20 million). At its peak, the film appeared on 2,017 screens during the week of September 9 and eventually grossed $33.4 million at theaters nationwide.[23] To broaden the film's potential impact, the producers released the film on DVD a mere ninety-one days after the film's release, making it available for purchase and online rentals. The producers also set low-cost exhibition rates to encourage conservative groups and churches to offer special screenings prior to the election.[24] The movie became the fourth-highest-grossing documentary of all time and the second-highest-grossing political documentary after *Fahrenheit 9/11*.

Yet despite such popularity with moviegoers the film differed from *Fahrenheit* in several important regards. In particular, the tremendous range of the film's wild-eyed conspiracy theories would prove too much for broad-based acceptance beyond far-right true believers, as the film conjured an Obama who was a dangerous socialist, anti-American, anti-Christian, anti-capitalist, Third-World other. In so doing, the film offered the well-trod narrative (employing the same arguments and same facts) that had been a staple of right-wing radio, blogs, and television for years, including Fox News, and Rush Limbaugh's and Glenn Beck's popular radio programs. It is a narrative embraced by the right wing of the Republican Party, but it is not an argument that a Republican candidate such as Mitt Romney could successfully employ as he pushed toward the ideological middle of a general-election campaign. While the film purportedly sought to establish what America would look like were Obama reelected, it instead covered old ground by tracing Obama's juvenile history through Third World colonial nations (Kenya and Indonesia) and making guilt-by-association connections with supposed American radicals, whom D'Souza calls "Obama's Founding Fathers"—Frank Marshall Davis, Bill Ayers, Edward Said, Roberto Unger, and Reverend Jeremiah Wright.[25] In short, there is not much here for the mainstream press to pick up and discuss, while those attracted to such a narrative had ample opportunity to engage with it over the previous four years.

The film's novel contribution was its narrative approach—taking Obama's reading of his book on tape *Dreams from My Father* and using Obama's voice to assist in the voice-of-God narration of D'Souza in his effort to psychologize Obama's relationship with his father. Through reenacted scenes, for instance, D'Souza made the direct connection between Obama the politician to Obama Sr. the anticolonialist "radical." "This is where Obama reconciles with his father," D'Souza argues about Obama's 1987 trip to his father's grave in Kenya. "He resolves not to be like his father but take his dream. Where the father failed, he will succeed. In doing so, perhaps he can become worthy of his father's love—the love he never got."[26] In another major departure from *Fahrenheit*'s approach, the film focused less on the president's actions in office—including policies such as rescuing Wall Street bankers, refusing to close Gitmo, or maintaining Bush-era tax cuts for the wealthy—but offered instead a highly stylized and creatively crafted message dependent on this largely uncontestable psychologizing of Obama as a young man.

Thus, while the film proved popular with conservatives drawn to this now-familiar fear-inducing narrative, it did not play as significant a role in shaping public discourse as had *Fahrenheit 9/11* in 2004.[27] Given its framing as a potentially damaging political narrative that might affect the outcome of the election—yet muted by its familiarity and incredulous conspiratorial approach—what we are left with is the realization that, as the fourth-largest-grossing documentary of all time, the film became another enormously successful media commodity in the what former Bush speechwriter David Frum dubbed the "conservative entertainment complex."[28] Frum's argument mirrors that of liberal journalist Alex Pareene, who has detailed how popular right-wing voices have transformed the conservative movement into "an elaborate moneymaking venture," and my own argument that cable "news" outlets such as Fox News (and MSNBC) should be seen as forms of "political-entertainment television."[29] In sum, the film may have had little effect in shaping public discourse surrounding the campaign, but it proved once again that conservatives (like liberals) will spend plenty of money on media products with distinct and strong ideological perspectives, however familiar yet fantastical.

2016 was a cultural event—not in the ways *Fahrenheit 9/11* turned out to be but cultural in the sense that this was a narrative that had become "True" in the minds of many conservative voters simply because of its repetition over time across right-wing media (adding film to the repertoire here). Thus its significance was demonstrated after the election when it became clear that many conservatives—from Fox News commentators to Mitt Romney himself—actually believed Romney was going to win the election right up until the moment he didn't. What more-clear-eyed conservative commentators pointed out was how Republicans had created an insulated media bubble where it was possible for ideas and beliefs to have no relationship to reality, specifically because the narratives told in these conservative media outlets are produced more for entertainment value than accurate critical assessments and information. D'Souza may have used these conservative narratives to produce one of the most popular documentaries of all time, but its political value or critical acumen proved less significant than its cultural ones.

SOCIAL MEDIA AS CIVIC-PERFORMANCE SPACE

Increasingly in the digital age a prime location for cultural expression is through social media. Indeed, it is the many manifestations of public expression and engagement that occur within these digital social spaces that we see how traditional electoral events such as presidential debates or even the party-nominating conventions become much broader cultural events. Seen through the lens of media specificity, events are first broadcast on television but are then taken up and given additional meaning, often within minutes of their real-life occurrence, through a rash of citizen commentary and a variety of performances in social media venues such as Twitter, Facebook, and Tumblr. But as the term itself suggests, political events become social or cultural events, with the event's ultimate meaning and electoral importance shaped by these cultural engagements. Whether such engagements had particular "effects" on the campaigns or the election's eventual outcome is impossible to gauge. Rather, the interest is in the rituals of engagement themselves and the opportunities available through such events for an expanded notion of what comprises meaningful citizenship. By citizens taking up these events as discursive objects, the events become more than just something to be consumed on television.

On Election Day 2012, for instance, there were 71.7 million Facebook posts related to the election, while Twitter experienced 31.7 million tweets. Election tweeting peaked at 327,453 tweets per minute at 11:19 P.M. EST when most of the news networks called the election for Obama, making it the most-tweeted event in U.S. political history.[30] Also on Election Day, Obama was mentioned ten million times on Facebook, including 4.1 million times between 11:00 P.M. and 12:00 A.M. Overall, the election was the most talked about event on Facebook in 2012.[31]

Perhaps more insightful is the way in which these social media venues served as performative venues for citizens during specific campaign events. During the October 3 presidential debate, Twitter received 10.3 million tweets related to the debate in general. When Romney declared that he would defund PBS and put Big Bird out of work, the comment received 825,168 mentions. Obama's reminder to Romney that the U.S. military had evolved beyond "horses and bayonets" received 426,675 mentions during the October 23 debate.[32]

When responding to a question about pay equity for women during the October 16 debate, Romney stuck his foot in his mouth when telling a story about his time as governor of Massachusetts. As he recounted noticing that there had been no women applicants for positions in his cabinet, he says he went to various women's groups and asked, "'Can you help us find folks?,' and they brought us whole binders full of women.'" The awkward choice of words proved quite humorous to many people, as the terms quickly became fodder for Twitter and Facebook posts. The Twitter hashtag #bindersfullofwomen was immediately born. The comment also led to the creation of a Binders Full of Women Facebook page, resulting in 220,000 "likes" overnight.[33] Citizens also displayed a particular craftiness in ridiculing Romney for his "binders" comment by descending upon Amazon.com and using the Customer Reviews section for an Avery Durable View Binder to write humorous critiques posed as user "reviews," such as this one:

5,302 of 5,486 people found the following review helpful

[5.0 out of 5 stars], A presidential candidate's choice is the choice for me, October 17, 2012

By Bazinga

As a woman, I'm not adept at making decisions that concern me. So when I need the right choice, I turn to the presidential candidate that KNOWS. One with prideful experience in this department. I don't want to be filed away in an inferior & confusing electronic doohickey that I couldn't possibly understand. Or heaven forbid, have a man ask for & listen to my ideas! I'd much rather rely on this top of the line, 1980s style, Avery Durable binder. It's the choice America can trust. My education, my ideas, my opinions, my choices, please PLEASE keep them safely stored away here and far away from the men that might fear them (I mean, want to use them to hire me somedaynever). I'd write more about this most useful product, but it's time I hurry home to make dinner.[34]

Citizens also employed the software program Photoshop to craft ridiculing and mocking mash-up pictures (often quite humorous) that are easily spread through social media, known as "memes." For instance, one popular meme was a picture of Big Bird on the set of *Sesame Street* holding a white binder that simply says "Women" on it, written in cursive, with a heart behind it. Obama's "horses and bayonets" comment became another popular meme, for instance, one which showed a painting of a confederate general riding a white horse leading his troops, and included the block-faced message, "PRESIDENT ROMNEY, YOUR ARMY IS READY."

In what media-studies scholars call our "participatory culture," citizens increasingly watch television while also using their computers, laptops, tablets, and smartphones to engage with other viewers.[35] Given this ability to contribute commentary (both humorous and serious) and critiques to a community of people, citizens are demonstrating their desire to engage with the campaign and electoral events. Thus, whereas Al Gore's repeated use of the word *lockbox* in a 2000 election debate resulted in satirical ridiculing on a television program such as *Saturday Night Live*, citizens themselves now join in the fun by satirizing and mocking such missteps immediately via social media. As such, they transform the event from something one watches on television into a broader event in which citizens have avenues available for centering the conversation on their own interests and supplying their own voices in making the event meaningful. There are no accurate measures for how much of this commentary is humorous and how much is serious (or both). But any casual observer or participant in such forums quickly realizes that comments, postings, or memes that have a humorous or satirical quality to them get spread much more often than those limited to polemics or ideological cheap shots. In short, we're all satirists now, even if by sharing those formulations constructed by others.

In many ways, the key ingredient of digital-media production is a speech act's "spreadability" (as opposed to "virality," a term suggesting contagion more than willful dissemination).[36] Spreadable media invites sharing, which invites more viewing. Media are now made for exhibition solely on video-sharing sites such as YouTube and Vimeo. A music video such as "Mitt Romney Style," a political parody version of Korean musical artist Psy's "Gangnam Style" video, garnered 34.6 million views on YouTube alone. Carly Rae Jepsen's "Call Me Maybe" music video was appropriated for an Obama parody called "Barack Obama Singing Call Me Maybe" that also had over thirty-four million views. *Epic Rap Battles of History (Season 2)*—a rap video series similar to *Celebrity Death Match*—pitted Barack Obama against Mitt Romney, resulting in over fifty million views. And these are just a few of the most-viewed parody videos that employed Obama, Romney, or both as vehicles for election parodies. Skimming through YouTube's related video catalog, an entire genre of election parodies exists. In short, election year is the time for satirical and parodic videos of the two major-party candidates, and given the nature of spreadable media, many of these videos garner more views than do the conventions or debates on television.

EVALUATING THE CULTURAL EVENT:
LOCATING THE REAL, THE FAKE, AND THE SURREAL

The 2012 presidential campaign demonstrated both how presidential elections have become cultural events as much as political ones and that the political and cultural are really inseparable. Documentary films, entertainment television, and social-media exchanges are all performative spaces for playing out the campaign, with engagements by media professionals, public intellectuals, and average citizens alike all contributing to the "meaning" of the election. What is more, campaign or electoral events are not distinct and isolated political events that are first described, debated, and made sense of by news media and pundits, then consumed by citizen-audiences. Instead, debates, advertisements, and party conventions become events through which citizens are actively involved in establishing what these events mean—whether through watching the Republican-primary debates as a reality-television program, attending to the intertextual narratives of right-wing media that have constructed Obama as dangerous other, learning about campaign finance through a lawyer's tutelage about how to create a Super PAC on an entertainment show, helping narrate campaign events in real time through Twitter and Facebook posts, or sharing and spreading campaign-related parody videos. Perhaps in the convergent, hypermediated digital era the engaged citizenry of the mid- to late-nineteenth-century partisan era of American politics (as described by Michael Schudson[37]) is being reinvented, offering new forms of popular involvement with campaign and electoral events that are less divorced from the rhythms of everyday life than has been the case for much of the last century.

What the 2012 presidential election also highlights is the challenge this era presents in maintaining a firm grasp on what is real and what is fake within these popular media genres and engagements. A fake pundit talk show hires a real lawyer to help create a real Super PAC that runs real yet fake advertisements but offers real education in the process. A documentary (by definition, a genre dedicated to reality) based on real books offers fake claims about a real president, offering fake education in the process. A series of real-party primary debates is hosted on real news channels yet resembles the surreal and concocted popular genre of television programming that goes by the moniker of reality television. And social media became the exchange medium for an array of citizen- and professionally produced parody (by definition, faked reality) videos and memes that offer fantastical yet real interpretations of events and candidates.

Perhaps the most surreal of all in this confused state of fake-real mediation was a fake narrative about a real speech given by President Obama that was largely created by Fox News (by definition, news being a genre dedicated to reality) that was then adopted by the Republican Party as one of their convention themes. On July 13, 2012, President Obama gave a speech making a case for the role of government in people's lives. Individual success in life, he argued, is dependent on more than just individual drive and determination but also needs things like education and infrastructure (from roads to the Internet), things that government—as agent of the people's will, needs, and desires—can and does supply. On July 16 Fox News presented a redacted version of Obama's speech in which the producers cut out certain key parts, crafting a sound bite that made it seem as if Obama had argued that individual business owners were not responsible for their own success because, as the video's new formulation put it, "You didn't build that."

As the media watchdog group Media Matters has detailed, "In the two days that followed Fox's initial misrepresentation of Obama's remarks, the network devoted forty-two segments and more than two hours of airtime to misrepresenting Obama's 'you didn't build that' remarks."[38] Media Matters also reports that at least four journalism outlets—the *Washington Post*, the Associate Press, FactCheck.org, and Politi-Fact.com—had debunked the fabricated narrative. Within days, though, Romney had incorporated the narrative into his campaign speeches as a critique of Obama, and within a month the Republican Party had decided to use a reformulated version of it as one of its nominating convention themes, We Built This. In short, a real speech became a fake speech through video editing, and its repeated invocation on a real news channel created a fake narrative that would go on to become a real rhetorical device and convention theme. And for good measure that convention's most memorable moment featured a real Hollywood director and actor, Clint Eastwood, conducting a fake dialogue with an empty chair on which an imaginary (fake) Barack Obama was supposedly sitting. In sum, precisely the locations for where we might expect or assume that reality is firmly established and adhered to—a news channel and a political convention—themselves became arenas for inauthenticity.

In conclusion, this election witnessed a popularization of the presidential campaign as a cultural event, but one in which traditional media markers for establishing verisimilitude have become much more contested, fluid, and altogether unstable. Thus, while campaigns will inevitably continue to be more fully integrated into citizens' daily lives through an array of media platforms and programming genres, those engagements cannot necessarily depend on established media conventions to connote truthfulness. Campaigns, already highly stylized events with dubious relationship to anything beyond their constructed nature, become all the more comprised of spaces where citizens will have to fend for themselves in determining who or what to believe in or trust.

NOTES

I extend my appreciation for the valuable research assistance of my graduate assistant, Tyler DeAtley.

1. Henry Jenkins, *Convergence Culture* (New York: NYU Press, 2007); see also Jeffrey P. Jones, "A Cultural Approach to the Study of Mediated Citizenship," *Social Semiotics* 16, no. 2 (2006): 365–83; Jeffrey P. Jones, *Entertaining Politics: Satirical Television and Political En-*

gagement (Lanham, Md.: Rowman & Littlefield, 2010); and Bruce A. Williams and Michael X. Delli Carpini, *After Broadcast News: Media Regimes, Democracy, and the New Information Environment* (New York: Cambridge University Press, 2011).

2. See Jeffrey P. Jones in both "The Shadow Campaign in Popular Culture," 195–216, in the *2004 Presidential Campaign: A Communication Perspective*, ed. Robert Denton, Jr. (Lanham, Md.: Rowman & Littlefield Publishers, 2005), and "Pop Goes the Campaign: The Repopularization of Politics in Election 2008," 170–90, in *The 2008 Presidential Campaign: A Communication Perspective*, ed. Robert E. Denton, Jr. (Lanham, Md.: Rowman & Littlefield Publishers, 2009).

3. The reasons explaining why are difficult to identify, but that is not a problem for just scholarship. Finding what works with audiences and voters is, of course, a guessing game on which the entertainment industry and political professionals alike spend much time and money.

4. Brian Stelter, "Republican Debates Are a Hot Ticket on TV," *New York Times*, October 16, 2011, www.nytimes.com/2011/10/17/business/media/republican-debates-are-a-hot -ticket-on-tv.html.

5. Brian Stelter, "Hiatus Over, GOP Series Looks Ready to Wrap Up," *New York Times*, February 22, 2012, www.nytimes.com/2012/02/23/us/politics/republican-debate-in-arizona -billed-as-the-season-finale.html.

6. Ali Gharib, "Herman Cain: I Don't Know the 'President of Ubeki-beki-beki-stan-stan,'" ThinkProgress.org, October 9, 2011, http://thinkprogress.org/security/2011/10/09/339879/ cain-uzbekistan-beki-beki-stan-stan/.

7. Felicia Sonmez, "Santorum Says He 'Almost Threw Up' after Reading JFK Speech on Separation of Church and State," *Washington Post*, February 26, 2012, www.washingtonpost .com/blogs/post-politics/post/santorum-says-he-almost-threw-up-after-reading-jfk-speech-on -separation-of-church-and-state/2012/02/26/gIQA91hubR_blog.html.

8. "Michele Bachmann: Look to China on Social Program Cuts," video, *HuffPost Politics*, accessed May 31, 2013, www.huffingtonpost.com/2011/11/12/michele-bachmann-us-china -socialist_n_1090688.html.

9. "Bachmann: 'The Devil Is in the Details' of Cain's 9-9-9 Plan," video, RealClearPolitics, accessed May 31, 2013, www.realclearpolitics.com/video/2011/10/11/bachmann_the_ devil_is_in_the_details_of_cains_9-9-9_plan.html.

10. Stephanie Condon, "Santorum Fights Charges He's a 'Fake' Conservative," CBS News, February 22, 2012, accessed May 31, 2013, www.cbsnews.com/8301-503544_162- 57383263-503544/santorum-fights-charges-hes-a-fake-conservative/.

11. Stelter, "Republican Debates Are a Hot Ticket."

12. Jeffrey P. Jones, "The 'New' News as No 'News': U.S. Cable News Channels as Branded Political Entertainment Television," *Media International Australia*, no. 144 (August 2012): 146–55.

13. Jeffrey P. Jones, Geoffrey Baym, and Amber Day, "Mr. Stewart and Mr. Colbert Go to Washington: Television Satirists Outside the Box," *Social Research* 79, no. 1 (2012): 33–60; Jones, *Entertaining Politics*, 224–32.

14. "Colbert Super PAC—Ham Rove's Secrets," video, Colbert Nation, accessed May 31, 2013, www.colbertnation.com/the-colbert-report-videos/398530/september-29-2011/ colbert-super-pac---ham-rove-s-comeback.

15. "Colbert Super PAC—Trevor Potter & Stephen's Shell Corporation," video, Colbert Nation, accessed May 31, 2013, www.colbertnation.com/the-colbert-report-videos/398531/ september-29-2011/colbert-super-pac---trevor-potter---stephen-s-shell-corporation.

16. "Colbert Super PAC—Trevor Potter & Stephen's Shell Corporation."

17. For a detailed examination of Colbert's Super PAC, its activities, and these segments, see Amber Day, "Shifting the Conversation: Colbert's Super PAC and the Measurement of Satirical Efficacy," *International Journal of Communication* 7 (2013): 414–429.

18. Jones et al., "Mr. Stewart and Mr. Colbert."

19. "Colbert Super PAC SHH!—Secret Second 501c4—Trevor Potter," video, Colbert Nation, accessed May 31, 2013, www.colbertnation.com/the-colbert-report-videos/421160/november-12-2012/colbert-super-pac-shh----secret-second-501c4---trevor-potter.

20. Jones, "The Shadow Campaign."

21. Dinesh D'Souza, *The Roots of Obama's Rage* (Washington, D.C.: Regnery Publishing, 2010).

22. Dinesh D'Souza, *Obama's America: Unmaking the American Dream* (Washington, D.C.: Regnery Publishing, 2012).

23. Nikki Finke, "Anti-Obama Pic #2 Political Documentary: Now Bigger Than 3 Michael Moore Movies," Deadline.com, www.deadline.com/2012/09/anti-obama-pic-2-political-documentary-now-bigger-than-3-michael-moore-movies/.

24. Ben Fritz, "'2016: Obama's America' Coming to DVD, Group Screenings This Week," *Los Angeles Times*, October 15, 2012, http://articles.latimes.com/2012/oct/15/entertainment/la-et-ct-obama-america-dvd20121015.

25. For a helpful review of the film, see Richard Brody, "Dinesh D'Souza's '2016: Obama's America,'" *New Yorker*, September 4, 2012, www.newyorker.com/online/blogs/movies/2012/09/dinesh-dsouzas-2016-obamas-america.html. As Brody articulates, perhaps the most insidious aspect of the film is its use of race as a means for subtle and not so subtle attacks on Obama.

26. *2016: Obama's America*, DVD directed by Dinesh D'Souza and John Sullivan (2012; Salt Lake City: Rocky Mountain Pictures).

27. Readers who prefer such conspiracy theories will no doubt attribute this to another right-wing conspiracy theory, the biases of a supposed "liberal media."

28. Alex Alvarez, "David Frum: Republicans Have Been Lied to and Exploited by a Conservative Entertainment Complex," Mediaite.com, November 9, 2012, www.mediaite.com/tv/david-frum-republicans-have-been-lied-to-and-exploited-by-a-conservative-entertainment-complex/.

29. Alex Pareene, "The Conservative Movement Is an Elaborate Moneymaking Venture," Salon.com, June 16, 2011, www.salon.com/2011/06/16/pay_play_rush/; Alex Pareene, "The Conservative Movement Is Still an Elaborate Moneymaking Venture," Salon.com, January 7, 2013, www.salon.com/2013/01/07/the_conservative_movement_is_still_an_elaborate_moneymaking_venture/; Jones, "The 'New' News as No 'News.'"

30. "Election Night 2012," Twitter, November 6, 2012, http://blog.twitter.com/2012/11/election-night-2012.html; Heather Kelly, "People Love Talking about the Election on Facebook," CNN, November, 8, 2012, www.cnn.com/2012/11/07/tech/social-media/election-day-chatter-facebook/index.html.

31. Kelly, "People Love Talking."

32. "Tracking the #Debates: Hempstead," Twitter, October 16, 2012, Twitter.com/gov/status/258422696071798784/photo/1/large.

33. Jenna Sakwa and Chenda Ngak, "'Binders Full of Women': The 'Big Bird' of the Second Presidential Debate," CBS News, October 17, 2012.

34. Bazinga, review of "Avery Durable View Binder with 12-Inch Slant Ring, Holds 8.5 × 11–Inch Paper, White, 1 Binder (17032)," Amazon, October 17, 2012, www.amazon.com/gp/cdp/member-reviews/A2XQBGLGN9C036/ref=cm_pdp_rev_more?ie=UTF8&sort_by=MostRecentReview#R300JT745JOIWZ.

35. Aaron Delwiche and Jennifer Jacobs Henderson, *The Participatory Cultures Handbook* (London: Routledge, 2013).

36. Henry Jenkins, Sam Ford, and Joshua Green, *Spreadable Media: Creating Value and Meaning in a Networked Culture* (New York: NYU Press, 2013).

37. Michael Schudson, *The Good Citizen: A History of American Civic Life* (New York: Free Press, 1998).

38. Melody Johnson, "'You Didn't Build That': How Fox News Crafted the GOP's Convention Theme," Media Matters for America, August 12, 2012, http://mediamatters.org/research/2012/08/21/you-didnt-build-that-how-fox-news-crafted-the-g/189468.

8

The New-Media Campaign of 2012

John Allen Hendricks

Mass communication technologies have played an important role in American politics since the beginning of the nation's history. Darrell M. West posited, "From the earliest days of the Republic, communications devices have been essential to political campaigns."[1] At the beginning of the nation's democracy, communication technology played a role when candidates were considering whether to be a candidate for the presidency. John Allen Hendricks and Shannon McCraw found that "George Washington was reluctant to serve a second term as president because of the critical and negative press" he had received.[2] A symbiotic relationship between politicians and the media has evolved. Jan Leighley asserts that "the public, the media, and political elites are interdependent."[3] As technology has advanced exponentially, particularly digital-media technology related to the Internet and specifically social media, the role that new media have played in the American political process has continued to be examined by scholars.

Not all scholars have found that the Internet will play a game-changing role in American politics. In 1999, not long after the Internet became mainstream, Richard Davis predicted that, "rather than acting as a revolutionary tool rearranging political power and instigating direct democracy, the Internet is destined to become dominated by the same actors in American politics who currently utilize other mediums."[4] Further, Davis asserted that "the Internet does not cause people to suddenly become politically active or even interested. Rather, American political behavior will remain essentially the same regardless of technological innovations designed to disseminate more political information."[5]

Conversely, Shanto Iyengar found that younger citizens were more politically engaged as a result of the Internet, stating that "it is clear that the Internet has dramatically increased participation. Young adults are the least likely to engage in traditional forms of political activity but the most likely to take advantage of technologically enhanced forms of participation."[6] Davis and Iyengar both acknowledged that the youth demographic was the only demographic in which the Internet, and new-media technologies, increased political participation.

The proliferation of new-media technologies throughout American history has required politicians to implement campaign-communication strategies that effectively reach the electorate using those technologies. West noted, "in this multifaceted situation, candidates must figure out how to reach voters who will decide key election contests."[7] Even political-communication scholars Dan Nimmo and Keith Sanders, as far back as 1981, asserted that "scholars can scarcely ignore the role played by the electronic media in the contemporary history of either democracies or totalitarian systems."[8]

Both democracies and totalitarian systems have potentially faced a game changer with new-media technologies related to the Internet. The spring of 2012 provided clear evidence of the Internet's ability to mobilize citizens and be used to strategize to the extent that dictators were toppled in several countries throughout the Middle East and North Africa. In a 2012 study Khang, Ki, and Ye found that as new-media technologies became more prevalent "social media have gained incremental attention among scholars, who have in turn been responding and keeping pace with the increased usage and impact of this new medium."[9]

Numerous observers of the role being played by social media in the presidential campaign emphasized that the technology had the ability to have a profound influence. Jeffrey Young, of the Voice of America, asserted that "political campaigns used to rely on speeches, rallies, and newspapers to reach and motivate voters. Then radio and TV made it possible to reach everyone quickly and simultaneously. Today, campaigns can spread their messages instantly—and, interactively—through the Internet's so-called 'social media.'"[10] Also, Amanda Michel and Ed Pilkington asserted that

> in the 2012 election cycle, both Mitt Romney's Republican campaign and Obama's have shifted markedly from text to video. They are increasingly attacking each other on screen and then rapidly rebutting each other also on screen. The online nature of the content allows it to be produced with lightning speed, and it is designed consciously with social-media sharing in mind.[11]

Moreover, Hajj Flemings of Blackenterprise.com believes that "it is no question that social media is changing everything and possibly predicting who will become the forty-fifth president of the United States of America."[12] Hence, this study examines the role that new-media technologies—specifically social-media technologies and the Internet—played in the 2012 American presidential campaign. President Barack Obama and former Massachusetts governor Mitt Romney both took full advantage of the Internet and social-media technologies.

In 2012 Obama's digital-campaign team outnumbered Romney's by a large amount with 750 on Obama's staff compared to 87 on Romney's staff.[13] Molly McHugh of DigitalTrends.com suggested that the role of social-media technologies in modern presidential campaigns is very important and plays an integral role throughout the course of the campaign. But the Romney campaign was not as active as the Obama campaign on social-media sites during the 2012 campaign. In fact, Obama posted four times more content than Romney did and utilized twice as many social-media platforms as did the Romney campaign.[14] McHugh stated, "The fact that campaigns now have Social Media directors is proof enough that this stuff matters—as in *could decide elections matters.*"[15]

Romney's early attempt to enter the social-media game got off to a rough start with a mistake that gave opponents something to pounce on: When the campaign released its first smartphone application, With Mitt, it misspelled *America* as "Amercia." Fox News reported, "after the 'Amercia' gaffe was discovered, Twitter users took great glee in imagining what 'Amercia' stood for and what policies Romney had planned for the nation, such as 'Amercia-n exceptionalism.'"[16] Moreover, when Romney's Twitter followers increased by more than one hundred thousand in a twenty-four-hour time frame, social-media experts and political observers accused the Romney campaign of buying the followers rather than actually attracting them with his campaign platform and political skills.[17]

During the Republican National Convention Romney's campaign released a branded version of Square—the mobile credit card–processing app that attaches to iPods, iPads, and Android-technology earphone jacks—to solicit donations from supporters. In addition to using the Romney Square app at the convention to sell campaign gear to those in attendance, more than five thousand supporters were given the device to use after the convention to solicit and raise funds for the Romney campaign. Romney supporters who were not at the convention were able to obtain a Square app on the Romney Web page to conduct their own fundraising on behalf of the Republican candidate.[18] Interestingly, the Romney campaign's digital director, Zac Moffatt, did not place high expectations on the Square app's ability to raise huge sums of cash for the campaign. Rather, the Romney campaign envisioned the Square app serving more as a tool to "engage" supporters and get them involved in the campaign. The campaign believed the app would be ideal to use at the homes of supporters during debate-viewing parties and other informal political gatherings. Sasha Issenberg reported that "by turning supporters and volunteers into donors, the campaign hopes it can entice them to get yet further involved later."[19]

TAILORING/TARGETING MESSAGES USING SOCIAL MEDIA

Mobile Devices

The 2012 presidential campaigns utilized technology to gain voter information and then tailor and target messages to specific demographics. After the Democratic and Republican conventions journalist Matt Massey observed that, "along with traditional media, social media is playing a much more prominent role in the marketing strategies of national and local political races. As marketers, the information and data fallout from both conventions are just now starting to come in, and one thing is clear: politics are becoming very personal."[20]

The use of mobile devices and smartphones is a common practice now in American culture with consumers using their smartphones to download applications (apps) to access all types of information. More than half of the entire American population has a mobile phone. Seizing on this vast audience, the 2012 presidential candidates utilized smartphone apps to communicate with the electorate. Mobile-phone usage is predicted to continue to be a dominant communication tool, especially where social-media apps are concerned. One study predicts that by 2016 there will be a 23 percent increase in mobile-phone use.[21]

Republican Mitt Romney's July 2012 release of a smartphone app designed to reveal who he had chosen as his vice presidential running mate was one means used by the candidates to gather information and data from voters to send future tailored and targeted messages. "Mitt's VP" sent a push notification informing users of Romney's running mate. However, in order to receive the notification, users were required to send the Romney campaign an e-mail address, phone number, and zip code. The app not only permitted users the opportunity to share their opinions about Romney's choice but also sent users directly to the campaign's website where they could make a campaign donation. In 2008 Barack Obama used mobile- and smartphone technology to also announce his running mate, but the technology was not as sophisticated as Romney's app in 2012. Obama simply sent a text message to voters informing them that Joe Biden was his vice presidential running mate. However, Felicia Sonmez of the *Washington Post* observed that "the 3 A.M. message arrived on users' mobile devices several hours after news of Obama's choice had already leaked out."[22] During the 2012 campaign Obama did release a smartphone app designed to allow supporters to organize events related to the campaign. YouTube emerged as a major player when it came to getting messages to the electorate. A YouTube app is found on more than 350 million devices, with those mobile devices uploading more than three hours of video per minute to the site. Moreover, in 2011 traffic from mobile devices tripled.[23]

Facebook

Facebook proved to be a good social-media technology for the two presidential candidates in 2012. It was the second-most-visited website in the United States (with YouTube being the third-most).[24] In October 2012 it was reported that Facebook had one billion users with six hundred million users accessing their Facebook accounts via smartphone.[25] Ryan Cohn of SocialFresh.com, a social-media consulting firm, suggested that, "whether through advertising, search, messaging, or community development, these two presidential campaigns are pioneering the use of social media unlike ever before."[26]

The Obama campaign paid to have advertisements placed in the newsfeed of Facebook users in the battleground states. The unique aspect of this was that Facebook users saw the Obama advertisements whether they had "liked" Obama's Facebook page or not and whether they were a Democrat or a Republican.[27]

However, not all social media strategies implemented by the Obama campaign on Facebook appeared to be prudent. Brittany Darwell of InsideFacebook.com noted the Obama campaign purchased sidebar ads on Facebook during the campaign. She believes that "this type of ad, which leads off Facebook and does not have a 'like' button or social context, is known among social marketers as the worst performing unit on Facebook. Not only do these ads cost more and have lower average click-through rates than others on the social network, when users do notice and interact with them there is no social amplification of this action. Users' friends won't see that they 'liked' the page or engaged with a post because there are no calls to action from the ad to do these things."[28]

Facebook's sponsored-results tool, released in August 2012, allowed marketers and specifically the political candidates to have a sponsored link appear in the drop-down menu of choices related to whatever topic Facebook users were searching for and interested in.[29] Facebook users might search for other Facebook pages or even applications that interfaced with Facebook. Unlike the Obama campaign, the Romney campaign took advantage of this new technology. By doing so, they had the ability to divert user traffic from the topics and search words that were originally typed into the Facebook search tool. Cleverly, when Facebook users searched for the terms "Barack Obama," "Joe Biden," "Democrats," and "Republicans" among other terms, they were not only provided the page that they had been seeking but also were shown as the very first link, clearly labeled "sponsored," a drop-down option from the menu that directed users to Romney and Paul Ryan's webpage.[30] In comparing the amount of activity between the two candidates on Facebook, one study found that during the month of June 2012 both Romney and Obama averaged two posts per day.[31] On Facebook parity between the two candidates existed.

Twitter

Originally known as "Twttr," the microblogging Internet platform was first introduced in 2006 and gained widespread popularity among the general public a year later. Twitter allows users to send short text messages of no more than 140 characters, known as "tweets," to followers who read those messages and have the ability to "retweet," forwarding those messages on to their own followers. Twitter was the eighth-most-visited website on the Internet during the 2012 presidential campaign.[32] The majority of Twitter users linked to the microblogging site from Facebook.[33] The social-media platform was in its infancy during the 2008 presidential campaign and the presidential primaries leading up to the 2008 election. Thus its use during the 2008 campaign was limited. However, by 2012 Twitter had established itself firmly as a social-media technology that technologically savvy individuals used regularly. As of October 2012 it was reported that Twitter had 140 million users.[34] With that many users, or potential voters, the candidates could not have ignored this social-media platform to communicate with the electorate.

Mitt Romney's campaign used Twitter heavily during the time leading up to the announcement of his vice presidential running mate. During the time period when the public and the media outlets were speculating as to who he would choose, the Romney campaign used "promoted tweets" that appeared whenever Twitter users conducted a search for possible vice presidential running mates.[35] The use of Twitter during the 2012 presidential campaign played a pivotal role in the overall narrative of the election. One campaign observer stated that "because Twitter democratizes the delivery of information, tweets can help a candidate by getting out a message that might not be seen on traditional media like newspapers and television."[36] Like all social media, Twitter allowed the candidates to communicate directly with supporters without having to go through traditional-media gatekeepers and agenda setters. Twitter was not only very inexpensive for the presidential candidates to use as a campaign communication tool but also served as a mass medium that could get messages out to voters immediately. In addition to its benefits during the 2012 campaign, Twitter was criticized for its lack of focus on substantive issues. Charlie Warzel of *Adweek* asserted that "it is the home of meaningless scooplets and high-profile dustups."[37]

The Obama campaign was ahead of the Romney campaign when looking at the number of followers and number of tweets for each candidate. As of November 1, 2012, just five days prior to the election, Obama had 21.5 million followers compared to Romney's 1.6 million followers. In terms of engagement and interactivity with the followers, Obama also was ahead of Romney, with 7,500 tweets compared to his challenger's 1,300 tweets. One report found that during several weeks in June 2012 Romney averaged only one tweet a day compared to Obama's daily average of twenty-nine.[38] By way of comparison, during the entire 2008 presidential campaign Barack Obama only tweeted 262 messages.[39] The numbers are a bit deceiving especially in terms of "engagement," as asserted by Zach Green of 140Elect, who serves as a consultant to political candidates on how to use Twitter effectively. He said that "Obama tweets ten times more often as Romney and gets additional support on Twitter from his campaign. But, Romney's tweets are more often shared and retweeted, suggesting his supporters are 'engaged.'"[40] Moreover, Obama had two official Twitter accounts, @BarackObama and @Obama2012, compared to Romney's one account, @MittRomney.[41]

YouTube

Social-media platform YouTube was another technology used by the presidential contenders to communicate with the electorate during the 2012 presidential campaign. Introduced in 2005, YouTube was the third-most-visited website on the Internet, both globally and in America during the 2012 campaign.[42] In 2011 YouTube had more than one trillion views, which equates to 140 views for every human in the world, received more than eight hundred million visitors a month, and showed viewers more than four billion hours of video.[43]

In order to attract some of those monthly visitors interested in politics, in October 2011 YouTube created a politics channel designed to direct viewers to not only content produced by the candidates themselves but also content created by individuals unaffiliated with the political campaigns. Although the YouTube political channel received impressive numbers of views during the Republican primary, it did not garner the type of video views that the 2008 campaign saw. Jennifer Preston of the *New York Times* noted that "while online video is playing an increasingly important role for candidates to get their message across, this campaign season has not yet produced the same number of hit viral videos, like the popular music video 'Obama Girl' that people saw this time four years ago."[44] As of November 1, 2012, the YouTube politics channel had 74,533 subscribers and more than ten million video views.[45] ABC News, the *Wall Street Journal*, Al Jazeera English, the social-news website Buzzfeed, and other mainstream networks partnered with YouTube to offer live-streamed coverage of the presidential and vice presidential debates and both political-party conventions.[46]

In June 2012 the YouTube Politics Channel released a list of the top-five political videos on the channel. Interestingly, they were chosen by YouTube not based on the number of views but rather on how much they engaged viewer commentary or sharing.[47] Four of the top five videos pertained to the Supreme Court ruling on the Patient Protection and Affordable Care Act, commonly known as "Obamacare." When comparing YouTube video views between Romney and Obama, the Democratic president had very impressive numbers. As of November 1, 2012, President Obama's YouTube channel had exceeded 262 million video views, with 254,807 subscribers, compared to Romney's channel's 29.3 million views and 27,633 subscribers.[48] Obama's YouTube channel was created in September 2006 while Romney's was created in August 2006. Amanda Michel and Ed Pilkington of the *Guardian* say that "the scale of viewing underlines the growing importance of video as a political communications tool, as well as Obama's own personal dominance in utilizing the form."[49]

As of November 2, 2012, the most-viewed video on Obama's YouTube channel, with nearly four million views, was "African Americans for Obama." During the thirty days preceding August 27, 2012, "people have spent more than twenty cumulative years watching official videos of Obama and Romney (that's two years longer than Justin Bieber has been alive)."[50] As of November 1, 2012, the most-watched video on Mitt Romney's YouTube channel, with nearly 1.4 million views, was "Doing Fine?"[51] The second-most-watched video on Romney's channel was "The American Comeback Team," the first video of Romney with Paul Ryan, his vice presidential running mate, which received more than 1.2 million views.[52]

Pinterest and Tumblr

Both of the presidential campaigns had pages at Pinterest, a site described as a "virtual pinboard" that allows users to organize and share their favorite things such as recipes, photos of clothes, and ideas about how to decorate homes, among other things.[53] In the United States, in terms of Internet traffic, Pinterest was ranked as the tenth-most-visited website during the 2012 election period and primarily reached the twenty-five- to thirty-four-year-old demographic.[54] Similar to Twitter's retweet function or Facebook's sharable content, Pinterest allows users to "pin" and "repin" items, which increases the number of views that the original post, or "pin," might have received. In June 2012 *Forbes* magazine reported that Pinterest was the third-largest social-media site, with 104 million visits, outpaced only by Facebook and Twitter.[55] The site was introduced to social-media users in 2010, so its popularity and adoption rate has been impressive and 2012 was the first U.S. presidential campaign in which Pinterest was used by the candidates. The majority of Pinterest users, more than 68 percent, are women, and nearly 30 percent of Pinterest users have a household income of more than $100,000 annually.[56]

Since Pinterest is known as a social-media site that appeals primarily to more women than men, the presidential spouses each had a Pinterest page. Michelle Obama's Pinterest page consistently remained ahead of Ann Romney's in the number of followers. As of November 5, 2012, just one day before the election, Mrs. Obama had 44,946 followers while Mrs. Romney had 13,916 followers. But in an effort to not leave any potential female supporter overlooked, candidates Obama and Romney themselves had Pinterest pages. President Obama's Pinterest page had 35,767 followers on November 5, 2012, compared to Governor Romney's 2,265. Like the first lady's page, President Obama's page had more followers than Governor Romney's.[57] On Pinterest users create boards with themes and then pin graphics of items related to that theme. President Obama's Pinterest page had twelve boards that included (1) Obama 2012 in Action, (2) In His Own Words, (3) Just the Facts, (4) Faces of Change, (5) The First Family, (6) Truth Team 2012, (7) Obama Art, (8) Obama 2012 Store, (9) Pet Lovers for Obama, (10) Joe Biden on the Road, (11) Snacks of the Campaign Trail, and (12) Dear Mitt Romney, while Governor Romney's Pinterest page had eleven boards that included (1) Republican National Convention, (2) #BuiltByUs, (3) Television, (4) Movies, (5) Books, (6) Romney Bus, (7) On the Road, (8) Mitt Gear, (9) Infographics, (10) Family, and (11) Your Support.

Alicia Cohen of *The Hill* asserted that "winning the Pinterest popularity contest might not mean much when it comes to the election, but the role of the spouses likely matters more on the female-centric site."[58] Ann Romney had nine boards, including (1) July 4th Recipes, (2) Crafts/DIY, (3) Things I Love, (4) Patriotic, (5) Inspiration, (6) Family, (7) Recipes, (8) Campaign, and (9) Books Worth Reading, while Michelle Obama had six boards—(1) Why We Vote, (2) People Who Inspire Me, (3) Recipe Ideas, (4) Around the White House, (5) Great Memories, and (6) Family. Ann Romney primarily posted recipes and photos of herself with comments about herself in the photos while Michelle Obama posted a photo of herself in a push-up competition with talk-show host Ellen DeGeneres. President Obama posted his family's chili recipe while Governor Romney posted recommended books. One of the governor's book recommendations, L. Ron Hubbard's

Battlefield Earth: A Saga of the Year 3000, drew some attention among political observers. One blogger succinctly summed up why the candidates and their wives would use Pinterest despite it not really being very conducive to politics: "I think that both women wanted the same thing from Pinterest: "to allow people to see their personable, relatable, human side."[59]

Perhaps most importantly Pinterest was used by both campaigns in 2012 to reach out to and communicate with the much-coveted women's vote. Political experts predicted the female vote would most likely determine the election's outcome.[60] Worth noting, throughout the presidential campaign Romney was accused of being out of touch with average Americans due to his incredible amount of wealth he had amassed over the tenure of his very successful business career. His personal net worth was estimated to be upward of a quarter of a billion dollars. Thus his Pinterest page was used to show citizens that, despite his wealth, he engaged in ordinary, average activities like most Americans. He wanted Pinterest users to know that his favorite television shows were *30 Rock*, *American Idol*, and *Modern Family* and that his favorite movies were *O Brother, Where Art Thou?*, the *Stars Wars* trilogy, and *Indiana Jones: Raiders of the Lost Ark*.

Tumblr, founded in 2007, provides Internet users a social-media platform to share almost anything they find interesting—including photos, videos, music, and text messages from computers and mobile phones—by customizing each page's colors and themes.[61] As of November 2012, Tumblr boasted 79.5 million blogs and 34.9 billion posts. In the United States, in terms of Internet traffic, Tumblr was ranked as the twentieth-most-visited website offering users a microblogging platform during the 2012 election period.[62] Like Pinterest, more women than men use Tumblr, and that demographic is skewed more toward the eighteen- to twenty-four-year-old range. Tumblr does not provide follower counts, so it is not possible to easily compare the reach and effectiveness of the Obama and Romney strategies using this social-media site.

CANDIDATE WEBSITES

The candidates not only used the Internet to distribute their campaign messages to the electorate via their websites, but they also used their websites to gather and compile personal data from the users of their Web pages and the social-media technologies they employed. Upon visiting Obama's website, before being able to access its content the visitor was required to provide an e-mail address and a postal zip code. Not only did prominent links on the Web page encourage visitors to make financial donations, but visitors were also provided with opportunities for engagement, like the ability to "call voters," "attend an event," "volunteer," provide "voting info," "remind friends to vote," "host an event," "make calls," or "start grassroots fundraising" by clicking a tab that would then send a link with directions for participating in the chosen activity. Importantly, the Obama Web page provided visitors with voter information that included the ability to "get voting info for your state," "check your registration status," "commit to vote," "find your polling location," and "volunteer for the election." President Obama's website also attempted to reach out to almost every voting demographic possible with more than twenty groups with dedicated links providing information on policy stances related to each demographic. The demographic links included (1) African Americans, (2) Asian Americans and Pacific Islanders, (3) Catholics, (4) Educators, (5) Environmentalists, (6) Jewish Americans, (7) Latinos, (8) LGBT Americans, (9) Native Americans, (10) Nurses, (11) Parents, (12) People of Faith, (13) People with Disabilities, (14) Rural Americans, (15) Seniors, (16) Small-Business Owners, (17) Sportsmen, (18) Veterans and Military Families, (19) Women, and (20) Young Americans. President Obama's website provided visitors the opportunity to connect with his campaign via (1) Facebook, (2) Flickr, (3) Google+, (4) Instagram, (5) Mobile App, (6) Pinterest, (7) RSS, (8) SMS, (9) Spotify, (10) Storify, (11) Tumblr, (12) Twitter, and (13) YouTube. Obama utilized six more social-media technologies to connect to his website than did Romney.

When visiting the Mitt Romney website, the first thing the visitor saw was a request to make a financial contribution and solicitation for personal information—name, address, phone number, and e-mail. To encourage electorate engagement and help with the campaign, the website provided opportunities for visitors to participate, including "find events," "make calls," and "fundraise." There was also a link for visitors to choose their state, which then provided information about voting, volunteering, and upcoming community events in each state. Like Obama's, Romney's website attempted to reach out to almost every voting demographic possible, with less groups, one fewer than the Obama site, with dedicated links providing information on policy stances related to each demographic. The demographic links included (1) Americans of Faith, (2) Asian Americans and Pacific Islanders, (3) Black Leadership Council, (4) Catholics, (5) Educators, (6) Energy Voters, (7) Farmers and Ranchers, (8) Former Obama Supporters, (9) Health-Care Professionals, (10) Jewish Americans, (11) Juntos con Romney, (12) Lawyers, (13) Polish Americans, (14) Public-Safety Professionals, (15) Romney Voters for Free Enterprise, (16) Sportsmen, (17) Veterans and Military Families, (18) Women for Mitt, and (19) Young Americans. The website provided visitors the opportunity to connect with his campaign via (1) Facebook, (2) Twitter, (3) Google+, (4) Flickr, (5) Spotify, (6) Tumblr, and (7) YouTube. Both Romney and Obama provided Spanish versions of their websites.

Data Collection

The 2012 presidential campaign utilized technology that allowed both presidential candidates to collect massive amounts of personal data on users who visited their websites. The data collection was worrisome for some observers who found that both the Obama and Romney campaigns leaked private data to third parties unbeknownst to users.[63] President Obama's Web page privacy policy notified visitors that personal information would be gathered by Obama for America (OFA). The website's disclosure stated:

the term "personal information" means information that specifically identifies an individual (such as a name, address, telephone number, mobile number, e-mail address, or credit card number) and information about that individual or his or her activities that is directly linked to personally identifiable information. Personal information does not include "aggregate" information, which is data we collect about the use of the Sites or about a group or category of services or users, from which individual identities or other personal information has been removed. This Policy in no way restricts or limits our collection and use of aggregate information.[64]

The Obama website distinguished "active collection" as opposed to "passive collection" when gathering personal information. For active collection, the Obama website disclaimer stated:

Personal information may be collected in a number of ways when you visit our Sites. We collect certain information you voluntarily provide to us, such as when you create an account or a profile, make a donation, make a purchase, send us an e-mail, or sign up to receive e-mail or text-message updates, fill out a form, connect through a social feed, sign up to be a volunteer or host an event, request information, apply for an internship, or use a voter-registration-form tool. Such information may include personal information, such as your name, mailing address, e-mail address, phone number, geographic location, and credit card information. We may also collect demographic information you may voluntarily provide from time to time, such as in response to questionnaires and surveys, including gender, ethnicity, education, and interest information. If this information is tied to personally identifiable information, it will be treated as personal information. Personal and demographic information may also be collected if you provide such information in connection with creating a profile or group, leaving comments, posting blog comments or other content, sending an e-mail or message to another user, or participating in any interactive forums or features on the Sites. In addition, from time to time we may collect demographic, contact, or other personal information you provide in connection with your participation in surveys, contests, games, promotions, and other activities on the Sites. We may also obtain information from other sources and combine that with information we collect on our Sites.[65]

As for passive collection of identification, the site said that:

When you use the Sites, some information is also automatically collected, such as your Internet Protocol (IP) address, your operating system, the browser type, the address of a referring website, and your activity on our Sites. If you access the Sites from a mobile device, we may also collect information about the type of mobile device you use, your device's unique ID, the type of mobile Internet browsers you use, and information about the location of your device (for information about how to opt out of this data collection, please see "What Choices Do You Have Regarding the Use of Your Information?" below). We treat this information as personal information if we combine it with or link it to any of the identifying information mentioned above. Otherwise, it is used in the aggregate only.

When President Obama released his "Are You In" mobile app, it also mined data from users, requiring them to provide their name, photo, gender, list of friends, date of birth, current city, e-mail address, and permission to post on a user's wall. During the Republican primary, Governor Tim Pawlenty released a similar app and requested the same information and the ability to post to users' Facebook wall as well as access users' newsfeeds.[66]

On Mitt Romney's website the privacy policy was not as aggressive as Barack Obama's. The first paragraph of the privacy policy stated that

> At Romney for President, Inc., we are committed to providing the highest level of protection for your online privacy and security. As you explore our website, we encourage you to provide us with information about yourself so we can contact you with the latest news about Governor Romney. However, you will always be able to decide how much, if any, personal information you'd like to provide. And you will always be able to unsubscribe from our e-mail database quickly and easily through the link provided at the bottom of every e-mail that we send.[67]

The Romney website, like Obama's, collected personal information such as IP addresses, browser types, computer operating systems, and Internet service providers using cookies. Both websites noted that Web browsers allowed users to disable cookies.

CANDIDATE MEMES AND SOCIAL MEDIA

Candidates work diligently to use social media to their benefit by employing many individuals to staff the Internet political-strategy departments. However, when something a candidate says or does seems odd or quirky to observers, the actions can "go viral," being shared rapidly across the Internet by users, leaving the campaigns very little control over the message. Moments during a political campaign when a candidate makes a mistake or states something in a manner that resonates with both supporters and opponents can go viral on social media. A viral photo or phrase is called a "meme." The second presidential debate produced a meme when Romney said that he would consider cutting federal funding to PBS and specifically said that, though he liked Big Bird, he would still consider cutting funding for *Sesame Street*. Before the debate had even ended, social-media sites were abuzz with images and statements in support of Big Bird. As *Politico* reporter Tony Romm observed, "There is a piece of information . . . and it begins to bounce around, essentially. It's shared, it's repeated. It reverberates."[68]

In an attempt to appeal to women voters, during the second presidential debate Republican Mitt Romney made reference to making a concerted effort to recruit women possessing impressive credentials and qualifications to work for his administration when he was governor of Massachusetts. Romney told voters that in that quest to fill positions he received "binders full of women" who were qualified. This remark by Romney was found to be both humorous and condescending to voters, and within minutes the candidate's unfortunate choice of words began trending on Twitter, Facebook, and Tumblr. Once again, before the debate had even concluded, twenty Facebook pages had been created referencing the "binders full of women" comment and a similar Twitter account had accumulated more than twelve thousand followers.[69] Facebook users shared and "liked" photos or memes that parodied what Romney had said by showing three-ring binders with photos of women on them and jokes about women in binders. One company even purchased the rights to the http address BindersFullofWomen.com, promising to use the Web address as an outlet to educate voters on Romney's record on women.[70]

The Republicans were not the only ones to get caught up in the social-media reverberation of memes. Tumblr teamed up with the *Guardian* to create live GIFs of gaffes or parodies as they occurred during the presidential and vice presidential debates in order to post immediately to social-media sites such as Tumblr. A GIF is a brief video that oftentimes is a looped video feed or sometimes a photo, but once they go viral they become a meme. Tumblr had numerous campaign memes that were not flattering to Vice President Joe Biden. For example, brief video clips were created of Joe Biden smiling at awkward times when Republican vice presidential running mate Paul Ryan was speaking during their debate. The constant reverberation of memes on Tumblr can be influential when Tumblr receives an average of fifteen billion page views monthly. Memes can be even more damaging when they are picked up and shared by users of Facebook and Twitter, which is oftentimes what happens.

Obama supporters on Pinterest criticized Romney for staying at "luxury" hotels as he traveled around the nation campaigning, thus, encouraging citizens to believe that the wealthiest individual to ever run for president only stayed in luxury hotels and could not identify with average Americans who could not afford to lodge at luxury hotels. The liberal Center for American Progress reviewed the reports that Romney filed with the Federal Election Commission (FEC) and posted, or pinned, nine luxury hotels that were listed in the FEC report, places Romney had stayed while campaigning. The meme on the Pinterest page only had 1,467 followers and likely did not have much influence on the campaign rhetoric. In all fairness, the meme did not show or discuss hotels Romney stayed at while campaigning that were not considered to be luxury hotels—such as the Marriott Hotel chain. Perhaps most notable of all memes during the 2012 presidential campaign was the "We Built That" meme pertaining to President Obama. During a speech in Virginia in July 2012 Obama said that

There are a lot of wealthy, successful Americans who agree with me—because they want to give something back. They know they didn't— Look, if you've been successful, you didn't get there on your own. You didn't get there on your own. I'm always struck by people who think, Well, it must be because I was just so smart. There are a lot of smart people out there. It must be because I worked harder than everybody else. Let me tell you something: there are a whole bunch of hardworking people out there. [Applause.]

If you were successful, somebody along the line gave you some help. There was a great teacher somewhere in your life. Somebody helped to create this unbelievable American system that we have that allowed you to thrive. Somebody invested in roads and bridges.

If you've got a business, you didn't build that. Somebody else made that happen. The Internet didn't get invented on its own. Government research created the Internet so that all the companies could make money off the Internet.[71]

From the speech, the phrase "you didn't build that" became a meme. On social-media sites there were photos of Obama with the quote under his image and videos of the speech were shared by Facebook users with links directly to the YouTube video. Governor Romney's campaign even built a huge wall with large letters reading, WE BUILT THAT, which served as the backdrop to many of his campaign speeches railing against Obama's policies and leadership. Obama was mocked throughout the campaign, with his photo and the quotation next to prominent innovators. One meme had a photo of God creating Earth posted along with the Genesis 1:1, "In the beginning, God created the heavens and the earth," with a photo of Obama saying to God, "You didn't build that. Somebody else made that happen."[72]

Memes and other social-media chatter spike when something substantial is happening on the campaign trail and in the news. Socialbakers.com, a social-media metrics firm, created the Twitter "Cheermeter," designed to measure the amount of tweets that each candidate received. The Cheermeter showed significant spikes in tweets for Romney from August 28 to 30, 2012, which was when the Republican National Convention was underway, with tweets averaging 348,021 per day. During the Democratic National Convention, from September 4 to 6, 2012, its tweets for Obama spiked, with an average of 1.28 million daily tweets. Also, the Cheermeter showed an increase in the number of tweets on October 3, 16, and 22, 2012, during the three presidential debates, each of which averaged 1.3 million tweets.

Aside from the conventions and the debates, there was only one additional significant spike in tweets on the Cheermeter, and that was on September 17, 2012, when the controversial "47 percent" remark by Governor Romney went viral on both social- and traditional-media outlets. During a private campaign fundraiser where he was secretly videotaped, Romney said that

> There are 47 percent of the people who will vote for the president no matter what. All right—there are 47 percent who are with him, who are dependent on government, who believe that, that they are victims, who believe that government has the responsibility to care for them, who believe that they are entitled to health care, to food, to housing. . . . My job is not to worry about those people. I'll never convince them they should take personal responsibility and care for their lives.[73]

On the day the story appeared on social media and traditional media, there were nearly a million tweets about Romney that day, compared to only 302,703 tweets about him the day prior. On November 5, 2012, the day before the election, there was a final spike in tweets about the candidates, with Obama receiving more than 1.4 million tweets and Romney receiving just a little over one million (see, again, table 8.1).

Facebook created an Elections page that measured presidential-candidate Facebook "likes" gained by day from October 6, 2012, to November 5, 2012. The metrics obtained from Facebook shows that on specific dates there were significant spikes in Facebook "likes" for the presidential candidates.

On October 9, 2012, Obama received more than 1.1 million "likes," compared to Romney's 96,922. On October 18, 2012, Romney received 185,032, compared to Obama's 46,375. On October 28, 2012, Romney received 264,986, compared to Obama's 79,651. On October 31, 2012, Romney received 166,204, compared to Obama's 56,440. And on November 2, 2012, just four days before the election, Romney received 92, 834 "likes," compared to Obama's 26,144. Aside from a heavy campaign schedule and a tightening of the race, there were no significant news items during the period between October 6 and November 5, 2012, that would explains Romney's lead in Facebook activity. Superstorm Sandy had wreaked havoc in the Northeast and caused both candidates to suspend campaigning for a day, which may have contributed to the metrics from October 28 through 31. Overall, during the final few weeks of campaigning, Governor Romney was acquiring more "likes" on Facebook than President Obama, which mirrored Romney's growing momentum as Election Day approached (see, again, table 8.2).

DISCUSSION

Indeed, new-media technologies, and specifically social-media sites, play an important role in the American political process in the twenty-first century. Although this technology is now standard in presidential campaigning, it has not overtaken traditional media such as television and radio. First, candidates still spend vast amounts of money on traditional-media advertising on both television and radio. Second, social media, despite its popularity, is perceived to be less reliable than traditional media. The lack of trust among Internet users toward social media most likely explains why nearly 60 percent of individuals surveyed indicated they watch local television news daily. Noteworthy though is that more than 50 percent of eighteen- to twenty-nine-year-olds got their news from Facebook, compared to only 5 percent of Internet users sixty-four years old and older. The older demographics' reluctance to rely on social media for news was not due to a lack of technological savvy, as 53 percent of this demographic went online in 2012, which was a 38 percent increase over online users during the 2008 presidential campaign.[74]

Social-media platforms permit candidates to achieve something they have aspired to do for many years—bypass the traditional media, the "gatekeepers," who have the ability to influence a campaign's rhetoric as well as which issues and themes are covered in a daily news cycle. Due to the astonishingly large number of people, and voters, using social-media technologies in 2012, the presidential campaigns were able to not only bypass traditional media but also shape and spin the messages that they wanted covered on traditional media such as television and radio news. An example of this included the incident where Romney's communications director found a blog that discussed a passage in President Obama's memoir where he discussed eating dog meat as a child when he lived in Indonesia. The Romney team tweeted about it and provided a link to the blog in the tweet. Afterward, almost every major news outlet in the nation reported on the story. One observer noted, "TV and press commentators can provide a filter for understanding political messages that no amount of direct marketing from Obama or Romney HQ can escape. But that doesn't appear to be stopping [the campaigns] from trying."[75]

It was not sufficient enough for candidates to just push messages out to the voters; rather, it was essential that candidates utilized social media to "engage" the voters to "share," "retweet," "forward," "pin," and "GIF" a campaign's message. A successful presidential campaign wants social-media users to help perpetuate the campaign's message. The Project for Excellence in Journalism asserted that "in 2012, in short, voters are playing an increasingly large role in helping to communicate campaign messages, while the role of the traditional news media as an authority or validator has only lessened."[76]

Now journalists pay less attention to the "spin room" and "spin doctors" during debates and campaign rallies and more attention to the social-media sites to see what users are saying and what topics are trending at the moment. Social-media memes and trending topics now drive the daily campaign news cycle, which has a substantial impact on the quality of news and the shelf life of a story:

> As more than one person has pointed out, this process has telescoped the political news cycle (and arguably every other news cycle) to the point where stories about a newsworthy moment or event emerge within minutes of it occurring, as it sweeps through Twitter and then becomes the fuel for real-time commentary by news pundits and mainstream channels like CNN. The news cycle—which used to last for days or even weeks in some cases—now has a half-life of about an hour.[77]

The demographics on social-media sites are not representative of the nation's demographics; thus, the daily news and news cycles might not always be representative of the interests and concerns of the nation's general population. For example, Twitter users tend to be younger, female, and more liberal than the nation's general population, while Facebook users tend to be more representative of all demographics.[78] Perhaps it is more important to consider that this change tends to focus on the trivial and less substantive issues—such as Big Bird and "binders full of women."[79] Finally, social-media sites make it easier to conceal the identities and true agendas of those who tweet, post, share, retweet, and create memes that potentially influence the decisions made on Election Day.

To be competitive candidates for the American presidency must have a technologically savvy social-media strategy. Regarding the 2012 presidential campaign and social media, Jay Samit of *Ad Age* asserted that, "in fact, any candidate or issue campaign that expects to succeed needs to make social engagement a critical part of their strategy, or they're doomed to fail."[80]

After the Republican primary concluded and former Massachusetts governor Mitt Romney officially became the Republican party's nominee, his campaign had to not only shift its message from the themes and issues of the primary to appeal to a broader demographic of voters, but it also had to enhance its social media, or digital, campaign strategy. And in the beginning Romney's campaign was far behind Obama's social-media strategy. Although never really completely catching up with the Obama campaign, the Romney campaign did improve its new media strategy drastically. As late as June 2012 technology experts were criticizing the Romney campaign's lack of technological knowledge and prowess. One observer stated that "the lack of basic knowledge and focus on best of breed interactive strategies within the Republican Party is frankly embarrassing."[81] But by Election Day the Romney campaign's social-media strategy was on par with Obama's, as great strides had been made by the Republicans to overcome the Obama campaign's four-plus-year head start to building and perfecting the use of new-media technologies.

Both presidential candidates mined data like never before. The combination of social-media popularity among the electorate and the technological ability to gather and collect personal information from the users of the social networks created a situation that allowed a national campaign to be run like a local one. The technology combined with the data that was mined permitted the two campaign camps to microtarget voters to encourage them to contribute financially and serve as volunteers for the campaigns. Social-media users even experienced targeted messaging on their Facebook newsfeeds and walls with information about candidate stances on issues that were judged to be of interest to them based on data mined. The Obama campaign's new-media team in Chicago was more advanced at data mining than Romney's team. According to Lois Romano of *Politico*, "the depth and breadth of the Obama campaign's 2012 digital operation—from data mining to online organizing—reaches so far beyond anything politics has ever seen, experts maintain, that it could impact the outcome of a close presidential election."[82]

Social-media technologies provide a platform for the electorate to be listened to by the politicians who oftentimes forget about them once they gain a powerful political office. New media provides an outlet for citizens to interact with and be engaged in political campaigns. Brian Solis of FastCompany.com emphasized that the 2012 presidential campaign needed to use new-media technologies as "bottom-up" instead of "top-down communication" as had been the case during the 2008 presidential campaign.[83]

Anecdotally, despite using social media at unprecedented levels, it appears that both presidential candidates in 2012 did not embrace Solis's advice, as much of the communication on social-media platforms was pushing candidate messages out to voters rather than focusing on creating a dialogue with and among the voters. Above all, social media played a significant role in electing the president in 2012, but the fact that new-media technologies shared the spotlight with traditional-media technologies cannot be ignored. Traditional media clearly remain important campaign tools for presidential candidates, as evidenced by the vast amounts of money spent in battleground states on advertising and the fact that candidates still spent time doing television and radio interviews in those media markets. Social media simply provided an additional outlet for presidential candidates to engage and communicate with the electorate.

APPENDIX

Table 8.1.   Twitter Cheermeter by Days

Date	Obama	Romney	Date	Obama	Romney
8/23/2012	165,932	191,814	9/30/2012	327,273	206,181
8/24/2012	197,761	157,653	10/1/2012	375,641	264,616
8/25/2012	194,605	157,295	10/2/2012	643,569	393,283
8/26/2012	245,649	225,246	10/3/2012	1,393,302	1,487,011
8/27/2012	277,142	344,817	10/4/2012	589,221	543,062
8/28/2012	416,791	657,454	10/5/2012	338,633	286,148
8/29/2012	447,866	582,494	10/6/2012	317,601	300,104
8/30/2012	596,198	867,538	10/7/2012	420,744	483,464
8/31/2012	292,353	216,730	10/8/2012	492,742	442,115
9/1/2012	330,916	193,113	10/9/2012	465,262	465,672
9/2/2012	430,539	246,987	10/10/2012	410,457	371,592
9/3/2012	629,911	296,310	10/11/2012	623,443	551,593
9/4/2012	1,290,666	431,020	10/12/2012	297,379	271,011
9/5/2012	1,203,341	363,069	10/13/2012	299,070	294,479
9/6/2012	1,352,207	405,003	10/14/2012	388,970	352,031
9/7/2012	397,449	220,008	10/15/2012	547,901	449,652
9/8/2012	312,112	261,402	10/16/2012	1302663	1,346,370
9/9/2012	420,118	291,457	10/17/2012	631479	638,036
9/10/2012	441,219	243,137	10/18/2012	567864	521,997
9/11/2012	633,987	432,287	10/19/2012	383564	346,038
9/12/2012	553,085	344,735	10/20/2012	383100	352,311
9/13/2012	453,100	292,059	10/21/2012	589144	480,225
9/14/2012	300,234	182,305	10/22/2012	1,233,325	1,149,178
9/15/2012	274,543	169,667	10/23/2012	771,440	541,847
9/16/2012	371,648	302,703	10/24/2012	824,511	501,409
9/17/2012	515,890	927,025	10/25/2012	749,304	477,524
9/18/2012	446,021	524,257	10/26/2012	537,119	361,159
9/19/2012	445,785	397,499	10/27/2012	553,566	456,243
9/20/2012	379,991	376,590	10/28/2012	668,001	590,102
9/21/2012	249,937	234,589	10/29/2012	639,978	564,116
9/22/2012	247,085	213,455	10/30/2012	657,053	500,588
9/23/2012	367,150	333,954	10/31/2012	779,269	493,871
9/24/2012	482,743	317,557	11/1/2012	428,739	263,818
9/25/2012	426,547	294,567	11/2/2012	741,194	588,413
9/26/2012	385,652	247,960	11/3/2012	923,715	749,061
9/27/2012	228,464	151,017	11/4/2012	531,837	463,939
9/28/2012	254,155	163,044	11/5/2012	1,429,809	1,096,123
9/29/2012	266,658	170,233			

Note: See figure 8.1 for a graph that corresponds to the above data. Reprinted with permission from www
.socialbakers.com/elections/cheermeter.

Figure 8.1   Twitter: Cheermeter by Day

Source: Retrieved from www.socialbakers.com/elections/cheermeter/. Reprinted with permission.

Notes:
1. Each circle represents a date, starting August 23, 2012, going through November 5, 2012.
2. The dark line represents Obama's daily tweeted mentions.
3. The gray line represents Romney's daily tweeted mentions.
4. See table 8.1 for daily metrics.

Table 8.2.   Facebook Likes by Day Metrics

Date	Romney	Obama	Date	Romney	Obama
2-Oct	97,577	17,589	19-Oct	155,033	38,207
3-Oct	85,219	30,257	20-Oct	141,085	37,274
4-Oct	134,394	91,320	21-Oct	122,861	32,156
5-Oct	189,382	135081	22-Oct	113,770	29,392
6-Oct	103,076	45,153	23-Oct	126,941	87,542
7-Oct	102,529	36,602	24-Oct	158,145	113,621
8-Oct	103,321	30,830	25-Oct	148,539	45,928
9-Oct	96,922	1,197,931	26-Oct	147,263	49,977
10-Oct	103,149	29,683	27-Oct		
11-Oct	135,414	49,704	28-Oct	264,986	79,651
12-Oct	145,958	58,893	29-Oct	119,683	30,358
13-Oct	157,417	40,617	30-Oct	117,469	36,167
14-Oct	125,393	29,903	31-Oct	166,204	56,440
15-Oct	36,808	23,917	1-Nov	16,887	5,521
16-Oct	56,441	27,313	2-Nov	92,834	26,144
17-Oct	131,970	55,550	3-Nov		30,790
18-Oct	185,032	46,375			

Note: See figure 8.2 for a graph that corresponds with data. Reprinted with permission from http://elections .insidefacebook.com.

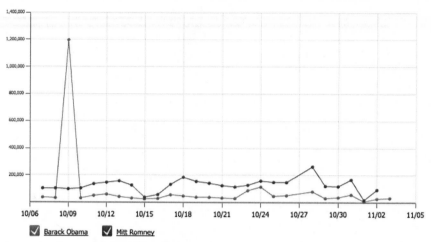

Figure 8.2.   Facebook Likes by Day Metrics

Source: Retrieved from http://elections.insidefacebook.com. Reprinted with permission.

Notes:
1. Each circle represents a date starting October 8, 2012, going through November 3, 2012.
2. The gray line represents Obama's daily Facebook likes.
3. The dark line represents Romney's daily Facebook likes.
4. See table 8.2 for daily metrics.

NOTES

1. Darrell M. West, *Air Wars: Television Advertising in Election Campaigns, 1952–2008*, 5th ed. (Washington, D.C.: CQ Press, 2010), 2.

2. John Allen Hendricks and Shannon K. McCraw, "Coverage of Political Campaigns," in *American Journalism: History, Principles, Practices*, ed. W. David Sloan and Lisa Mullikin Parcell (Jefferson, N.C.: McFarland, 2002), 181.

3. Jan E. Leighley, *Mass Media and Politics: A Social Science Perspective* (Boston: Houghton Mifflin, 2004), 8.

4. Richard Davis, *The Web of Politics: The Internet's Impact on the American Political System* (New York: Oxford University Press, 1999), 5.

5. Davis, *The Web of Politics*, 172.

6. Shanto Iyengar, *Media Politics: A Citizen's Guide*, 2nd ed. (New York: W. W. Norton, 2011), 123.

7. West, *Air Wars*, 2.

8. Dan D. Nimmo and Keith R. Sanders, "Introduction: The Emergence of Political Communication as a Field," in *Handbook of Political Communication*, ed. Dan D. Nimmo and Keith R. Sanders (Beverly Hills, Calif.: Sage, 1981), 25.

9. Hyoungkoo Khang, Eyun-Jung Ki, and Lan Ye, "Social Media Research in Advertising, Communication, Marketing, and Public Relations, 1997–2010," *Journalism and Mass Communication Quarterly* 89, no. 2 (2012): 290.

10. Jeffrey Young, "Internet, Social Media Prominent in U.S. Presidential Race," *Voice of America*, August 13, 2012, www.voanews.com/articleprintview/1485372.html.

11. Amanda Michel and Ed Pilkington, "Obama Passes YouTube Milestone as Online Videos Remake Campaigning," *Guardian*, July 24, 2012, www.guardian.co.uk/world/2012/jul/24/obama-youtube-milestone-online-videos.

12. Hajj Flemings, "Social Media Guide to the 2012 Presidential Election," Blackenterprise.com, September 6, 2012, www.blackenterprise.com/technology/social-media-guide-2012-presidential-election/.

13. Katie Rogers, "Obama Bests Romney in the Social Media Campaign, Research Shows," *Guardian*, August 15, 2012, www.guardian.co.uk/media/2012/aug/15/obama-bests-romney-when-it-comes-to-social-media.

14. "Obama Leads but Neither Candidate Engages in Much Dialogue with Voters," Journalism.org, August 15, 2012, www.journalism.org/analysis_report/how_presidential_candidates_use_web_and_social_media.

15. Molly McHugh, "How Social Media Is Sinking Mitt Romney," DigitalTrends.com, September 27, 2012, www.digitaltrends.com/social-media/how-social-media-is-sinking-mitt-romney/.

16. "Romney Campaign Spells 'America' Wrong in New iPhone App," Fox News, May 30, 2012, www.foxnews.com/politics/2012/05/30/romney-campaign-spells-america-wrong-in-new-iphone-app/.

17. McHugh, "How Social Media Is Sinking Mitt Romney."

18. Alex Fitzpatrick, "Romney Campaign Fundraisers for Success with Square," Mashable.com, August 31, 2012, http://mashable.com/2012/08/31/mitt-romney-square/.

19. Sasha Issenberg, "Mitt Romney's Square Deal: Not about the Money," Slate.com, August 30, 2012, www.slate.com/blogs/victory_lab/2012/08/30/mitt_romney_s_square_app_mobile_donations_are_about_more_than_money_.html.

20. "Politics: Now It's Personal; Social Media in Politics," MassyMedia, September 11, 2012, www.masseymedia.com/blog/politics-now-its-personal-social-media-in-politics/.

21. "Mobile Users to Consume 8 Times More Social Media in 2016," *OSP Magazine*, June 4, 2012, www.ospmag.com/osp-central/ospcentralinternationalupdate/mobile-users-consume-8-times-more-social-media-2016.

22. Felicia Sonmez, "Romney Camp Releases 'Mitt's VP' Mobile App," *Washington Post*, July 31, 2012, www.washingtonpost.com/blogs/election-2012/post/romney-camp-releases-mitts-vp-mobile-app/2012/07/31/gJQAl4CZMX_blog.html.

23. "Statistics," YouTube, http://www.youtube.com/t/press_statistics.

24. "Top Sites in the United States: The Top 500 Sites in the United States," Alexa, November 2012, www.alexa.com/topsites/countries/US.

25. Craig Smith, "(Oct 2012 Update) How Many People Use the Top Social Media, Apps & Services?" *Digital Marketing Ramblings*, October 4, 2012, http://expandedramblings.com/index.php/resource-how-many-people-use-the-top-social-media/.

26. Ryan Cohn, "Who Is Winning the Presidential Election on Facebook? Obama or Romney," SocialFresh.com, October 22, 2012, http://socialfresh.com/obama-vs-romney-facebook-strategy/.

27. McHugh, "How Social Media Is Sinking Mitt Romney."

28. Brittany Darwell, "Does Romney Have a Better Facebook Strategy Than Obama," InsideFacebook.com, August 28, 2012, www.insidefacebook.com/2012/08/28/does-romney-have-a-better-facebook-strategy-than-obama/.

29. Josh Constine, "Facebook Officially Launches 'Sponsored Results' Search Ads," Techcrunch.com, August 22, 2012, http://techcrunch.com/2012/07/19/facebook-sponsored-results/.

30. Brittany Darwell, "Does Romney Have a Better Facebook Strategy than Obama."

31. "How the Presidential Candidates Use the Web and Social Media: Degree of Digital Effort; Obama Far Outweighs Romney," Journalism.org, August 15, 2012, www.journalism.org/analysis_report/degree_digital_effort_obama_far_outweighs_romney.

32. "Top Sites in the United States."

33. "Twitter.com."

34. Smith, "(Oct 2012 Update)."

35. Emily Schulthesis, "Mitt Romney Makes Most of VP App," *Politico*, August 9, 2012, http://dyn.politico.com/printstory.cfm?uuid=E4ACDA9C-C40C-4C93-AA60-3AE24CA2A8DD.

36. Rob Lever, "Twitter Shakes Up U.S. Election Campaign," *Agence France Presse*, August 27, 2012, www.google.com/hostednews/afp/article/ALeqM5gR38L1LQyI7ZD8OucG50yzJZXrrQ?docId=CNG.ae3c582c70c925b75f92dbef50d564c5.691.

37. Charlie Warzel, "The 140-Character-or-Less Campaign," *Adweek*, May 7–13, 2012, 24, www.adweek.com/news/technology/140-character-or-less-campaign-140067.

38. "How the Presidential Candidates Use the Web."

39. Frederic I. Solop, "'RT @ BarackObama WE Just Made History': Twitter and the 2008 Presidential Election," in *Communicator-in-Chief: How Barack Obama Used New Media Technology to Win the White House*, ed. John Allen Hendricks and Robert E. Denton, Jr. (Lanham, Md.: Lexington Books, 2010).

40. Lever, "Twitter Shakes up U.S. Election Campaign."

41. "How the Presidential Candidates Use the Web."

42. "Top Sites in the United States."

43. "Statistics."

44. Jennifer Preston, "New Politics Channel on YouTube," *New York Times*, October 6, 2011, http://thecaucus.blogs.nytimes.com/2011/10/06/youtube-launches-new-politics-channel/.

45. "YouTube Politics," YouTube, accessed November 1, 2012, www.youtube.com/politics.

46. Nicole Enberg, "YouTube Launches New 'Election Hub' Channel with ABC News Digital and Other News Partners," press release, ABC News, August 22, 2012, http://abcnews.go.com/blogs/headlines/2012/08/youtube-launches-new-election-hub-channel-with-abc-news-digital-and-other-news-partners/; Leslie Meredith, "YouTube Launches 2012 Elections Hub," FoxNews.com, August 23, 2012, www.foxnews.com/tech/2012/08/23/youtube-launches-2012-elections-hub/.

47. Elizabeth Flock, "Angry 'Obamacare' Videos Top YouTube's Politics Channel," *U.S. News and World Report*, June 29, 2012, www.usnews.com/news/blogs/washington-whispers/2012/06/29/angry-obamacare-videos-top-youtubes-politics-channel-.

48. "mittromney's channel," YouTube, accessed November 1, 2012, www.youtube.com/user/mittromney; "BarackObama.com," YouTube, accessed November 1, 2012, www.youtube.com/user/barackobamadotcom.

49. Michel and Pilkington, "Obama Passes YouTube Milestone."

50. Ramya Raghavan, "Videos Mentioning Obama or Romney Top 2 Billion Views," YouTube Trends, August 27, 2012, http://youtube-trends.blogspot.com/2012/08/videos-mentioning-obama-or-romney-top-2.html.

51. Chris Taylor, "Hidden Cam Clip Has More Views Than Official Romney Videos on YouTube," Mashable.com, September 18, 2012, http://mashable.com/2012/09/18/romney-youtube-video-views/.

52. Raghavan, "Videos Mentioning Obama or Romney."

53. "About," Pinterest.com, accessed November 3, 2012, http://pinterest.com/about/.

54. "Top Sites in the United States."

55. Stephanie Chandler, "Pinterest Power: How to Use the Third Largest Social Media Site to Promote Your Business," Forbes.com, June 13, 2012, www.forbes.com/sites/work -in-progress/2012/06/13/pinterest-power-how-to-use-the-third-largest-social-media-site-to -promote-your-business/.

56. Christine Erikson, "13 'Pinteresting' Facts about Pinterest Users [INFOGRAPHIC]," Mashable.com, February 25, 2012, http://mashable.com/2012/02/25/pinterest-user-demo graphics/.

57. Alicia M. Cohn, "Study: President Obama, Ann Romney Winning at Pinterest," *The Hill*, October 30, 2012, http://thehill.com/blogs/twitter-room/other-news/264909-study -president-obama-ann-romney-winning-at-pinterest.

58. Cohn, "Study: President Obama."

59. Olivia Roat, "Politics, Pinterest, and Publicity: How Michelle Obama and Ann Rom- ney Use Pinterest," *MainStreetHost.com Blog*, August 1, 2012, http://blog.mainstreethost.com/ politics-pinterest-and-publicity-how-michelle-obama-and-ann-romney-use-pinterest.

60. Brie Jackson, "Women Voters May Hold the Key to 2012 Presidential Race," WBTW News 13, October 29, 2012, www2.wbtw.com/news/2012/oct/29/women-voters-may-hold -key-2012-presidential-race-ar-4844170/.

61. "Tumblr Lets You Effortlessly Follow Anything," Tumblr.com, www.tumblr.com/ about, retrieved November 3, 2012.

62. "Top Sites in the United States."

63. Natasha Singer, "Romney and Obama Campaigns Leaking Web Site Visitor Data," *New York Times*, November 1, 2012, http://bits.blogs.nytimes.com/2012/11/01/romney-and -obama-campaigns-leaking-web-site-visitor-data/.

64. "Organizing for Action Privacy Policy," BarackObama.com, accessed November 2, 2012, www.barackobama.com/privacy-policy?source=footer-nav.

65. "Organizing for Action Privacy Policy."

66. Michael L. Sifry, "Election 2012: It's Not Facebook; It's the Data, Stupid," Tech- President.com, April 20, 2011, http://techpresident.com/blog-entry/election-2012-its-not -facebook-its-data-stupid.

67. "Privacy Policy," MittRomney.com, accessed November 2, 2012, www.mittromney .com/privacy.

68. Young, "Internet, Social Media Prominent."

69. David Zurawik, "Going Deeper Than Big Bird and Binders on Twitter and TV Debates," *Baltimore Sun*, October 22, 2012, http://articles.baltimoresun.com/2012-10-22/entertainment/ bal-twitter-debates-big-bird-binders-20121019_1_social-media-binders-hashtags.

70. Elise Viebeck, "'Binders Full of Women' Goes Viral," *The Hill*, October 16, 2012, http://thehill.com/blogs/healthwatch/other/262445-romneys-binders-full-of-women-remark -goes-viral.

71. "You Didn't Build That," Know Your Meme, http://knowyourmeme.com/memes/ events/you-didnt-build-that.

72. "You Didn't Build That."

73. Rick Ungar, "Romney Fail: Caught on Video Revealing Extraordinary Contempt for 47 percent of Americans," *Forbes*, September 17, 2012, www.forbes.com/sites/rickun- gar/2012/09/17/romney-fail-caught-on-video-revealing-extraordinary-contempt-for-47-per- cent-of-americans/.

74. James Rainey, "Voters Still Tuned in to Traditional New Media, Poll Finds," *Los Angeles Times*, August 24, 2012, http://articles.latimes.com/2012/aug/24/nation/la-na-media-poll-20120824.

75. Michel and Pilkington, "Obama Passes YouTube Milestone."

76. "How the Presidential Candidates Use the Web."

77. Mathew Ingram, "What Tumblr Can Tell Us about the Future of Media," *Business Week*, October 29, 2012, www.businessweek.com/articles/2012-10-29/what-tumblr-can-tell-us-about-the-future-of-media.

78. Karlin Lillington, "Romney All Thumbs When It Comes to Social Media," *Irish Times*, November 1, 2012, www.irishtimes.com/newspaper/finance/2012/1101/1224325975699.html.

79. Ingram, "What Tumblr Can Tell Us."

80. Jay Samit, "Three Ways Social Media Will Make or Break 2012 Election Campaigns," *Ad Age*, June 23, 2012, http://adage.com/article/digitalnext/social-media-make-break-2012-election-campaigns/228367/.

81. Al DiGuido, "Social Media: GOP Needs to Bring 'A Game' to Mitt Romney's Online Profile," Humanevents.com, June 19, 2012, www.humanevents.com/2012/06/19/social-media-gop-needs-to-bring-a-game-to-mitt-romneys-online-profile/.

82. Lois Romano, "Obama's Data Advantage," *Politico*, June 9, 2012, www.politico.com/news/stories/0612/77213.html.

83. Brian Solis, "A Social Democracy: The White House Learns to Listen," FastCompany.com, June 14, 2011, www.fastcompany.com/1759871/social-democracy-white-house-learns-listen.

9

Explaining the Vote in the Election of 2012: Obama's Reelection

Henry C. Kenski and Kate M. Kenski

> Put simply, identity matters in politics, oftentimes more than anything else. We can view political battles in budgetary terms, or in terms of cultural hot-button issues, but one of the most important elements of voting is seeing yourself in the person you elect. It looks to me like Barack Obama convinced would-be GOP voters who never would have supported him to stay home rather than support this "other fellow," Mitt Romney.
>
> —Jay Cost[1]

> But it's clear that Obama's team was generations more advanced than Romney's. In a close race, turnout makes a difference; the investments Democrats have put into their technological tools have paid off and will continue to do so.
>
> —Reid Wilson[2]

The 2012 election continued the spirited clashes between Republicans and Democrats that had characterized the presidential elections of 2000, 2004, and 2008. From 1968 through 1992 Republican candidates dominated presidential elections, with the exceptions of 1976 when Jimmy Carter won a narrow victory and in 1992 and 1996 when Democrat Bill Clinton won twice. In both 1992 and 1996 Independent third-party challenger Ross Perot prevented Clinton from winning a popular-vote majority (he won 43 percent in 1992 and 49 percent in 1996). Republicans returned to the White House with the victories of George W. Bush in 2000 (victory in the electoral college without a popular-vote majority) and a narrow 51 percent to 48 percent reelection win in 2004.

The elections of 2008 and 2012 featured decisive victories for African American Democrat Barack Obama, as he became the first Democratic candidate since Franklin Roosevelt to win a majority of the popular vote twice. Obama won the popular vote by 53 percent to Republican John McCain's 46 percent in 2008, with an electoral margin of 365 to 173 and by an impressive margin of more than 9.5 million votes,[3] a much stronger performance than President George W. Bush's three million–vote margin over Senator John Kerry in 2004.[4] Obama's first election was a decisive victory but not a landslide. He faced great obstacles in 2012 in part due to mediocre job ratings, consistently in the 45 percent to 48 percent range, and a very weak economy, with forty-two consecutive months of an unemployment rate of 8 percent or more. But Obama went on to wage an effective campaign that made the electoral framing a choice between two candidates rather than a referendum on his record. He ended up winning the popular vote by a 51 percent to 48 percent margin and the electoral vote by 332 to 206. Both Obama victories underscored a Democratic revival in presidential elections.

The study of political-campaign communication focuses on the messengers, the messages, the channels of communication (print, radio, television, social media, etc.), the audience, and the effects. The purpose of this chapter is to explain the presidential vote in 2012 by utilizing a framework that draws on key factors in the political communication to explain the vote. We focus on (1) the overall political environment, (2) the rules of the game and the electoral college, (3) the salience of party identification, (4) the messenger, (5) the messages and campaign strategy, (6) the channels of communication, and (7) and the audience or the demographic base of the presidential vote, with special attention given to the roles of gender and race/ethnicity in recent elections and the 2012 campaign. We begin first with observations on the overall political environment.

THE OVERALL POLITICAL ENVIRONMENT

The overall political environment has become even more polarized since Bush's re-election in 2004. His second term saw a decline in his job ratings, the economy, Iraq, and presidential management of problems like the aftermath of Hurricane Katrina.[5] Similarly, the Republicans in Congress stumbled badly with fiscal management, failed to deliver reforms, and grappled with ethical problems. A "trifecta of Iraq, congressional corruption, and Bush's unpopularity cost them their ruling majority in Congress."[6] Republicans lost thirty-one House seats and six Senate seats in Congress in 2006 as the Democrats took control.

A political and economic scenario emerged making Democrats heavy favorites to win the presidency in 2008, even before examining the respective strengths and weaknesses of the candidates. The worst economic environment in terms of public confidence fell during the post–World War II era. The average consumer confidence measured for the presidential party in power winning is ninety-six, and for the presidential party in power losing is seventy-two. To place the 2008 presidential contest in perspective, consumer confidence was an abysmal fifty-eight on the day of the election.[7] In the 2008 report "Obama's Road to the White House: A Gallup Review," analysts Saad, Jones, and Newport concluded that what was an essentially close presidential contest evaporated after the economic meltdown in mid-September. Specifically they noted that "McCain's lead came to an abrupt halt with the onset of the Wall Street crisis in mid-September. By September 17 the Republican nominee again trailed Obama by a few percentage points, and while the race briefly closed to a tie later in the month, McCain never regained the lead." The Gallup team called the economic crisis the "economic game changer."[8]

Another key change in the political environment in 2008 was the image of the Republican Party, held in low regard since 2006, making it difficult for both its members of Congress and its presidential candidates to attract voters. "Voters no longer think lean government, smart and strong defense, and good old-fashioned family values when they think Republican. They think reckless spenders, misguided war, and hypocrisy."[9] Entering the 2008 campaign, the GOP was still saddled with a negative image and recorded low scores on the generic ballot question in surveys by virtually all polling organizations. RealClearPolitics reported that the average spread on the generic congressional ballot when one averaged many different polls in fall 2008 was an 11.5 percent Democratic advantage (52.1 percent to 40.6 percent). Party image was a big constraint on Republican prospects, and in 2006, with low GOP scores in a large number of polls when respondents were asked which party they trusted most to handle problems.[10]

In 2008, a presidential-election year, the public expected the party controlling the White House to have a strong record on the central issues of peace and prosperity. Todd and Gawiser's comparison of the 2004 exit-survey data with the 2008 exit survey confirms the stunning decline in voter perception of Bush's governance. In 2004 voters believed the country was moving in the right direction by a 49 percent to 46 percent margin, but in 2008 they felt the opposite, with a striking 75 percent saying the country was moving in the wrong direction and only 20 percent saying it was moving in the right direction. Although Bush struggled throughout 2008 with job ratings 1 percent or 2 percent short of a majority, the exit survey in 2004 indicated 53 percent of voters approved of his job performance compared to 46 percent who disapproved. In 2008, his disapproval escalated to 71 percent, and his approval was only 27 percent. His Iraq policy had 51 percent approval and 45 percent disapproval in 2004, but in 2008 some 63 percent recorded disapproval and 36 percent approval. The largest single candidate trait cited by voters was change, and those favoring change supported Obama 89 percent to 9 percent over McCain. Obama emerged as the candidate of change.[11]

The midterm election of 2010 constituted a hostile political environment that impacted on the Democratic Party. This election is summarized well in Sean Trende's persuasive book, *The Lost Majority*. Trende reminds us how quickly our politics can change and how subject they are to events. He argues that Obama and the Democrats underestimated the fragility of their coalition and misread the scope of their election mandate. Enacting policies that lacked strong public support (health-insurance reform, cap-and-trade energy, massive deficit spending, etc.) cost the Democrats, who ended by losing a net of sixty-three seats in the House and six seats in the Senate. Republicans captured the House of Representatives and missed reaching a fifty-seat tie in the Senate because of choices made by Republican primary voters in Colorado, Nevada, and Delaware, who had selected candidates with little chance of winning the general election. All of the negative environmental factors previously mentioned in 2008 were also present, with a weak economy and high unemployment, a substantial drop in the president's job rating, a weak party image and support for the Democrats in the polls, substantial Democratic losses among working class and suburban voters, and a lower nonwhite turnout.[12] This negative election resulted in the worst showing in House midterm elections since 1938.

The negative environment continued in 2011 and 2012. President Obama had to defend to a doubtful public—increasingly unconvinced that a real recovery had taken hold—an economic record that had kept unemployment above 8 percent for forty-two consecutive months.[13] James Campbell wrote an interesting essay in August 2012 that placed Obama's overall economic record in historical context. He presented data traditionally used by presidential-election scholars to predict the election outcomes, including economic growth in the second quarter of election years from 1948 to 2012. Eleven presidents were listed, with the best being Richard Nixon in 1972, with 9.8 percent GDP, and the two lowest at tenth and eleventh places being Barack Obama in 2012 at 1.5 percent and Jimmy Carter with –7.9 percent real GDP growth in 1980. Campbell then used a larger aggregate figure of mean economic growth from the beginning of a president's second year to the second quarter of the election year for ten presidential administrations (total of ten quarters). Kennedy/Johnson was best at 5.2 percent real GDP growth, followed by Reagan with 4.1 percent in 1984. Barack Obama was ranked eight with real GDP growth at 2.1 percent, with Bush 1992 and Nixon/Ford 1976 tied for ninth and last place with real GDP growth at 1.5 percent. Campbell emphasized the economic vulnerability of Obama but also predicted that the key was "whether Mitt Romney will be seen by voters as an acceptable alternative to President Obama."[14] In short, there are two parts to a successful message for a challenger: The first is to make the case against the economic record of the incumbent, but also essential is to establish yourself as an acceptable alternative. It was the latter that Romney failed to do, and so Obama escaped defeat despite having one of the weakest economic records among presidents since 1948.

Other negative factors in the environment included the president's job ratings, which had hovered below 48 percent for most of 2012. Trende notes that Obama's approval had been below 48 percent about 80 percent of the time in Gallup polls taken since that January 1. Coming down the stretch in 2012, his approval tended to be in the 46 percent to 48 percent range, which was on the bubble for reelection. Also, the public's perceptions of both parties were negative, and a CBS News poll in August, for example, found the GOP with a 35 percent favorable rating and a 53 percent unfavorable rating. Democrats fared slightly better, with 43 percent favorable and 47 percent unfavorable.[15]

Trende notes that this disparity may have played a role in the conventions of the two parties. The Democratic convention was more like a challenger convention, with each speaker attacking Romney and reintroducing Obama. The attacks covered a wide a variety of issues, including cultural issues, designed to increase enthusiasm among Democratic core support groups. The Republican convention speakers by contrast did little to bash Obama and focused more on positive themes and on trying to reintroduce and rebrand their party and preempt attempts to link Romney and Ryan to the unpopular Bush administration. Given the negative public perceptions about their party, Republican speakers were trying to inoculate the ticket against the potentially devastating question, Do you really want to put the Republicans in charge? The Republican Party's image had declined since the successful midterm election of 2010, and time and convention effort were devoted to bettering that image.[16] In summary, the political environment since 2006 has become increasingly negative. It advantaged the Democrats in the 2006 midterm and the 2008 presidential races, while the 2010 midterm benefitted Republicans. In 2012 it was still negative and hurt both presidential candidates and both parties, but it hurt the Republican Party image more than it did the image of the Democratic Party.

RULES OF THE GAME: THE ELECTORAL COLLEGE AND THE POPULAR VOTE

Americans do not vote directly for president but instead cast their ballots for a slate of electors committed to a presidential ticket. Each state has a number of electoral votes equal to its representation in Congress. California, for example, has fifty-three representatives and two senators and therefore has fifty-five electoral votes. A small state like Wyoming has only one House member and two senators for three electoral votes. The District of Columbia has three electoral votes as a result of a constitutional amendment. There are 538 total electoral votes, and these votes in most states are counted on the basis of a winner-take-all rule: the ticket winning the state's popular vote receives all of the state's electoral votes. There are two exceptions—Maine (four electoral votes) and Nebraska (five electoral votes). Both award the ticket winning the state's popular vote two electoral votes and then give one electoral vote for each of the state's congressional districts. It takes a majority or 270 electoral votes to win the presidency. Prior to 2008, no candidate had captured a single electoral vote by winning a congressional district while losing a state until Obama carried a Nebraska congressional district while losing the state and earning one electoral vote in 2008. No such event occurred in 2012.

In presidential elections Democrats historically are consistently stronger in the East and the Pacific West, while Republicans have had an edge in the South, the mountain West, and the rural Midwest. The larger Midwestern states are often competitive and historically battlegrounds for both party tickets.[17] Recent political conditions and demographic factors have changed so that it is now easier for the

Democratic Party to forge an electoral-college majority. After the 2008 election Democratic strategist Mike Berman observed that the "Democrats have carried eighteen states plus D.C. in five straight presidential elections, totaling 248 electoral votes, just twenty-two short of the 270 to win. In contrast, Republicans have carried thirteen states in five straight elections, totaling a mere ninety-five electoral votes." If one adds to the list states where the Democrats won in four of the five elections from 1992 to 2008, their potential electoral vote increases to 264.[18] Victory is not impossible, but it is as a steeper climb for Republican candidates today. Given the clear electoral propensity of so many states, both party tickets focus on battleground or potential swing states. The list of swing states changes a little, of course, from election to election, depending on the candidate matchups, issues of the day, and the existing political environment.

The political landscape in 2008 was such that fourteen states were considered competitive in early summer, but six were dropped by the fall, replaced by two wild-card states and traditionally Republican Indiana. The final list included Colorado, Florida, Indiana, Missouri, Montana, Nevada, New Hampshire, New Mexico, North Carolina, Ohio, and Virginia. These eleven states were competitive or swing states in 2008. Barack Obama won nine of them, and McCain captured only two—Missouri and Montana.[19]

Obama's ambitious campaign strategy in 2008 paid off in the swing states as he won the three Republican-oriented southern states, Florida, North Carolina, and Virginia with the help of an increased African American turnout and support from upscale white voters. He also pulled upsets in three western states that Bush carried narrowly in 2004—Colorado, Nevada, and New Mexico. Finally, he also moved Ohio, Indiana, and Iowa into the Democratic column. It was an impressive victory in which nine states changed their votes from 2004. In 2004, only three states changed, as Iowa and New Mexico switched to Bush and New Hampshire to Kerry.[20]

There was considerable consensus among analysts and pundits that there were seven definite swing states in the battle for the presidency in 2012. They were New Hampshire in the East, Florida and Virginia in the South, Iowa and Ohio in the Midwest, and Colorado and Nevada in the West. Different analysts added four or five other states to this list. We believe that a most thoughtful and credible list was developed by RealClearPolitics, which is printed in table 9.1.[21] The other four potential swing states identified were Michigan, North Carolina, Pennsylvania, and Wisconsin. These were the eleven toss-up or swing states in 2012. Table 9.1 identifies the ten states and D.C. as solid Obama, with 154 total electoral votes. Another sixteen states, primarily small or medium sized in electoral votes—with the exception of Texas and its thirty-eight electoral votes—with 128 total electoral votes, are classified as solid Romney. There would be very few challenges by analysts to the other four categories, likely Obama (four states, thirty electoral votes), leans Obama (two states, seventeen electoral votes), likely Romney (six states, fifty-two electoral votes), and leans Romney (one state, Arizona, with eleven electoral votes).

Table 9.1.   Battle for the White House, 2012

Likely Obama (30)	Leans Obama (17)	Toss-Up (146)	Leans Romney (11)	Likely Romney (52)
CT (7)	MN (10)	CO (9)	AZ (11)	GA (16)
ME (4)	OR (7)	FL (29)		IN (11)
NJ (14)		IA (6)		MT (3)
NM (5)		MI (16)		MO (10)
		NV (6)		SC (9)
		NH (4)		SD (3)
		NC (15)		
		OH (18)		
		PA (20)		
		VA (13)		
		WI (10)		

Solid Obama (154)		Solid Romney (128)	
CA (55)		AL (9)	
DC (3)		AR (6)	
IL (20)		KS (6)	
MA (11)		LA (8)	
RI (4)		NE (5)	
DE (3)		OK (7)	
HI (4)		TX (38)	
MD (10)		WV (5)	
NY (29)		AK (3)	
VT (3)		ID (4)	
WA (12)		KY (8)	
		MS (6)	
		ND (3)	
		TN (11)	
		UT (6)	
		WY (3)	

Source: "Battle for White House," RealClearPolitics, accessed November 5, 2012, www.realclearpolitics.com/ epolls/2012/president/2012_elections_electoral_college_map_race_changes.html.

The many major campaign decisions and money allocated by Obama and Romney indicate that this was the battleground picture for the making of the president in 2012. Some analysts suggest that the 2012 campaign most resembled the Bush reelection campaign of 2004. Both had presidents with mediocre job ratings in the 45 percent to 48 percent range that were right on the reelection bubble, and both presidents had a mixed economic record at best. Both had adequate but uncharismatic challengers from Massachusetts. Both relied heavily on attack or negative advertising to damage and to frame the overall image of their challengers before the latter could frame themselves. Obama started a little earlier in the spring and Bush in the summer of the election year. Finally, both disregarded to a great extent the national polls to focus on voting publics in the critical swing states, and both executed successful campaign strategies.

In 2012 the Obama campaign strategy proved most effective. In early spring Obama campaign manager Jim Messina "proposed an unorthodox strategy" of moving early and blasting Romney on television in the critical swing states. This helped Obama win his reelection battle despite continuing economic anxieties, as it defined Romney early in the campaign.[22]

Obama waged an early attack-oriented campaign during the presidential-nomination contests. With limited media attention, he was able to target his advertising attacks on Romney in the critical swing states. Obama was unopposed on the Democratic side except for unknown or minor candidates while Romney had to win a divisive and competitive nomination contest. In analyzing the role of money in the Republican-nomination race on April 25, 2012, CNNMoney reported that Romney spent $76.6 million, not only far more than any other campaign but more than the combined spending of Ron Paul, Rick Santorum, and Newt Gingrich. The article ends with the interesting observation that only "one candidate has a jump on Romney in that category: President Obama. The Obama reelection campaign has brought in $191 million and already spent less than half—$89 million—of that total."[23] Although basically unopposed, the Obama campaign by late April had already outspent Mitt Romney and was on the attack.

This endeavor continued throughout the summer. One anonymous pro-Romney supporter observed in early August that Romney was picking up in red states where there was no attack advertising and voters were responding to national news. In the swing states, however, he felt that Obama's ad blitz was helping the president to build up solid margins with only Colorado close and a slight Romney lead in North Carolina.[24] The Obama campaign continually claimed publicly that they had the lead in the critical swing states.

Our research led us to conclude that these Obama claims were not simply political spin. They were correct empirically. We consulted RealClearPolitics to obtain lists of the numerous polls conducted in the eleven swing states[25] and examined them to see where the two candidates stood after the Republican and Democratic conventions in early September. Obama led in nine of the eleven states, and there were conflicting polls in North Carolina and Virginia, one favoring Obama and the other Romney. There were numerous state polls in October through November 4 with some house effects (slight bias) that advantaged one of the candidates, particularly firms identified as either Republican or Democratic but also house effects for some of the independent firms. Thus in most states there were some polls favoring Obama and others Romney. A careful examination of all October and early November polls suggests that in seven swing states at least three-fourths of the polls favored Obama. There was greater division among the polls in Colorado, Florida, and Virginia, but in these states a number favored Obama at the end. Most polls in North Carolina favored Romney or had the two candidates tied.

RealClearPolitics computes final averages—*RCP averages*—for polls in each state for the final phase of the campaign (the last ten to fourteen days depending on when the polls were in the field). In ten of the eleven states Obama was ahead, with only North Carolina favoring Romney (+2.2 percent). At the end in the states where there was more of a split in the polls, Obama had the higher RCP averages in Colorado (+4.7 percent), Florida (+.9 percent), and Virginia (+3.0 percent). Our conclusion is that Obama had an early lead in the swing states by early September with the possible exceptions of North Carolina and Virginia. He continued his dominance in the swing states even when Romney took a slight lead in some of the national polls after the first presidential debate in October. Campaigns matter, and Obama waged a stronger campaign in the swing states than did Romney.

PARTY IDENTIFICATION AND THE PRESIDENTIAL VOTE

A central factor in voting is party identification, a psychological concept that is measured by asking respondents if they think of themselves as a Democrat, Republican, Independent, or something else. Usually about 25 percent to 30 percent select Independent, although about a half or three-fifths have partisan leanings. About 70 percent of the electorate identifies with one of the two major parties, and as the exit surveys in the past four presidential elections reveal, the partisan identifiers cast close to 90 percent of their vote for their party's candidate. Party identification taps voter perception of their leanings at the present time. It should not be confused with party registration. Sometimes people register with one party but do not bother to change their registration or simply stay registered with the party to which their families historically have belonged. This is more of a problem in the South, where some older southerners think of themselves as Alabama Democrats or Mississippi Democrats and continue to identify as Democrats while voting Republican in presidential elections because the Democratic candidate may be viewed as too liberal.

Because of the potency of party identification, the two parties conduct massive registration drives in order to have an advantage over the other party. Because 90 percent of partisans vote for their party's candidate, and Independents often split, an edge in party identification is money in the electoral bank. It is an important step before addressing the candidate choices and issue menu in a given election. Because of the Republican image problems so evident in the election of 2006 and in many polls in 2007 and 2008, Obama encouraged Democrats to run up strong advantages in new party registrations to increase Democratic Party identification. Massive party-registration drives were successful in swing states, which created a Democratic edge.[26]

At the national level in 2008, Democrats had a striking 39 percent to 32 percent advantage in party identification, compared to parity in party identification 37 percent to 37 percent in 2004 and a slight Democratic 39 percent to 35 percent advantage in 2000.[27] Given past trends in which each party captures around 90 percent of its identifiers, this represented a dramatic change. Todd and Gawiser observed following the 2008 election that "this constituted the fewest Republicans in twenty-eight years. Much of the electorate may not have looked all that different from 2004, but the likelihood is that the members of the electorate was dramatically different."[28]

There was continual speculation and debate during the 2012 over what the party-identification distribution would be, and many opinion polls of likely voters differed in large part because of the party-identification distributions in the sample. Some Democratic and independent pollsters believed that Democrats would continue to have a 6 percent to 7 percent edge, while Republican and some independent pollsters felt it would be no more than 2 percent to 3 percent Democratic. This dispute continued through Election Day and was resolved by the national exit survey, which concluded that the party division had changed very little, with 38 percent identifying as Democratic, 32 percent Republican, and 29 percent as Independent or something else.[29] The 2012 identification profile helps to explain Obama's reelection.

To overcome such a disparity in party identification, Romney would have had to substantially pick up substantial crossover votes from the Democrats, which has not happened since the Reagan era, and/or win over a disproportionate percentage of Independents. A crossover vote was improbable because of strong support for Obama and the historical record of partisan voting for both parties. The highest presidential percentage of defections for Democrats was in 1972 when 33 percent cast ballots for Nixon over McGovern. The highest defection for Republican voters was in 1964 when 20 percent voted for Johnson over Goldwater.[30]

The historical record also shows that the Republican candidate received a majority of the Independent vote from 1952 to 2004. The exceptions were 1964, with Independents favoring Johnson, and 1992 and 1996, when Bill Clinton won by pluralities (39 percent to 30 percent, and 43 percent to 35 percent). John Kerry, the Democrat, narrowly won the Independent vote 49 percent to 48 percent in 2004, while Barack Obama captured Independents comfortably 52 percent to 44 percent in 2008. It is notable that that while McCain won Independents in eleven of thirteen southern states, the two southern states where Obama won the Independents were the heavily contested swing states of Florida, by 52 percent to 45 percent, and Virginia, 49 percent to 48 percent.[31] The 2012 exit data show more partisanship and even less crossover voting, as Obama won 92 percent of the Democrats and Romney only 7 percent. Romney took 93 percent of the Republicans compared to 6 percent for Obama. Romney did win the Independents by a small 50 percent to 45 percent margin, although the percentages were disappointing for Republicans as some pre-election polls had Romney with double-digit leads with this group.

Table 9.2 contains data on both the overall vote and the Independent vote in the eleven swing states in both 2012 and 2008. The data underscore that Romney did better than McCain in all eleven states with a range of 1 percent (Florida, New Hampshire, and Ohio) to 4 percent (Wisconsin). The numbers, however, were not strong enough to win. Obama won ten of the eleven states, with Romney's

Table 9.2. Swing States: 2012 and 2008 National Exit Poll Profiles, Comparison of All Voters (%) and Independents (%)

All Voters						
	2012			2008		
	% of the Vote	*Obama*	*Romney*	*% of the Vote*	*Obama*	*McCain*
National	100	51	48	100	53	46
CO	100	51	47	100	53	45
FL	100	50	49	100	51	48
IA	100	52	47	100	54	44
MI	100	54	45	100	57	41
NV	100	52	46	100	55	43
NH	100	52	46	100	54	45
NC	100	48	51	100	50	49
OH	100	50	48	100	52	47
PA	100	52	47	100	55	44
VA	100	51	48	100	53	46
WI	100	53	46	100	56	42

Independents						
	2012			2008		
	% of the Vote	*Obama*	*Romney*	*% of the Vote*	*Obama*	*McCain*
National	29	45	50	29	52	44
CO	38	45	49	39	54	44
FL	33	50	47	29	52	45
IA	34	55	41	33	56	41
MI	30	48	49	29	52	42
NV	34	43	51	32	54	41
NH	43	52	45	45	59	39
NC	29	42	57	27	39	60
OH	31	43	53	30	52	44
PA	20	45	50	18	58	39
VA	29	43	53	27	49	48
WI	31	49	48	29	58	39

Sources: "Battleground State Polls," RealClearPolitics, www.realclearpolitics.com/epolls/2012/president/battleground_states.html, and "National Election Results," Decision 2012, http://elections.nbcnews.com/ns/politics/2012/all#.UaZUJ5X8_a5 (individual state 2012 demographic data from aforementioned source derived by adding state code at the end—e.g., for Colorado use http://elections.msnbc.msn.com/ns/politics/2012/colorado/president/#.UKP); Chuck Todd and Sheldon Gawiser, *How Barack Obama Won* (New York: Vintage Books, 2009); all 2008 exit-poll data are from Todd and Gawiser.

sole victory being North Carolina (51 percent to 48 percent). Romney also out-performed McCain and won the Independent vote nationally, 50 percent to 45 percent compared to McCain's 52 percent to 44 percent loss to Obama. Similarly, Romney did better than McCain in nine of the swing states, matched him in Iowa, and trailed McCain by 3 percent in North Carolina, where Romney nevertheless topped Obama in the Independent vote 57 percent to 42 percent. Romney won the Independent vote in seven of the swing states, with Obama carrying Independents in four states—Florida, Iowa, New Hampshire, and Wisconsin. Overall, this was a Republican improvement, but the numbers were not strong enough to offset the overall Democratic advantage in party identification. To make a serious run at the incumbent, Romney needed to carry all eleven swing states with a double-digit edge among Independent voters.

Table 9.3 summarizes the vote in the eleven swing states for both Democratic and Republican identifiers. The proportion of Democratic identifiers went down slightly in seven of the states, remained the same in Virginia, and increased in three states, the most notable being a 3 percent increase in Colorado. More important than change in the proportion of the vote was the increase in partisan voting. Nationally Democratic identifiers went from 89 percent for Obama in 2008 to 92 percent in 2012. Moreover, in every single swing state in 2012 the percentage of Democrats voting for Obama was higher than those in 2008. The highest partisan Democratic distributions were in Colorado and New Hampshire, at 96 percent, and Iowa, Michigan, Nevada, and Wisconsin, at 95 percent. The lowest were in North Carolina and Pennsylvania, still an impressive 91 percent in both. In short, while crossover voting in recent swing-state elections has never been high, it was at a historic low level for Democrats in 2012.

Table 9.3 documents very miniscule drops in the percentage of Republican in seven of these states compared to 2008, with two remaining the same and two with slight increases. Like their Democratic counterparts there was an increase in partisanship among Republicans nationally with 90 percent for McCain to 93 percent for Romney. Increased Republican partisan voting occurred in all eleven states, with North Carolina and Michigan the highest at 96 percent and Florida the lowest at 92 percent. The data on both parties underscores the partisan nature of the environment and the limited potential for swing-state crossover voting.

In developing campaign strategies historically, candidates have embraced partisan reinforcement, mobilization (registering, contacting, and turning out more partisans), winning Independents—particularly those with partisan leanings—and crossover voting. Given current trends, it appears that the crossover voting of the past may be gone with the political wind. Mobilization of partisans seems to be the most promising strategy. Consider a hypothetical 2 percent increase in the proportion of the vote for one of the political parties. Assume that 90 percent of the vote is a partisan vote and that that party would experience a net increase of 1.6 percent in its vote. Assume a hypothetical increase of 2 percent in the Independent vote, and an extremely generous 60 percent of the vote for one party. The net increase in the vote

Table 9.3. Swing States: 2012 and 2008 National Exit Poll Profiles, Comparison of Democratic and Republican Voters (%)

| | **Democrats** | | | | | |
| | 2012 | | | 2008 | | |
	% of the Vote	Obama	Romney	% of the Vote	Obama	McCain
National	38	92	7	39	89	10
CO	33	96	3	30	92	7
FL	35	90	9	37	87	12
IA	33	95	4	34	93	6
MI	40	95	4	41	93	6
NV	37	95	4	38	93	6
NH	30	96	4	29	92	8
NC	39	91	8	42	90	9
OH	38	92	7	39	89	10
PA	45	91	9	44	90	10
VA	39	94	6	39	92	8
WI	36	95	4	39	95	5

| | **Republicans** | | | | | |
| | 2012 | | | 2008 | | |
	% of the Vote	Obama	Romney	% of the Vote	Obama	McCain
National	32	7	93	32	9	90
CO	29	5	94	31	13	87
FL	33	8	92	34	12	87
IA	33	7	93	33	9	90
MI	30	4	96	29	10	89
NV	29	6	93	30	11	88
NH	27	6	94	27	11	89
NC	33	4	96	31	4	95
OH	30	5	94	31	8	92
PA	35	7	93	37	13	87
VA	32	6	94	33	8	92
WI	32	5	95	33	10	89

Sources: "2012 Election President: Live Results," RealClearPolitics, accessed November 9, 2012, www .realclearpolitics.com/elections/live_results/president/; "Presidential Election Results," MSNBC, accessed November 9, 2012, http://elections.msnbc.msn.com/ns/politics/2012/all/president/#.UKP (individual state 2012 demographic data from aforementioned source derived by adding state code at the end—e.g., for Colorado use http://elections.msnbc.msn.com/ns/politics/2012/colorado/president/#.UKP); Chuck Todd and Sheldon Gawiser, *How Barack Obama Won* (New York: Vintage Books, 2009); all 2008 exit-poll data are from Todd and Gawiser.

for that party would be only 0.4 percent. Although maximizing the Independent vote is a laudable goal, there is a larger political payoff for mobilizing additional political identifiers. Two recent examples of successful mobilization were by George W. Bush in 2004 and Barack Obama in 2008. In 2004 Bush focused on increasing the vote of white evangelicals more likely to support him and added 3.2 million Republican voters to the electorate. In 2008 Barack Obama concentrated on increasing the number of African American voters and added 3.5 million Democrats to the list.[32]

THE MESSENGER

At the heart of every campaign communication are the messengers or candidates and their messages, and the issues and candidate traits they invoke to persuade the audience or voters to support them. Analysts quite frequently draw too strong a line between issues and personality/character in campaigns when the reality is that American elections have always been image-oriented and issue-involved. The two concepts are like two overlapping concentric circles. Candidates use issues, for example, to demonstrate personal qualities, like commitment to change, experience, competence, leadership, vision, trust, and empathy. Voters may lack detailed issue knowledge themselves, but they can observe campaign behavior and assess how candidates fare on important personal traits. Alternatively, voters may focus on the issues identified by the candidate to assess if he or she really cares about people like themselves or is biased toward other groups.[33] For analytical purposes, we analyze messengers and candidate issues separately.

In the 2012 book *The Candidate: What It Takes To Win and Hold The White House*, Popkin explores in great detail many past campaigns and what it takes to be an effective presidential candidate. Among the most desirable traits he identifies are the ability to persuade voters he or she is one of them, to convince voters that he or she understands their lives and shares their values, to show vision on how he or she would lead the country the next four years, to state how he or she would lead us there with a demonstration of ability to oversee a large campaign, and to show people how he or she could command the ship of state.[34] Before voters respond to a message, they develop a gut appraisal of the messenger. If they have serious reservations about the messenger, they are unlikely to be persuaded by the campaign messages. The election of 2012 was no different, and once again voters expressed concern about candidate traits and issues. Most of the empirical data used to make observations comes from the election exit surveys for 2012, 2008, and 2004.

First, at the heart of the communication process dating back to Aristotle is the fact that both the messenger and the message are important. There has to be source credibility for individuals to accept the message sent. Our previous research demonstrated that the Democratic presidential candidates Gore and Kerry had a slight advantage on the messages and issues in 2000 and 2004 but Bush had an edge as the messenger. This is illustrated by looking at voter preferences on candidate traits as well as voter preferences on issues.[35] One can also find in the 2004 exit survey that voters by 53 percent to 46 percent had a favorable view of Bush but by 51 percent to 47 percent an unfavorable view of Kerry.[36] This question was asked in the 2012 exit survey, and 53 percent had a favorable opinion of Obama and 46 percent were unfavorable. By contrast, 50 percent had an unfavorable opinion of Romney with 47 percent favorable.[37] Voters thus gave a higher rating to Obama over Romney as a messenger.

Second, the 2012 exit-survey data show that Obama had a strong advantage in 2012 as a messenger compared to Romney.[38] We previously mentioned his edge in voter perceptions of favorability. After struggling to reach a majority most of the year, Obama's job-approval exit-poll rating was 54 percent favorable and 45 percent unfavorable. At the national level, the question Who is in touch with voters like you? found voters favoring Obama 53 percent to 43 percent for Romney. This is the Popkin concern that the candidate be perceived as one of us and one who shares our values. When asked who is to blame for current economic problems, some 53 percent blamed Bush and only 38 percent Obama, despite Obama's weak economic record.

Finally, candidate perceptions influence who voters trust on policy. Voters trusted Obama over Romney on Medicare by a 52 percent to 44 percent margin. The economy was Romney's strongest issue, but even here Obama had a slight advantage. Voter perception marginally favored Romney by 49 percent to 48 percent on who could handle the economy. This was tempered by the fact that 4 percent of the 49 percent who chose Romney voted for Obama while only 1 percent of the 48 percent who selected Obama voted for Romney. The end result was a slight overall edge for Obama. Similarly by 49 percent to 47 percent voters felt Romney would better handle the deficit, but 3 percent of the 49 percent selecting Romney voted for Obama compared to only 1 percent of the 47 percent selecting Obama voted for Romney. Again, neither a perception that he could better handle the economy nor the deficit was strong enough to help Romney overcome Obama.

The third observation concerns swing states. Table 9.4 presents the national data and the data for the eleven swing states for answers to the questions (1) Who is more in touch with people? (2) Who is to blame for current economic problems? (3) Who can better handle Medicare? and (4) Who can better handle the economy? The question of who can better handle the deficit was not included. Most of the swing states are close to or only a little above or below the national averages for these four questions. The voters in all eleven swing states favored Obama over Romney on who was in touch with people like them. North Carolina even favored Obama on the in-touch question, but by a lower 49 percent to 47 percent margin. Only ten of the states were asked the blame question, and all ten blamed Bush over Obama. Similarly, only ten were asked who can better handle Medicare, and all ten chose Obama. There was more division on who could better handle the economy, with five states giving a slight edge to Romney, four favoring Obama, and two that were tied. Although Romney did slightly better in swing states on the economy, like the national distributions, a small net percentage of voters who selected one candidate defected to the opposite candidate on the electoral ballot, benefitting Obama. Overall, Obama had the edge as a messenger in the swing states.

Table 9.4.   2012 National and Swing State Exit Poll Profiles: Who Is More in Touch, Who's to Blame for Current Economic Problems, Who Can Better Handle the Economy, and Who Can Better Handle Medicare? (% of All National and Swing-State Voters)

	Who is more in touch with people like you?			Who's to blame for current economic problems?	
	Obama	Bush		Obama	Bush
National	53	43	National	38	53
CO	51	42	CO	36	51
FL	49	46	FL	42	51
IA	55	41	IA	37	53
MI	55	39	MI	34	57
NV	51	44	NV	38	52
NH	55	42	NH	38	57
NC	49	47	NC	40	49
OH	50	46	OH	40	51
PA	56	41	PA	N/A	N/A
VA	52	45	VA	43	52
WI	52	45	WI	41	54

	Who can better handle the economy?			Who can better handle Medicare?	
	Obama	Romney		Obama	Romney
National	48	49	National	52	44
CO	46	49	CO	N/A	N/A
FL	45	51	FL	50	46
IA	49	46	IA	51	44
MI	53	43	MI	54	42
NV	46	49	NV	53	42
NH	50	47	NH	51	46
NC	47	51	NC	49	46
OH	46	50	OH	49	46
PA	52	45	PA	49	47
VA	49	49	VA	54	43
WI	49	49	WI	51	47

Sources: "2012 Election President: Live Results," RealClearPolitics, accessed November 9, 2012, www .realclearpolitics.com/elections/live_results/president/; "Presidential Election Results," MSNBC, accessed November 9, 2012, http://elections.msnbc.msn.com/ns/politics/2012/all/president/#.UKP (individual state 2012 demographic data from aforementioned source derived by adding state code at the end—e.g., for Colorado use http://elections.msnbc.msn.com/ns/politics/2012/colorado/president/#.UKP).

Romney was hurt throughout the campaign by his more formal and wooden style, and his propensity for verbal gaffes made him look out of touch with average voters. Continual attacks by his Republican opponents for the nomination and by Obama throughout the year on his wealth, his job record at Bain Capital, and his initial reluctance to release tax returns hurt his image and drove up his negatives. Being wealthy alone may not have been a fatal flaw, but he said things that reinforced a distance from the average American. It reinforced the out-of-touch wealthy-person image when he said that "some of his best friends own NASCAR teams [and] corporations are people and [made] a $10,000 wager. But in terms of verbal miscues nothing damaged Romney as badly as his caught-on-tape moment at a fundraiser full of wealthy donors on the 47 percent of Americans who don't pay income taxes."[39] In the final analysis, Obama tops Romney as a campaign messenger.

THE MESSAGE

Messages are essential components of the communication process. They are essential in presenting the overall campaign narratives as well as positioning candidates on the issues. In 2012 there was much media discussion as to whether this campaign would be a referendum on Obama or it would simply be seen as a choice between two candidates. In reality all campaigns are a mixture of both, but particular campaigns may be weighted more heavily to one of these campaign frames with less support for the other. The challenger Romney sought to make it a referendum on Obama's record, while Obama tried to discredit Romney as an acceptable alternative so that it would be seen as a choice between two candidates.

Dan Balz emphasizes that Obama wanted to make the election a choice but not one on his record. He sought to discredit Romney as a wealthy candidate who favored the rich, destroyed jobs while at Bain Capital, etc. Some Democrats said that even before the convention the Obama campaign had done a good job drawing sharp contrasts with Romney. Obama's support of the auto bailouts, his decision to send the Navy SEALs team to kill Osama bin Laden, and his claims that he had helped to set the foundation for economic recovery were all part his narrative on accomplishment claims. His weakness was an economic record of unemployment at 8 percent or higher for forty-two consecutive months.[40]

The narrative Obama chose to deal with the state of the economy involved blaming Bush for the bad economy (tax cuts for the rich, etc.) and stressing that he had inherited a terrible economic situation and still needed more time to deal with it. Although the message was heavily criticized as ineffective, Obama nevertheless used the argument that things could have been worse. He even went so far as to claim that had he not done what he did the country could have plunged into a depression. What hurt politically was the persistence of unemployment and slow economic growth. One Democratic strategist said in early September that "his most convincing defense of his economic record is contrast and comparison with the other side's proposals moving forward. If he is defending his record, he is not doing what he needs to do."[41] Obama tended to follow this advice and did not opt for refutation but rather a counterargument that involved a comparison and contrast between the two candidates.

Obama was on the attack in early spring and all summer with his advertising, his messages of the day, his conference calls, and his tweets attempting to discredit Romney as an acceptable alternate to manage the economy. Although voters dislike negative ads, studies show they nevertheless process information from these ads when evaluating candidates. Contrast ads can do more to move voters than straight personal attacks or purely positive ads.[42]

The basic advantages of attack ads have stood the test of time and were established almost twenty years ago in Pfau and Kenski.[43] The advantages are that attack messages generate more attention, are more likely to be remembered than positive ads, and are effective if the message appears credible and is perceived as not going over the top. Attack messages, however, need an immediate response if they are frequent because a lingering negative message if not dealt with could become believable to some voters even if it is false. Finally, an effective approach to attack advertising is to inoculate and frame your own message before the attack occurs. Even if there are weaknesses in your background or issues positions, you are far better off framing them before your opponent does.

Bill Clinton in 1992 and George Bush in 1988 took many strong attacks before their respective party conventions, but both responded and turned their campaigns around. Neither, however, had taken the kind of pounding on the airwaves that Mitt Romney absorbed in the summer of 2012 by the Obama campaign. Much of what voters knew about Romney came from negative ads and attacks by Democrats and earlier by his Republican rivals during the primaries and caucuses. Romney spent little money after the primaries to rebut these ads or tell his own story.[44] He had exhausted his money in the nomination fight and spent considerable time from mid-April raising money, which he believed he could not spend until he was the party's official nominee. As noted earlier, the failure to respond early was a critical mistake as Obama's attacks moved his numbers up in the swing states and made the case that Romney was an unacceptable alternative.

Romney's core message from the very beginning of his campaign involved jobs and the economy and his credentials as a businessman, governor, and Olympic organizer to address the problem. Obama could not fix the problem, but Romney could. His strategy and message was to make the election a referendum on Obama's economic record, focusing on unemployment at 8 percent or more for forty-two consecutive months, slow economic growth, and trillion dollar deficits. After his selection of Paul Ryan as his vice presidential running mate, Romney also opted to fight for Medicare reform and called for a return of the $716 billion dollars he said that Obama transferred out of Medicare to pay for the new health-care reform entitlements.[45]

Some critics claimed that in developing his economic message from the nomination to the start of the general election Romney failed to provide a vision. Simply pointing out Obama's failed economic policies was not enough. It was a little late, but that vision was provided in the first general-election debate where Romney clearly dominated Obama. Jay Cost observes that it provided an emphasis on growth, prosperity, income, and jobs that is reminiscent of the visions provided by past successful Republican presidents like McKinley, Coolidge, and Reagan and that his message tied the importance of probusiness economic policies to mass prosperity. Helping businesses grow creates jobs, raises income, and spreads prosperity to all citizens.[46] This vision, however, should have been put forth at the beginning of the Republican nomination race in January.

A debate critique by some conservatives of Romney was his failure to take the Bush blame game head on because of his strategy to distance himself from the Bush administration. This strategy abandoned the opportunity to address the deficit issue and the Bush blame game thematic. Moore notes that it is hard for conservatives to defend the Bush record in spending, prescription-drug benefits for Medicare, the biggest increase in education in twenty years, the biggest transportation bill, etc. It is true that the deficit was falling rapidly until the Democrats took over Congress after the 2006 midterm. In the first debate and in response to a Bush question Romney could have noted that the deficit had fallen in fiscal year 2007 to $161 billion, and as a share of GDP the deficit had fallen to 1.2 percent. After the Democratic takeover, the deficit soared to $459 billion in 2008 and then to $1.4 trillion in 2009. Bush deserves some of the blame, but the Democratic Congress proved even more damaging to our country's finances. Specifically Moore notes that "the deficit the past four years has averaged 7 percent of GDP and $1 trillion a year. It would have been nice if Mr. Romney had told that to the nationwide audience on Tuesday night."[47]

It might have helped him address the persistent Obama attack that Bush was to blame for the state of the economy, as this Obama message resonated in 2012.

Finally, we note that the Obama attacks were effective not only on candidate traits and perception of the messenger but also on messages. In his attacks on Romney as an out-of-touch plutocrat, Obama claimed that Romney's policies would help the wealthy. The success of his message attacks is confirmed by the data in table 9.5. At the national level in the 2012 exit poll, two questions asked were: (1) Who do Obama's policies generally favor? and (2) Who do Romney's policies generally favor? Of the 86 percent of voters who commented on Obama policies, only 10 percent said the rich, 44 percent the middle class, and 31 percent the poor. Thus, three-quarters of the voters regarded him as not favoring the rich. Of the 89 percent of voters who commented on Romney policies, 53 percent said the rich, followed by 34 percent the middle class, and only 2 percent the poor. Hence over half believed his policies benefitted the rich, and only one-third said they favored the middle class.

The table also contains comparable data for nine of the eleven swing states. The conclusion is the same. In all nine swing states, Obama's policies were viewed as disproportionately favoring the middle class and the poor, the highest state being New Hampshire with 91 percent expressing an opinion and 49 percent saying middle

Table 9.5.   2012 National and Swing State Exit Poll Profiles: Which Groups Are Favored by Obama's and Romney's Policies? (% of All National and Swing-State Voters)

	Who do Obama's policies generally favor?				Who do Romney's policies generally favor?		
	Rich	Middle Class	Poor		Rich	Middle Class	Poor
National	10	44	31	National	53	34	2
CO	n/a	n/a	n/a	CO	n/a	n/a	n/a
FL	8	44	32	FL	53	35	2
IA	11	47	28	IA	54	35	1
MI	8	46	32	MI	56	34	n/a
NV	9	44	30	NV	56	34	1
NH	9	49	33	NH	55	38	1
NC	8	40	29	NC	47	35	4
OH	10	43	36	OH	56	35	1
PA	n/a	n/a	n/a	PA	n/a	n/a	n/a
VA	9	46	34	VA	53	38	1
WI	12	48	32	WI	54	38	1

Source: "2012 Election President: Live Results," RealClearPolitics, accessed November 9, 2012, www .realclearpolitics.com/elections/live_results/president/; "Presidential Election Results," MSNBC, accessed November 9, 2012, http://elections.msnbc.msn.com/ns/politics/2012/all/president/#.UKP (individual state 2012 demographic data from aforementioned source derived by adding state code at the end—e.g., for Colorado use http://elections.msnbc.msn.com/ns/politics/2012/colorado/president/#.UKP).

class and 32 percent saying the poor. The lowest was North Carolina with only 77 percent offering an opinion, with 40 percent saying Obama's policies favored the middle class and 29 percent saying the poor. Obama's messages identifying him as more supportive of the middle class and the poor were effective. Turning to perceptions of who would be favored by Romney's policies, voters in all nine states said his policies were most supportive of the rich, with highs of 56 percent in Michigan, Nevada, and Ohio, and the low in North Carolina, with 47 percent. Only low single-digit percentages selected the poor, while virtually all of the middle-class percentages in the nine states were close to the national percentage of 34 percent. Thus Obama's attack messages were effective in persuading voters that Romney's policies would favor the rich. Romney did not inoculate against the Obama attacks before they were launched. Moreover, Romney waited too long to respond and was unsuccessful in his use of refutation and counterargument to mitigate the electoral impact of these attacks. In 2012 the message advantage went to Obama.

CHANNELS OF COMMUNICATION

The electoral environment is changing with respect to which channels of communication voters utilize to get information on presidential campaigns. General news-consumption habits of the country are changing rapidly. A September 2012 study by the Pew Research Center presented data from 1991 to 2012 to assess news consumption from 1991 to 2012. In it TV news consumption dropped 13 percent from 68 percent in 1991 to 55 percent in 2012, newspapers declined 27 percent from 56 percent to 29 percent, and radio fell 21 percent from 54 percent to 33 percent. Online was nonexistent in 1991, so the study used 2002 and found an increase in online use from 24 percent to 39 percent. Television, newspapers, and radio are increasingly less important to the citizenry with respect to general news consumption.[48]

Analyzing the trends, Pew's Andrew Kohut writes that "the transformation of the nation's news landscape has already taken a heavy toll on print news sources, particularly print newspapers. But there are now signs that television news—which so far has held onto its audience through the rise on the Internet—also is increasingly vulnerable, as it may be losing hold on the next generation of news consumers."[49]

The Pew Research Center released another study in late October 2012 comparing where people turned for campaign news in January 2012 and compared it to where they turned for campaign news in October 2012. Most sources gained or remained the same. Cable news was the single largest source, but the Internet gained the most. The study did percentage breakdowns within news-source categories. People turned to television cable news for campaign news by 36 percent in January and 41 percent in October. They turned to local news by 32 percent in January and 38 percent in October, to network news 26 percent in January and 31 percent in October, to cable-news talk shows 15 percent in January and 18 percent in October, and finally to late-night comedy shows 9 percent in January and 12 percent in October. Cable news is clearly the leader, followed by local news and network news.[50]

The study also finds that 25 percent turned to the Internet in January for campaign news and 36 percent in October. Looking at print sources, local newspapers were 20 percent in January and 23 percent in October, and national newspapers were at 8 percent in January and 13 percent in October. Radio sources did not show a change over ten months. NPR was 12 percent in both January and October, and talk-radio shows were 16 percent in both January and October. Social media doubled but still remained limited. Facebook was 6 percent in January and 12 percent in October, Twitter 2 percent in January and 4 percent in October, and YouTube 3 percent in January and 7 percent in October. Again, cable news was still first, but the "biggest gains have come on the Internet—both to the websites of traditional news sources and those native to the Web."[51]

A key concern in channels of communication is the tone of the coverage and whether it is more positive or negative for a candidate. In 2008 the media-coverage advantage went to Obama. According to the Center for Media and Public Affairs (CMPA), Barack Obama received the most positive coverage in the twenty-year history of these studies with 68 percent positive evaluations from the four major networks. Robert Lichter, director of the nonpartisan center for Media and Public Affairs at George Mason University, noted that "Obama's positive press is the strongest since we began monitoring election news in 1988." By contrast, he points out that only 33 percent of Senator McCain's coverage was positive, the worst of any candidate since George H. W. Bush received only 29 percent positive coverage in 1988.[52]

The situation differed substantially in 2012. More comprehensive media research was done in 2012 by the Pew Research Center's Project for Excellence in Journalism in various studies in which the analysis was produced through two forms of coding media content. One involved computer-assisted coding of more than eleven thousand news outlets. The second involved human coding of fifty-two key news outlets covering print, broadcast, cable, audio, and online means of distribution. The first 2012 study focused on the nomination process and covered the period from January 2 to April 15.[53] They found that horse-race coverage (focus on campaigns and winning and losing) still dominated, but it was only 64 percent in 2012 compared to 80 percent for the Republicans and 80 percent for the Democrats in 2008. The coverage was largely negative for all of the candidates. The public was offered a mixed view of Romney, one that emphasized his wealth and his record as a private equity executive and focused on the difficulties he'd had as a campaigner in persuading conservative voters to accept him. He fared better than most of the candidates in that he had more positive than negative coverage for one week after an early January New Hampshire–primary victory and also for the weeks after his primary victories in Michigan and Arizona in late February to mid-April when he clinched the nomination. In this time frame, the media spent considerable coverage on Romney's momentum and the mathematical inevitability of his winning the nomination. For most of the primary and caucus season, "the tone of Romney's news coverage vacillated primarily between mixed and unflattering." The public was exposed to mostly a negative portrayal of Obama, and his positive coverage never exceeded his negative coverage in any singe week from early January to mid-April. The negative portrayal "in substantial part is a function of the fact that for many months he has been the target of multiple Republican candidates attacking his record and his competence as they sought to take his job."[54]

The Pew Research Center did another study covering the preconvention period from May 29 to August 5. The coverage of both Obama and Romney was highly negative, and neither had the edge. The study found that 72 percent of the Obama-narrative coverage was negative, as was 71 percent of Romney's narrative. Five of the six top narratives for both candidates were negative. Half of all the assertions about Obama focused on whether his administration helped to fix the recession or made it worse. Most of the coverage (36 percent) suggested he had failed to do enough. This was twice as much as the counterargument that the economy would have been weaker had it not been for his policy actions (16 percent). The Romney media coverage included a number of sizable and negative themes. The largest was that he was a callous "vulture capitalist," which made up 14 percent of the assertions. The theme that he was a rich elitist was almost as large (13 percent). The notion that he was a weak, gaffe-prone campaigner was also substantial (11 percent), as was asking if his policies would hurt the economy (10 percent). One explanation for the substantial coverage of both, the study concludes, is that campaigns now play a much larger role in shaping the news. 58 percent of the statements about the record and character of the candidates on the twelve most prominent websites, for example, were made by campaigns and surrogates. Outside experts had the smallest coverage online and were responsible for making only 2 percent of the statements. The positive arguments of both candidates received little coverage.[55] The media in 2012 were simply part of the overall negative environment.

According to the Pew Research Center, the negative media coverage continued into the autumn, the one exception to the negative pattern falling in the final days of the campaign from October 29 to November 5. At this time there was a surge in the positive coverage of Obama, and the negative coverage of Romney was accompanied by a drop in attention for Romney. Obama's positive coverage exceeded his negatives by 10 percent, and he was aided by the positive assessments of his response to Superstorm Sandy. Romney's coverage was 17 percent more negative than positive.[56] Overall, the media coverage in 2012 was disproportionately negative, and it was simply a manifestation of the negative political environment.

THE AUDIENCE

Explaining the vote requires an analysis of voter-support demographics for both level of support (percentage of the vote) and the percentage changes from the previous election. Most demographic groups do not divide evenly between the two parties but have historic tendencies to favor either the Democratic or Republican ticket.[57] Table 9.6 shows the demographic compositions and distributions of the vote for both 2012 and 2008. The 2008 election was not a good Republican year, and McCain registered lower percentages in virtually all voter-demographic categories when compared to Bush. McCain's strongest support came from Republican identifiers (90 percent), conservatives (78 percent), and white evangelicals (74 percent).[58]

The problem for McCain was that Obama ran strongly across the board and did not allow many openings. Of particular significance is that the party-identification distribution favored the Democratic candidate 39 percent to 32 percent, compared to 37 percent parity in 2004. Obama captured 89 percent of the Democrats to McCain's 90 percent of Republicans. This meant there was very little voter crossover. Although both candidates appealed to Independents, Obama dominated in the end by a 52 percent to 44 percent margin. Obama also increased the Democratic margins both for black and Hispanic voters. The percentage of African Americans voting moved from 11 percent in 2004 to 13 percent in 2008. Youth voters (the much-written-about eighteen- to twenty-nine-year-old group) did not make a major jump in turnout, inching up from 17 percent of the vote in 2004 to 18 percent in 2008, but their margin of Democratic support was a stunning 66 percent to 32 percent, compared to 54 percent to 45 percent in 2004. Obama also won back the Catholic vote by 54 percent to 45 percent, a vote Bush had carried 52 percent to 47 percent in 2004.

Table 9.6. Demographic Comparison of 2012 and 2008 Presidential Vote

Category	% of 2012 Vote	2012 (%) Obama	2012 (%) Romney	% of 2008 Vote	2008 (%) Obama	2008 (%) McCain	Republican Difference
Total Vote	100	51	48	100	53	46	+2
Urban	32	62	36	30	63	35	+1
Suburban	47	48	50	49	50	48	+2
Rural	21	39	59	21	45	53	+6
Right Track	46	93	6	20	27	17	−11
Wrong Track	52	13	84	75	62	36	+48
Obama Job Approval	54	89	9	NA			NA
Obama Job Disapproval	45	3	94	NA			NA
Democrats	38	92	7	39	89	10	−3
Independents	29	45	50	29	52	44	+6
Republicans	32	6	93	32	9	90	+3
Liberal	25	86	11	22	89	10	+1
Moderate	41	56	41	44	60	39	+2
Conservative	35	17	82	34	20	78	+4
White	72	39	59	74	43	55	+4
Black	13	93	6	13	95	4	+2
Hispanic	10	71	27	9	67	31	−4
Men	45	45	52	47	49	48	+4
Women	55	53	44	53	56	43	+1
Married	60	42	56	66	47	52	+4
Unmarried	40	62	35	34	65	33	+2
18–29 years	19	60	37	18	66	32	+5
30–44 years	27	52	45	29	52	46	−1
45–59 years	38	47	51	37	50	49	+ 2
65 years plus	16	44	56	16	45	53	+3
Protestant	29	37	62	54	45	54	+8
Catholic	25	50	48	27	54	45	+3
White Evangelical	26	21	78	26	24	74	+4
Weekly Church	42	39	59	40	43	55	+4
Union Household	18	58	40	21	59	39	+1

Sources: Henry C. Kenski and Kate M. Kenski, "Explaining the Vote in the Election of 2008," in *The 2008 Presidential Campaign: A Communication Perspective,* ed. Robert E. Denton, Jr. (Lanham, Md.: Rowman & Littlefield, 2009), 195.

The data in table 9.6 show that Romney improved on McCain's performance by low single-digit percentages in most demographic categories with the exception of right-track, Democrats, Hispanics, and voters thirty to forty-four years of age. Obama received correspondingly low single-digit percentage drops in various demographic categories but emerged in the end with a solid 51 percent to 48 percent victory. Romney's largest gains were best with wrong-track voters, Protestants, rural voters, and voters eighteen to twenty-nine years of age (a group that he still lost decisively). The problem was that these gains were not large enough to overcome Obama's edge in various categories. Take the Independents, for example: Romney won them 50 percent to 45 percent, compared to McCain's loss of Independents by a 52 percent to 44 percent margin. The 5 percent Independent edge in the national exit survey, not to mention the eleven swing-state surveys, was simply not big enough to constitute a serious electoral threat. Some of the polls in October showed Romney with double-digit margins among Independents that did not hold up on election day.

Looking at the various categories, we see much continuity with 2008. In 2012 Obama retained urban voters by a healthy 62 percent to 36 percent margin, while Romney improved the GOP percentage among rural voters to 59 percent versus 39 percent. Romney captured suburban voters narrowly (50 percent to 48 percent), whereas they narrowly favored Obama in 2008. The latter was a disappointment for Republicans as some analysts thought that Romney was the type of Republican candidate who could run well in non-Southern suburban areas, like Bush 41 had in 1988. The suburban vote gain was simply too small.

Republicans had the advantage on right track/wrong track this time, whereas Obama had the advantage in 2008. We note, however, that the 46 percent saying right track in 2012 (much improved over 2011) was considerably higher than the 20 percent saying right track in 2008. Obama's job approval increased in the final weeks of the campaign, and he ended up with a 54 percent to 45 percent advantage, with approvers favoring him disproportionately and disapprovers opposing him decisively. As noted earlier, one of the most important factors in this election is that the party-identification distributions changed little and favored the Democrats 38 percent to 32 percent. Partisan voting increased for both parties with 92 percent of Democrats favoring Obama and 93 percent of the Republicans Romney. As noted earlier, Independents swung from Obama to Romney by a narrow 50 percent to 45 percent. The liberal voter percentage distribution increased from 22 percent in 2008 to 25 percent in 2012. Moderates dropped 3 percent overall to 41 percent of all voters, while conservatives improved by 1 percent to a total of 34 percent. As usual, a high 86 percent of liberals supported the Democrat, while a high 82 percent of conservatives voted Republican. The moderates once again voted for Obama 56 percent to 41 percent, although it was a 4 percent drop in support from 2008.

As the Obama campaign team predicted, the white vote dropped from 74 percent in 2008 to 72 percent in 2012. The black vote was 13 percent in both elections but really was about 0.2 percent higher in 2012. The Hispanic vote moved from 9 percent in 2008 to 10 percent in 2012. Among whites, Romney captured 59 percent compared to McCain's 55 percent. The black vote's Obama support was 2 percent lower in 2012 but still registered at a stunning 93 percent. The Hispanic vote was 4 percent more for Obama in 2012 than it had been in 2008 with a sizable Obama advantage of 71 percent to 27 percent. This was one group where Romney did poorly, and his policy positions dating back to the primaries hurt him.

Obama lost men 52 percent to 45 percent, compared to a narrow male edge in 2008 of 49 percent to 48 percent. The gender-gap advantage with women continued to favor Obama and by a margin of 55 percent to 44 percent. Although Romney picked up a few percentage points with both groups, the marital gap continued, with married voters voting Romney 56 percent to 42 percent and unmarried voters or singles Obama 62 percent to 35 percent. It is also important to note that unmarried voters as a percentage of the total vote rose by 6 percent compared to 2008, which clearly benefitted Obama.

In comparison to McCain in 2008, Romney made small gains in the age categories of eighteen to twenty-nine years, forty-five to fifty-nine years, and sixty-five years plus but dropped by 1 percent with the thirty to forty-four-year-old group. Voters eighteen to twenty-nine years voted Obama 60 percent to 37 percent, as did voters thirty to forty-four years by a lower 52 percent to 45 percent margin. Voters forty-five to fifty-nine years narrowly favored Romney 51 percent to 47 percent, while seniors in the sixty-five years plus group gave Romney the largest margin at 56 percent to 44 percent.

Romney made gains among the various religious groups, winning Protestants 62 percent to 37 percent, white evangelicals 78 percent to 21 percent, and those who attend church weekly 59 percent to 39 percent. Obama dropped 4 percent from 2008 but nevertheless carried Catholics narrowly 50 percent to 48 percent, largely due to his stronger support from Hispanic and other nonwhite Catholics. Overall 25 percent of all voters were Catholic, but the exit survey showed (not in the table) that 18 percent of all voters were white Catholics who favored Romney by a 59 percent to 40 percent margin. Union household members were 18 percent of the vote in 2012 and predictably went for Obama and by a 58 percent to 40 percent margin.

The 2012 demographic breakdowns underscore the continuity of the two party coalitions. Romney's best categories were Republican identifiers, conservatives, white evangelicals, Protestants, voters who attend church weekly, whites, rural voters, married voters, and seniors. Obama's most supportive groups were blacks, Democratic identifiers, liberals, Hispanics, urban voters, the unmarried, youth eighteen to twenty-nine years of age, union households, and moderates. Although the percentages of support for both Obama and Romney on gender were not as high as some of the groups just cited, it is notable that the gender gap has reverted to more of its historical pattern, with males voting Republican 52 percent to 45 percent and women Democratic 55 percent to 44 percent.

We also looked at select demographics in the eleven swing states, and they primarily followed the patterns in the national sample. In nine of the eleven swing states Romney captured males, but he but lost them narrowly in Colorado and Michigan. Obama won the female vote in all eleven states and actually exceeded or tied his national percentages in eight of these states. The female vote in the swing states was even stronger than his overall 55 percent to 44 percent national distribution. The age patterns held, with Romney winning seniors in nine of the states but only tying 50 percent to 50 percent in Iowa and losing them in New Hampshire 55 percent to 44 percent. The youth vote was available in ten of the states, and Obama won in all ten. In fact, his youth percentages topped his national percentage in eight of the ten states. Romney won the white vote in nine of the swing states but lost it by identical 51 percent to 47 percent margins in both Iowa and New Hampshire. The vote was available for black voters in eight states, and Obama won by even higher percentages than his national 93 percent share in six of them.[59]

The Hispanic vote was available for nine states, and Obama captured all of them, but by a slightly lower percentage than his 71 percent national share in seven of them. One state where Obama excelled with Hispanics was Colorado, where he won 75 percent to 23 percent, compared to his 61 percent share of the Colorado Hispanic vote in 2008. Hispanics were particularly important in Obama victories in Nevada (70 percent) and Florida (60 percent). Ten states had data on white evangelicals, and Romney won all ten of them, and his national share of the white evangelical vote was 78 percent, an improvement over McCain in 2008 at 73 percent. Despite a ten-state sweep of white evangelicals, Romney's winning percentages were a little low in both Iowa (64 percent to 28 percent) and Ohio (70 percent to 29 percent). His victory margin was impressive in Virginia (82 percent to 18 percent), but he was hurt in this state by a decline in the proportion of evangelicals at 23 percent and down from 28 percent in 2008. In short, the swing-state patterns for the most part followed the national patterns. When they did not, it was usually worked to the disadvantage of Romney who did not always carry all of the swing states in some demographic categories like whites and seniors.[60]

Moving on to gender, scholars and the media have long been concerned about a gender gap.[61] The gender gap, or differences in how men and women vote, exists and emerges during presidential elections. An equally important marital gap is also manifest in recent elections, with Republican candidates like Romney winning married voters 56 percent to 42 percent, Bush 57 percent to 42 percent, and McCain by a smaller 52 percent to 47 percent margin. Kerry carried the unmarried 58 percent to 40 percent, but Obama improved the support levels for single voters to 65 percent to 33 percent in 2008 and 62 percent to 35 percent in 2012.

Gender was a key demographic variable in explaining the vote in 2004 and 2008. Gender has attracted media and scholarly attention since the election of Ronald Reagan in 1980.[62] Beginning in 1980, differences seemed more apparent between men and women on party identification, presidential job approval, issues, and candidate choice. There is a tendency of men overall to be more Republican and women more Democratic. On issues, women are less inclined than men to favor the use of force in foreign policy and to express more support for domestic issues like education, health care, the environment, and financial support for the poor. In presidential elections, men have been more supportive of Republican candidates than have been women.[63]

A historical overview of gender in presidential elections is presented in table 9.7. These data demonstrate that the differences between how men and women voted from 1952 to 1976 are minimal. Of interest, however, is that both sexes voted Republican in 1952, 1956, and 1972. Despite media emphasis on Kennedy's youthful image and physical attractiveness, women nevertheless preferred Nixon in 1960 (51 percent to 49 percent), while men favored Kennedy (52 percent to 48 percent). In 1968 women supported Humphrey (45 percent to 43 percent) and men Nixon (43 percent to 41 percent). In 1976 females leaned toward Ford (51 percent to 48 percent), while men opted for Carter (53 percent to 45 percent). Although these differences grew in the latter three elections, the margins of difference were not great.

Larger percentage differences emerged in 1980 and were labeled in mass media as the gender gap. The data in table 9.7 confirm the existence of a gap, but the more significant point in 1980 is that Reagan was preferred by both sexes, although more by men than women. In 1980 Reagan had a 15 percent advantage with men and a 5 percent edge with women, while in 1984 his male margin was a striking 28 percent and 10 percent with women. In 1988 Bush led among men by 12 percent and among women by 4 percent. There was a gap in these three elections, but it did not threaten the Republican presidential ticket since it was favored by both sexes.

Table 9.7.   Gender and the Presidential Vote, 1952–2012 (% Vote by Gender)

	Males (%)			Females (%)		
Year	Democrat	Republican	Other	Democrat	Republican	Other
1952	47	53	0	42	58	0
1956	45	55	0	39	61	0
1960	52	48	0	49	51	0
1964	60	40	0	62	38	0
1968	41	43	16	45	43	12
1972	37	63	0	38	62	0
1976	53	45	1	48	51	0
1980	38	53	7	44	49	6
1984	36	64	0	45	55	0
1988	44	56	0	48	52	0
1992	41	37	22	46	38	16
1996	43	44	10	54	38	7
2000	42	53	3	54	43	2
2004	44	55	0	51	48	0
2008	49	48	3	56	43	1
2012	45	52	3	55	44	1

Sources: Gallup polls from 1952 to 1992 in Harold Stanley and Richard Niemi, *Vital Statistics on American Politics*, 4th ed. (Washington, D.C.: CQ Press, 1994), 77–79; 1996 and 2000 Voter News Service exit polls reported in Henry Kenski and Kate M. Kenski, "Explaining the Vote in a Divided Country: The Presidential Election of 2004," in *The 2004 Presidential Campaign: A Communication Perspective*, ed. Robert E. Denton, Jr. (Lanham, Md.: Rowman & Littlefield, 2005), 301–42; 2004 and 2008 reported by CNN.com and reported in Henry Kenski and Kate M. Kenski, "Explaining the Vote in a Divided Country: The Presidential Election of 2004," in *The 2004 Presidential Campaign: A Communication Perspective*, ed. Robert E. Denton, Jr. (Lanham, Md.: Rowman & Littlefield, 2005), 301–42; 2012 reported in "Presidential Election Results," MSNBC, accessed November 9, 2012, http://elections.msnbc.msn.com/ns/politics/2012/all/president/#.UKP.

The 1992 race was a three-way race with an Independent Ross Perot pulling 19 percent of the total vote. In this matchup Bill Clinton won both a plurality of males 41 percent to 37 percent and a larger margin with females 46 percent to 38 percent. In 1996 there was a gap, but Clinton surpassed Dole with both men (4 percent) and women (8 percent). Clinton's campaign strategy in 1996 sought to capture both sexes and to win as many white males as possible. This election, however, recorded the largest gender gap in U.S. history, as men favored Dole by a slim 1 percent and women favored Clinton by a striking 16 percent. In 2000 Bush was able to increase the Republicans' male advantage from 1 percent to 11 percent, while Gore experienced a drop in the Democratic female edge from 16 percent to 11 percent. The gender gap was alive and well in 2000.

By contrast the Kerry campaign in 2004 was unable to exploit the traditional gender gap effectively, and only 51 percent of females chose him compared to 48 percent for Bush, who increased his female support by 5 percent from 2000. Bush won males 55 percent to 44 percent in 2004, increasing his male support by 2 percent from 2000. John Kerry's pollster Mark Mellman observed that a major constraint on capturing women in 2004 was that the Bush campaign was so successful in getting an increased number of women to be concerned with the national-security issue.[64]

In 2008 Obama carried males narrowly 49 percent to 48 percent but made major inroads with women with a 56 percent to 43 percent advantage. As we previously noted, Romney carried males 52 percent to 45 percent and Obama scored higher with females 55 percent to 44 percent overall. The norm since 1980 is that women are less Republican than men in the vote, but some candidates are sufficiently strong to carry both groups. This is what Obama did in 2008 but not 2012. A good performance in gender voting is carrying these groups by a margin of 10 percent or more. Obama was especially strong with females, as he registered victory margins of 13 percent in 2008 and 11 percent in 2012. Romney did win males, but only by a margin of 7 percent.

A further consideration is race and ethnicity by gender, as such a data disaggregation captures a more complex gender reality. Table 9.8 contains data that note the overall gender vote for 2008 and 2012 but then disaggregates the data by white men, white women, Latino men, Latino women, black men, and black women. Both white men and white women were Republican in both elections, with the males registering higher levels of support of 57 percent compared to women at 53 percent in 2008, and 62 percent among men contrasted to 56 percent for women in 2012. Black men and black women recorded lopsided percentages for Obama, as the Republican candidates were not competitive. Black women were more supportive of Obama than were black men, narrowly in 2008 by 96 percent compared to 95 percent for women and far more decisively in 2012 with 96 percent for women compared to only to 87 percent for men.

Latino men and women were solid Obama supporters in the two-thirds to three-fourths range but nowhere near the astronomical levels of Obama's African American support. Latino women were slightly more supportive than Latino males of Obama

Table 9.8. The Presidential Vote in 2008 and 2012 by Race and Gender (%)

Category	% of 2008 Total Vote	2008 (%)		% of 2012 Total Vote	2012(%)	
		Obama	McCain		Obama	Romney
Total Vote	100	53	46	100	51	48
White Men	36	41	57	34	35	62
White Women	39	46	53	38	42	56
Latino Men	4	64	33	5	65	33
Latino Women	5	68	30	6	76	33
Black Men	5	95	5	5	87	11
Black Women	7	96	3	8	96	3

Sources: CNN.com/Election 2008 reported Henry Kenski and Kate M. Kenski, "Explaining the Vote in 2008," in *The 2008 Presidential Campaign: A Communication Perspective*, ed. Robert E. Denton Jr., 244–90, (Lanham, Md.: Rowman & Littlefield, 2009); and 2012 reported "Presidential Election Results," MSNBC, accessed November 9, 2012, http://elections.msnbc.msn.com/ns/politics/2012/all/president/#.UKP.

in 2008 (68 percent compared to 64 percent for men) and decisively more support-ive in 2012 (76 percent women and 65 percent for men). In both elections and for all three race, ethnic, and gender groups women were a larger proportion of the total vote than were their male counterparts. For whites, both males and females voted Republican, but males were more Republican than were females. For both Latinos and blacks, both males and females were Democratic, but women were more Demo-cratic than were men. In all three race, ethnic, and categories cases, women were less Republican than were men.

CONCLUSIONS

The 2012 presidential race resulted in an impressive victory for Barack Obama. He won in a very negative political environment, despite middling job ratings until Election Day and a weak economy with high 8 percent–plus unemployment and sluggish economic growth. The battle for the White House narrowed to a focus on eleven swing states, and Obama won ten of them, topping his 2008 performance of winning nine of eleven swing states. Party identification was once again salient, and the Democrats had a 38 percent to 32 percent edge, scarcely different from the 2008 margin of 39 percent to 32 percent. There was an increase in partisan voting with 92 percent of Democratic identifiers supporting Obama and 93 percent of Republican identifiers backing Romney. Independents swung to Romney by only a narrow 5 percent margin.

Obama dominated the race both as a messenger and on the message. He was seen by voters as being more in touch with them, while Romney was viewed as a less-empathetic wealthy candidate. Obama's campaign strategy worked, and so the election was seen as more of a choice between candidates rather than as a referendum on his record. Voters perceived Obama's policies as favoring the middle and lower classes and Romney's policies as favoring the rich. Obama's message established Romney as an unacceptable alternative. Once again Obama proved to be a master in the use of attack advertising, and 2012 probably surpassed the most impressive past attack campaigns—namely Johnson in 1964 and Bush in 1988. In 2008 Obama excelled with attack messages on McCain's age and in a message tying McCain to the unpopular Bush 43, to suggest a McCain presidency would be a third term for Bush policies. In campaign parlance, it was the McBush strategy.[65]

In 2012 Obama's strategy was to attack early and define Romney for voters who knew little about him. It built support for Obama in the eleven swing states and advanced the message that Romney was an unacceptable alternative who favored the wealthy. The ads moved Obama's numbers so that by September that there were fewer persuadable voters and those who were undecided and did not like Obama's job performance would be more inclined to stay home and not vote. Obama benefitted because Romney had no inoculation strategy, and three months of strong negative advertising received little response or rebuttal. Obama made Romney an unacceptable alternative. It appears that many Republicans and others less supportive of Obama simply stayed at home rather than voting.[66]

The data show that the channels of communication are changing. Newspapers and radio consumption is declining, and television is fighting to hold its own with difficulties attracting the younger generation. Cable television leads the market, while mainstream network television has experienced a considerable drop in audience. The most impressive growth the past ten years has been the Internet.

The Pew Research Center's studies of positive and negative tone underscore a very negative tone in the coverage of the 2012 presidential race that handicapped both candidates. The demographic group support patterns did not change dramatically from 2008, but there was more partisan voting, and white voters increased their support for Romney, as did nonwhites for Obama. The Independent vote shifted from Obama in 2008 to Romney in 2012, but only by a narrow 50 percent to 45 percent margin. The demographic patterns played out quite significantly in the eleven swing states and the few cases where they did not advantaged Obama.

We make several concluding observations about the future. The first is that the Republican Party needs to address its internal divisions and find a candidate who resonates better with American voters. It needs to attract new party members to reduce the salient 38 percent to 32 percent advantage Democrats have in party identification and to capture the Independent vote by a double-digit margin. This means finding a candidate who would be a better messenger and who could resonate with and motivate both Republicans and Independents. Republicans must improve on both messenger and message. On the latter, Republicans need to move beyond their macroeconomic positions and hone more targeted messages that show how voters would benefit from those policies and how the policies would create jobs and spread economic prosperity. Although Republicans are unlikely to win a majority of the vote from groups like Hispanics and single women, more attractive policy messages might gain a small percentage increase in their votes. Democrats, on the other hand, need to find a strong successor to Obama, perhaps someone like Hillary Clinton.

Second, Republicans need to confront the Democratic edge in technical skill and campaign talent. Obama's campaign ran a far superior technological operation and turnout endeavor. Project ORCA, the Romney voter-turnout system, was a dud. It was never pretested. The password given to volunteers didn't work, and the program crashed on Election Day. As already mentioned, Democrats far surpassed Republicans in utilizing new media technologies and "get-out-the-vote" efforts. He also notes that Democrats have a large number of capable campaign managers to deploy in campaigns and that the Republican Party only has a few. In Romney's high command, only two people had experience as campaign managers, and both were involved in older gubernatorial races in which their candidates had lost.[67] We would also add to this list the poor performance of Republican polling in the swing states and inaccuracy of their sample distributions.

Finally, there is the question about voter turnout and minority voters. Shortly after the 2012 elections Sean Trende observed the problem of the missing white voters, with at least seven million or more not turning out. He lauded the Obama turnout among blacks, a tad better by 0.2 percent from 2008, and the increased vote for Hispanics and Asians of about 1 percent. He argues, however, that "most importantly, the 2012 elections actually weren't about a demographic explosion with nonwhite voters. Instead they were about a large group of white voters not showing up." Thus "the increased share of the minority vote as a percent of the total vote cast is not the result of a large increase in minorities in the numerator [but] a function of many fewer white voters in the denominator."[68]

Future research must determine why so many chose not to vote. Trende rules out Romney's Mormonism and his moderate past as an explanation for the missing voters, noting that the decline didn't seem to be concentrated in southern states with high percentages of white evangelicals. He then looks at his home state Ohio with all absentee votes counted and fairly complete electoral returns. Trende's Ohio county and geographical analysis shows a good turnout in Democratic counties and urban areas, as well as Republican suburban counties in the southeast. The big drop occurred in the rural portions of Ohio, especially in the southeast. These are areas hit hard by the recession with high unemployment and almost no economic growth. They were also areas where voters were unhappy with Obama. Trende believes that Obama's negative ad campaign that stressed Romney's wealth and tenure at Bain Capital may have turned off voters about the Republican nominee as well. Self-inflicted wounds like Romney's 47 percent gaffe did not help. Given a choice between two unpalatable options, voters simply decided to stay home.[69]

Voter turnout was a problem, with a 5 percent national drop in the vote. The GOP turnout effort could have been better, but the truth is that Republicans need more than better get-out-the-vote efforts. Strassel observes that Obama's vote was down in virtually every battleground state and that in the end Romney topped McCain in every battleground state but Ohio. Romney's project ORCA turnout operation was a dismal failure, and it is tempting to rationalize that better turnout could have made the difference. Even with higher GOP turnout in key states, even with Obama shedding voters, Obama won with a mobilization strategy. He tapped new minority voters in numbers that beat even Romney's better turnout. In Florida 238,000 more Hispanics voted than in 2008, while Obama's margin of victory in Florida was only 78,000. In Ohio where Romney won Independents by 10 percent, the African American turnout increased by 178,000 votes with the president winning 96 percent of them. Obama's margin of victory in Ohio was only 103,000.[70]

The turnout argument is important, but Strassel argues that it is not enough and that Republicans would be better off fighting aggressively for an increased piece of the minority vote, particularly Hispanics. Republicans may never win a majority of the Hispanics, but the GOP could increase its percentages somewhat with a different tone and a policy platform that addresses their problems. Elections are won by the candidate and the message but also by the ground game. What is mind-boggling, Stassel argues, is that the Republicans had no Hispanic ground game. "The GOP doesn't campaign in those communities, doesn't register voters there, doesn't knock on doors. So while preelection polling showed Hispanics were worried about Obama policies, in the end the only campaign they heard from—by e-mail, at their door, on the phone—was the president's."[71]

In swing and competitive states where the Hispanic vote is a key, there is a big difference between a presidential candidate who only gets 27 percent of the vote and one who can win 33 percent to 35 percent. One can argue about the details, but Republicans need a plan to appeal more effectively to the Hispanic community. Modest Hispanic and minority voter shifts toward Republicans coupled with a strategy to identify and appeal to the missing white voters could return the Republican Party to a stronger political force. As Strassel succinctly puts it, "the key to winning turnout is having more people to turn out in the first place."[72]

NOTES

1. Jay Cost, "Morning Jay: Barack Obama and the Triumph of Identity Politics," *Weekly Standard*, November 8, 2012, accessed December 12, 2012, www.weeklystandard.com/blogs/morning-jay-barack-obama-and-triumph-identity-politics_662010.html.

2. Reid Wilson, "Republicans Confront Democrat Edge in Tech Skills, Campaign, Talent," *National Journal*, December 6, 2012, www.nationaljournal.com/columns/on-the-trail/republicans-confront-democrat-edge-in-tech-skills-campaign-talent-20121206.

3. Dave Leip, "2012 Presidential Election Results," *Dave Leip's Atlas of U.S. Presidential Elections*, accessed January 14, 2009, http://uselectionatlas.org/RESULTS/index.html.

4. Henry Kenski and Kate M. Kenski, "Explaining the Vote in a Divided Country: The Presidential Election of 2004," in *The 2004 Presidential Campaign: A Communication Perspective*, ed. Robert E. Denton, Jr. (Lanham, Md.: Rowman & Littlefield, 2005), 301–42.

5. Henry Kenski and Kate M. Kenski, "Explaining the Vote in 2008," in *The 2008 Presidential Campaign: A Communication Perspective*, ed. Robert E. Denton, Jr. (Lanham, Md.: Rowman & Littlefield, 2009), 244–90.

6. Lou Cannon and Carl M. Cannon, *Reagan's Disciple: George W. Bush's Troubled Quest for a Presidential Legacy* (New York: Public Affairs, 2008).

7. Neil Newhouse, *The 2008 Election: The Outcome*, a presentation to Republicans Associated for Mutual Support, November 20, 2008, Washington, D.C., Public Opinion Strategies, 1–59.

8. Lydia Saad, Jeffrey M. Jones, and Frank Newport, "Obama's Road to the White House: A Gallup Review," Gallup, November 5, 2008, accessed January 11, 2009, www.gallup.com/poll/111742/Obamas_Road_White_House_Gallup_Review.aspx?.

9. Jim VandeHei and Mike Allen, "Six Ways the GOP Can Save Itself," *Politico*, May 15, 2008, accessed January 15, 2009, www.politico.com/news/stories/0508/10370.html.

10. Kenski and Kenski, "Explaining the Vote in 2008."

11. Chuck Todd and Sheldon Gawiser, *How Barack Obama Won* (New York: Vintage Books, 2009).

12. Sean Trende, *The Lost Majority* (New York: Palgrave McMillan, 2012).

13. Dan Balz, "8 Questions: Dan Balz on the Democratic National Convention in Charlotte," *Washington Post*, September 2, 2008, accessed September 2, 2012, www.washingtonpost.com/wp-srv/special/politics/8-questions-democratic-convention.

14. James E. Campbell, "Can President Obama Survive His Economic Record?" *Sabato's Crystal Ball*, August 9, 2012, www.centerforpolitics.org/crystalball/articles/can-president-obama-survive-his-economic-record/.

15. Sean Trende, "A Tale of Two Conventions," RealClearPolitics, September 7, 2012, accessed September 19, 2012, www.realclearpolitics.com/articles/2012/09/07/a_tale_of_two_conventions_115375.html.

16. Trende, "A Tale of Two Conventions."

17. Michael Barone, *Our Country: The Shaping of America from Roosevelt to Reagan* (New York: Free Press, 1990).

18. Todd and Gawiser, *How Barack Obama Won*, 47.

19. Kenski and Kenski, "Explaining the Vote in 2008."

20. Kenski and Kenski, "Explaining the Vote in 2008."

21. "Battle for White House," RealClearPolitics, accessed November 5, 2012, www.realclearpolitics.com/epolls/2012/president/2012_elections_electoral_college_map_race_changes.html.

22. "Winning a Second Term Decisively," *Hotline*, November 7, 2012.

23. Charles Riley, "Romney Campaign Spent $18.50 per Vote," CNNMoney, April 25, 2012, accessed October 12, 2012, http://money.cnn.com/2012/04/25/news/economy/Romney-campaign-spending-vote/index.htm.

24. Jay Cost, "Morning Jay: Is Obama's Ad Blitz Moving the Polls?" *Weekly Standard*, August 3, 2012, accessed August 3, 2012, www.weeklystandard.com/blogs/morning-jay-obamas-ad-blitz-moving-polls_649254.html.

25. "Battleground State Polls," RealClearPolitics, accessed December 6, 2012, www.realclearpolitics.com/epolls/2012/president/battleground_states.html. From this source we tracked the polls in eleven swing states by using state codes—for example, Colorado was retrieved from "Colorado: Romney vs. Obama," RealClearPOlitics, accessed December 6, 2012, www.realclearpolitics.com/epolls/2012/president/co/colorado_romney_vs_obama-2023.html.

26. Kenski and Kenski, "Explaining the Vote in 2008."

27. Kenski and Kenski, "Explaining the Vote in 2008."

28. Todd and Gawiser, *How Barack Obama Won*, 45.

29. "Exit Polls: National and State," MSNBC, 2012, "Presidential Election Results: National Results," Decision 2012, http://elections.nbcnews.com/ns/politics/2012/all/president/#.UaZPpJX8_a4; "Presidential Election Results: Colorado," Decision 2012, National and state data were retrieved on November 9, 2012, from http://elections.msnbc.msn.com/nspolitics/2012/allpresident/#.ukp. Individual state demographic data come from this source by adding state codes as below—for example, Colorado was retrieved from http://elections.nbcnews.com/ns/politics/2012/colorado/president/#.UaZQuJX8_a4.

30. Kenski and Kenski, "Explaining the Vote in 2008."

31. Kenski and Kenski, "Explaining the Vote in 2008."

32. Jay Cost, "Can Obama Sustain Enthusiasm with African Americans?" *Weekly Standard*, October 22, 2012, www.weeklystandard.com/blogs/morning-jay-can-obama-sustain-enthusiasm-african-americans_655182.html.

33. Samuel L. Popkin, *The Reasoning Voter: Communication and Persuasion in Presidential Campaigns* (Chicago: University of Chicago Press, 1994).

34. Samuel L. Popkin, *The Candidate* (New York: Oxford University Press, 2012).

35. Kenski and Kenski, "Explaining the Vote in a Divided Country."

36. Kenski and Kenski, "Explaining the Vote in 2008."

37. "Exit Polls: National and State."

38. "Exit Polls: National and State."

39. "Winning a Second Term Decisively," *Hotline*, November 7, 2012.

40. Balz, "8 Questions: Dan Balz on the Democratic National Convention in Charlotte."

41. Balz, "8 Questions: Dan Balz on the Democratic National Convention in Charlotte."

42. Balz, "8 Questions: Dan Balz on the Democratic National Convention in Charlotte."

43. Michael Pfau and Henry C. Kenski, *Attack Politics: Strategy and Defense* (New York: Greenwood, 1990).

44. Dan Balz, "8 Questions: Dan Balz on the Republican National Convention in Tampa," *Washington Post*, August 27, 2012, www.washingtonpost.com/wp-srv/special/politics/8-questions-republican-convention/question1/index.html.

45. Balz, "8 Questions: Dan Balz on the Republican National Convention in Tampa."

46. Jay Cost, "Morning Jay: Mitt Romney and Modern Conservatism," *Weekly Standard*, October 19, 2012, accessed October 27, 2012, www.weeklystandard.com/blogs/morning-jay-romney-gets-heart-modern-conservatism_654946.html.

47. Stephen Moore, "The Bush Blame Game," *Wall Street Journal*, October 18, 2012, accessed October 18, 2012, http://online.wsj.com/article/SB10000872396390443684104578064413840921872.html.

48. Chris Cillizza, "The Rapidly Changing Media Landscape and What It Means for Politics—in 1 Chart," *Washington Post*, October 1, 2012, accessed October 10, 2012, www.washingtonpost.com/blogs/the-fix/wp/2012/10/01/the-rapidly-changing-media-landscape-and-what-it-means-for-politics-in-1-chart/.

49. Cillizza, "The Rapidly Changing Media Landscape."

50. "Internet Gains Most as Campaign News Source, but Cable TV Still Leads," Pew Research Center, October 25, 2012, accessed October 30, 2012, www.pewtrusts.org/our_work_report_detail.aspx?id=85899425772.

51. "Internet Gains Most as Campaign News Source."

52. Jennifer Harper, "Obama's Positive Press Sets Record," *Washington Times,* December 6, 2008, A3, www.washingtontimes.com/news/2008/dec/06/obamas-positive-press-sets-record/.

53. Pew Research Center, "How the Media Covered the 2012 Primary Campaign," Journalism.org, April 23, 2012, accessed August 31, 2012, www.journalism.org/analysis_report_topline_19.

54. Pew Research Center, "How the Media Covered the 2012 Primary Campaign."

55. Pew Research Center, "The Master Character Narratives in Campaign 2012," Journalism.org, August 23, 2012, accessed October 30, 2012, www.journalism.org/analysis_report/master_narratives.

56. Pew Research Center, "The Final Days of the Media Campaign 2012," Journalism.org, November 19, 2012, www.journalism.org/analysis_report/final_days_media_campaign_2012.

57. Barone, *Our Country*; and Henry C. Kenski and Lee Sigelman, "Where the Votes Come From: Group Components of the 1988 Senate Vote," *Legislative Studies Quarterly* 28, no. 3 (1993): 367–90.

58. Kenski and Kenski, "Explaining the Vote in 2008."

59. "Exit Polls: National and State."

60. "Exit Polls: National and State."

61. Michael X. Delli Carpini and Ester R. Fuchs, "The Year of the Woman? Candidates, Voters, and the 1992 Election," *Political Science Quarterly* 108, no. 1 (1993): 29–36; Thomas B. Edsall and Richard Morin, "Clinton Benefited from Huge Gender Gap," *Washington Post*, November 6, 1996, B7; Henry C. Kenski, "The Gender Gap in a Changing Electorate," in *The Politics of the Gender Gap: The Social Construction of Political Influence*, ed. Carol Mueller (Newbury Park, Calif.: Sage, 1988), 38–60; Kate Kenski and Kathleen Hall Jamieson, "The 2000 Presidential Campaign and Differential Growths in Knowledge: Does the 'Knowledge Gap' Hypothesis Apply to Gender as Well as Education?," paper presented at the Annual Meeting of the American Political Science Association in San Francisco, 2001; Kate Kenski and Kathleen Hall Jamieson, "The Gender Gap in Political Knowledge: Are Women Less Knowledgeable Than Men About Politics?," in *Everything You Think You Know about Politics . . . and Why You're Wrong*, ed. Kathleen Hall Jamieson (New York: Basic Books, 2000), 83–89; and Daniel Wirl, "Reinterpreting the Gender Gap" *Public Opinion Quarterly* 50 (1986): 316–30.

62. See all sources in note 61.

63. Kenski and Kenski, "Explaining the Vote in 2008."

64. Mark Mellman, "The Women's Vote in 2004," comments at the Annenberg Public Policy Center Election Debriefing, Philadelphia, December 3, 2004.

65. Kate Kenski, Bruce Hardy, and Kathleen Hall Jamieson, *The Obama Victory* (New York: Oxford University Press, 2010).

66. Jay Cost, "Morning Jay: Barack Obama and the Triumph of Identity Politics," *Weekly Standard*, November 8, 2012, accessed December 12, 2012, www.weeklystandard.com/blogs/morning-jay-barack-obama-and-triumph-identity-politics_662010.html.

67. Wilson, "Republicans Confront Democrat Edge."

68. Sean Trende, "The Case of the Missing White Voters," RealClearPolitics, November 8, 2012, accessed December 6, 2012, www.realclearpolitics.com/articles/2012/11/08/the_case_of_the_missing_white_voters_116106.html.

69. Trende, "The Case of the Missing White Voters."

70. Kimberly A. Strassel, "The GOP Turnout Myth," *Wall Street Journal*, November 22, 2012, accessed November 28, 2012, http://online.wsj.com/article/SB100014241278873243 52004578133120431803606.html.

71. Strassel, "The GOP Turnout Myth."

72. Strassel, "The GOP Turnout Myth."

Index

campaign, 80–86; types of attack ads in
2012, 86–88
American Dream, 2012 presidential
campaign and, 5–17; conventions and,
17–19; Democrat views of, 12–17;
differences between the parties, 3;
narrative and, 17–19; Obama and, 37,
38; presidential elections and, 2–5;
Republican views of, 5–12
attack ads, 2012 presidential campaign and,
86–88, 174–76, 187
Axelrod, David, 92, 109
Ayers, Bill, 123

Bachmann, Michele, 66, 67, 117, 119
Bain Capital, 11, 82, 88, 89, 91, 97, 98,
103, 104, 111, 173; Romney and, 35,
36
Balz, Dan, 35, 173
Barbour, Haley, 106
Beck, Glen, 123
Benoit, William, 59; essential speech
acts, 58–59; image repair strategies of,
99–100
Berman, Mike, 162
Biden, Joe, 5, 12, 14, 15, 34, 49, 51, 136,
137, 145; convention speech, 15
Big Bird, 125, 126, 144, 148
bin Laden, Osama, 14, 15, 173, 174
Blair, Tony, 28
Blitzer, Wolf, 104
Blomquist, David, 87
Boehner, John, 106, 107
Buchanan, Pat, 69
Burke, Kenneth, 99
Bush, Barbra, 25, 26, 27, 28, 29, 30, 31
Bush, George H. W., 72
Bush, George W., 3, 4, 14, 27, 28, 30, 31,
33, 46, 66, 69, 82, 116, 122, 124, 157,
158, 159, 161, 170, 171, 173, 174, 175,
178, 184, 185; Hurricane Katrina and,
158; Iraq and, 158
Bush, Jenna, 25
Bush, Laura, 24, 25, 27, 28, 29, 30, 33

Cain, Herman, 66, 67, 117, 119
campaigns, nomination phase, 24

Campbell, James, 160
candidate films, conventions and, 32–34
candidate websites, 141–42
candidate wives, conventions and, 23–38
Carter, Jimmy, 32, 47, 69, 72, 157, 160
Carville, James, 37
Castro, Julian, 12, 13, 14, 19; convention
speech, 12–14
channels of communication, 2012
presidential campaign and, 176–79
Christie, Chris, 6, 7, 8, 57, 67; convention
speech, 7–8
Cleveland, Grover, 72
Clinton, Bill, 3, 12, 14, 15, 26, 32, 34,
47, 68, 71, 87, 157, 166, 174, 185;
convention speech, 14
Clinton, Chelsea, 26
Clinton, Hillary, 24, 25, 26, 27, 28, 29, 31,
100, 188
CNN, 148
Cohen, Alicia, 140
Cohn, Ryan, 136
Colbert, Stephen, 10, 121, 122; super PAC
segments and, 120–22
Commission on Presidential Debates, 46,
52–53
conventions: 2012 presidential campaign
and, 1–19; candidate films and,
32–34; Democratic convention, 12–17;
narrative of 2012, 17–19; Republican
convention, 5–12; spouses and, 23–38;
women's speeches and, 25–31; women's
speeches, strategies of, 25–31
Cooper, Anderson, 90
Cost, Jay, 187
coverage, tone of in 2012, 177–79
Crowley, Candy, 49, 53

Darwell, Brittany, 137
Davis, Frank, 123
Davis, Richard, 133, 134
debates: 2012 first debate, 47–49; 2012
presidential, 47–53; 2012 presidential
debates, audiences of, 50, 54; 2012
presidential debates, Fox News and, 51;
2012 presidential debates, interruptions
during, 50, 51, 54; 2012 presidential

About the Editor and Contributors

Gwen Brown is adjunct professor in the Department of Communication and Journalism at Rider University and professor emerita in the School of Communication at Radford University, where she taught courses on communication theory, rhetorical analysis, and political communication from 1988 to 2010. Brown has presented numerous papers to professional meetings in both communication and political science and has published in the *Journal of Communication and Religion, Academic Questions*, and *National Review Online*. She has contributed "Deliberation and Its Discontents: H. Ross Perot's Antipolitical Populism" to Andreas Schedler's edited collection *The End of Politics? Explorations into Modern Antipolitics* and "'A More Perfect Union': Barack Obama's Failed *Apologia* and Successful Use of Identity Politics" to Robert Denton Jr.'s *Studies in Identity Politics in the 2008 Presidential Campaign*. Along with Matthew Franck, she published a chapter on the film *How Green Was My Valley* in Sidney A. Pearson Jr.'s collection *Print the Legend: Politics, Culture, and Civic Virtue in the Films of John Ford*. With Matthew Franck and Sandra French she published "Framing the Stem-Cell Debate: George W. Bush and Bioethics" in Robert E. Denton Jr.'s *The George W. Bush Presidency: A Rhetorical Perspective*.

Robert E. Denton, Jr., holds the W. Thomas Rice Chair of Leadership Studies in the Pamplin College of Business and is professor in the Department of Communication at Virginia Polytechnic Institute and State University (Virginia Tech). He served as the founding director of the Rice Center for Leader Development from 1996 to 2007. He currently serves as head of the Department of Communication, a position he previously held from 1988 until 1996. He has degrees in political science and communication from Wake Forest University and Purdue University. In addition to numerous articles, essays, and book chapters, he is author, coauthor, or editor of twenty-three books. The most recent titles include *The George W. Bush Presidency: A*

Rhetorical Perspective (2012), *Political Campaign Communication: Principles and Practices*, 7th ed. (with Judith Trent and Robert Friedenberg, 2011), and *Communicator-in-Chief: How Barack Obama Used New Media Technology to Win the White House* (coedited with John Allen Hendricks, 2010).

Scott W. Dunn is assistant professor at Radford University, where he teaches political communication and communication theory and coordinates the oral-communication component of the university's core curriculum. He studies the content and effects of political-campaign messages and news coverage of campaigns. He has a PhD from the University of North Carolina at Chapel Hill and master's and bachelor's degrees from Virginia Tech.

Jason A. Edwards is associate professor of communication studies at Bridgewater State University. He is author of *Navigating the Post–Cold War World: President Clinton's Foreign Policy Rhetoric* and *The Rhetoric of American Exceptionalism: Critical Essays*. Additionally, he has authored over thirty articles and book chapters appearing in venues such as *Rhetoric and Public Affairs, Communication Quarterly, Southern Journal of Communication, Presidential Studies Quarterly,* and *The Howard Journal of Communications*. He is currently working on a book that traces the rhetorical contours of American foreign-policy rhetoric and is in the early stages of a book project involving religion, rhetoric, and politics.

John Allen Hendricks is chair of the Department of Mass Communication and holds the rank of professor at Stephen F. Austin State University (SFA) in Texas. He served as director of the Division of Communication and Contemporary Culture at SFA from 2009 to 2012, which included the academic units of media studies, communication studies, Latin, Greek, and philosophy. He holds a doctorate from the University of Southern Mississippi, a master's degree from the University of Arkansas at Little Rock, and a bachelor's degree from Southern Arkansas University; all of the degrees are in mass communication. In addition to numerous articles, essays, and book chapters, Hendricks is the author or editor of eight books. The most recent titles include *Presidential Campaigning and Social Media* (coedited with Dan Schill), *Techno Politics in Presidential Campaigning: New Voices, New Technologies, and New Voters* (coedited with Lynda Lee Kaid), and *Communicator-in-Chief: How Barack Obama Used New Media Technology to Win the White House* (coedited with Robert E. Denton Jr., 2010), which was awarded the National Communication Association Applied Research Division's 2011 Distinguished Scholarly Book Award.

Rachel L. Holloway is associate professor of communication and serves as associate dean of Undergraduate Academic Affairs in the College of Liberal Arts and Human Sciences at Virginia Tech. Holloway has served as a university administrator since 2002. Her research investigates rhetorical and media strategies used in political and corporate campaign discourse. Holloway is author of numerous book chapters and coeditor of *Images, Scandal, and Communication Strategies of the Clinton Presidency*. Her scholarly work appears in *Rhetorical and Critical Approaches to Public Relations II* (2009), *Studies in Communication Science, Business Research Yearbook*, and *Political Communication*.

Jeffrey P. Jones is director of the Peabody Awards at the University of Georgia. His research focuses on the intersection of popular culture and politics. He is author of *Entertaining Politics*, 2nd ed. (2010), coeditor of *Satire TV: Politics and the Comedy in the Network Era* (2009) and *The Essential HBO Reader* (2008), as well as author of numerous articles and book chapters on media and politics.

Henry C. Kenski is professor emeritus in the Department of Communication at the University of Arizona. He has a doctorate in political science from Georgetown University. Kenski is coauthor with Michael Pfau of *Attack Politics: Strategy and Defense* (1990) and author of *Saving the Hidden Treasure: The Evolution of Ground-water Policy* (1991). He has written numerous articles and book chapters on different facets of political communication, including the media, political advertising, political campaigns, political rhetoric, public opinion, and voting behavior. He currently teaches as an adjunct professor in the Department of Communication at the University of Arizona.

Kate M. Kenski is associate professor in the Department of Communication and School of Government and Public Policy at the University of Arizona where she teaches political communication, public opinion, and research methods. She received her doctorate in communication from the University of Pennsylvania. She has published over thirty articles, books, and book chapters on political communication. Her book *The Obama Victory: How Media, Money, and Message Shaped the 2008 Election* (coauthored with Bruce W. Hardy and Kathleen Hall Jamieson) has won several awards, including the PROSE Award for 2010 Best Book in Government and Politics, the 2011 International Communication Association Outstanding Book Award, and the 2012 National Communication Association Diamond Anniversary Book Award.

Craig Allen Smith is professor emeritus of Communication at North Carolina State University. His works include *Presidential Campaign Communication: The Quest for the White House* (2010), *Persuasion and Social Movements*, 6th ed. (2012), with Charles J. Stewart and Robert E. Denton, Jr.; *The White House Speaks: Presidential Leadership as Persuasion* (1994) with Kathy B. Smith; *Political Communication* (1990); and numerous journal articles and book chapters.

John C. Tedesco is professor in the Department of Communication at Virginia Tech. His recent interests include political advertising, new media, and political efficacy. He is author or coauthor of numerous academic articles and book chapters. His work has appeared in such journals as *American Behavioral Scientist, Journalism Studies, Communication Research Reports, Communication Studies, Journal of Broadcasting and Electronic Media, Journal of Advertising*, and *The Harvard International Journal of Press/Politics*, to name a few. In addition, Tedesco is coeditor of three books, most recently *The Internet Election: Perspectives of the Web in Campaign 2004* (2006).

Joseph M. Valenzano III is assistant professor and basic course director at the University of Dayton. Prior to his current appointment he served as assistant professor-in-residence and basic course director at the University of Nevada, Las Vegas where his program received the 2009 Program of Excellence award from the Basic Course Division of the National Communication Association. His research interests are on the intersection of religion, politics, and mass media, and his work has appeared in the *Southern Journal of Communication, Journal of Media and Religion, Communication Quarterly*, and the *Journal of Language and Politics*. He also has coauthored a public speaking textbook, *The Speaker: The Tradition and Practice of Public Speaking*.

Ben Voth is chair of communication studies at Southern Methodist University and director of Debate and Speech programs. He publishes in both academic and major press outlets. His research and teaching specialization focuses on equipping people to have a voice. He has published numerous book chapters and journal articles on the various rhetorical impacts of argument, including topics such as humor and argument and public advocacy surrounding problems such as genocide. He consults with organizations such as The United States Holocaust Memorial Museum in Washington, D.C., to improve public communication among holocaust survivors who volunteer there. He coached numerous national champions in speech and finalists in NDT policy debate. He completed a master's degree in communication at Baylor University and a doctorate at the University of Kansas. He is an officer in the American Forensics Association and on the editorial board of Argumentation and Advocacy.